British Columbia
A Celebration

British Columbia
A Celebration

Edited by George Woodcock

Photographs by J. A. Kraulis

Hurtig Publishers
Edmonton

In affectionate and admiring recollection of
Roderick Haig-Brown and Ethel Wilson.
Tout passe; l'amitié reste.

               George Woodcock

For my sister, Ilze

            J. A. Kraulis

Hurtig Publishers Ltd.
10560 – 105 Street
Edmonton, Alberta

Canadian Cataloguing in Publication Data
Main entry under title:
British Columbia, a celebration

  ISBN 0-88830-239-8

   1. British Columbia.   I. Woodcock,
George, 1912–   II. Kraulis, J.A., 1949–
FC3811.B76   971.1   C83-091229-0
F1087.B76

Design/David Shaw & Associates Ltd.
Composition/Attic Typesetting Inc.
Separations/Great Western Graphics Corp.
Manufacture/D.W. Friesen & Sons Ltd.

Printed and bound in Canada

Contents

Acknowledgements / 6

Introduction   *George Woodcock* / 9

PART ONE: Time in Its Place

From *Out of the Silence*   *Bill Reid* / 33
With Captain Cook in Nootka Sound   *John Ledyard* / 34
Pacific Door   *Earle Birney* / 36
Three Indian Tales   *Franz Boas (Translated by*
    Dietrich Bertz) / 36
On the Rocks in Queen Charlotte Sound
    George Vancouver / 38
Lure   *Susan Musgrave* / 40
Chief Jammisit's Dance   *Jacinto Caamaño*
    (Translated by Harold Grenfell) / 41
From *George, Vancouver: a discovery poem*
    George Bowering / 42
A Walk at Cape Mudge   *George Vancouver* / 43
Indian Graveyard, Vancouver Island   *Robin Skelton* / 44
Massacre at Nootka Sound   *John R. Jewitt* / 44
The Myth of the Man Who Changed His Face
    Charles Hill-Tout / 47
Source   *Robin Skelton* / 48
Alexander Mackenzie Reaches the Pacific
    Roy Daniells / 49
Myth of the Wolves and the Corpse
    Charles Hill-Tout / 52
Fraser's River   *Charles Lillard* / 52
The Perils of the Fraser Canyon   *Simon Fraser* / 53
Skating Down Trout   *Kevin Roberts* / 56
First Winter on the Columbia   *David Thompson* / 56
Matq, or the Fire Myth   *Charles Hill-Tout* / 58
Lake   *Dale Zieroth* / 59
The Headwaters of the Columbia   *Paul Kane* / 60
Day after day the sun   *Patrick Lane* / 61
Fort Victoria—Fur Traders and Indians   *Paul Kane* / 62
In the Gulf   *Robin Skelton* / 64
A Reminiscence of 1850   *Dr. John Sebastian Helmcken* / 81
On the Old Trail   *Bruce Hutchison* / 84
Old Cariboo Wagon Road North   *Eric Ivan Berg* / 87
From *Hope: The Colours of Time.*
    A Drama for Voices   *Michael Mercer* / 88
The Black Canyon of the Ominica
    William Francis Butler / 90
The Birth of Vancouver   *Margaret Ormsby* / 93
November Walk near False Creek Mouth   *Earle Birney* / 96

PART TWO: Place & Persons

Touring B.C.   *Dale Zieroth* / 129
Ebb Tide   *Marjorie Pickthall* / 129
Salt Water and Tideflats   *Roderick Haig-Brown* / 130
On the Cape Scott Trail   *Tom Wayman* / 133
Mike   *M. Wylie Blanchet* / 134
Petroglyphs   *Ken Cathers* / 136
Blue Heron   *Ken Cathers* / 136
The Old Men of Telegraph Creek   *Edward Hoagland* / 137
The Forest Jungle   *Emily Carr* / 139
Target Practice at Findlay Creek   *Dale Zieroth* / 139
Sailing to the Logging Camps   *M. Allerdale Grainger* / 140
Swan Song   *Gary Geddes* / 143
The Last Spar-Tree on Elphinstone Mountain
    Peter Trower / 144
A Summer Journey   *Emily Carr* / 145
Encounter with an Archangel   *George Woodcock* / 146
Prospector   *Patrick Lane* / 150
The Mountains; The Valley   *Peter Trower* / 151
Wild Horses   *Patrick Lane* / 151
Canadian Pacific Camp   *Daphne Marlatt* / 152
What Do I Remember of the Evacuation?
    Joy Kogawa / 153
Fog   *Ethel Wilson* / 154
Social Credit Elected in B.C.   *Lionel Kearns* / 157
They Are Burning   *Fred Wah* / 157
The Medicine Cross   *Hugh Brody* / 157
From "Some Objects of Wood and Stone"
    Margaret Atwood / 160
The Cariboo Hores   *Al Purdy* / 160
From Flores   *Ethel Wilson* / 177
A Drowning at François Lake   *Andrew Wreggitt* / 180
Mist on the River   *Hubert Evans* / 181
Ito Fujika, The Trapper   *Howard O'Hagan* / 183
Nausikaa, Vancouver Island   *Theresa Kishkan* / 187
Bushed   *Earle Birney* / 187
At Sechelt   *Dorothy Livesay* / 188
Seashelter   *Dorothy Livesay* / 188
Ted's Wife   *Audrey Thomas* / 189
Finches Feeding   *P. K. Page* / 193
By the River   *Jack Hodgins* / 194
Christ Walks in This Infernal District Too
    Malcolm Lowry / 196
Blue River; Clearwater   *Tom Wayman* / 197
Autumn   *Rona Murray* / 197
Hagar's Escape   *Margaret Laurence* / 198
November Day on Howe Sound   *George Woodcock* / 201
Closeted   *David Watmough* / 202
Lardeau/Summer, 1964   *Fred Wah* / 205

Notes on Contributors / 206

Acknowledgements

The editor wishes to extend grateful acknowledgement to copyright-holders for permission to include material in this collection. Every effort has been made to contact copyright owners. If there have been errors or omissions, the publisher would be grateful for any information enabling suitable acknowledgement to be made in future editions.

"From *Out of the Silence*" by Bill Reid, from *Out of the Silence*, photographs by Adelaide de Menil, text by William Reid. Copyright 1971 Amon Carter Museum. Reprinted by permission of Amon Carter Museum (Forth Worth, Texas) and the author.

"With Captain Cook in Nootka Sound" by John Ledyard, from *A Journal of Captain Cook's Last Voyage to the Pacific Ocean* (1783).

"Pacific Door" by Earle Birney, from *The Collected Poems of Earle Birney*, vol. I, used by permission of The Canadian Publishers, McClelland and Stewart Limited, Toronto.

"Three Indian Tales" by Franz Boas, translated by Dietrich Bertz, from "Indian Folktales from British Columbia" in *The Malahat Review*, no. 60, October 1981, pages 64–66 and 73–74. These folktales were selected from a major work by Dr. Franz Boas first published in its entirety in Germany as *Indianische Sagen von der Nord-Pacifischen Küste Amerikas* in 1895 and translated into English by Dietrich Bertz for the B.C. Indian Language Project in the 1970s as *Indian Myths and Legends from the North Pacific Coast of America*. Reprinted by permission of Dietrich Bertz and the B.C. Indian Language Project.

"On the Rocks in Queen Charlotte Sound" by George Vancouver, from *A Voyage of Discovery to the North Pacific Ocean and Round the World*, vol. I (1798).

"Lure" by Susan Musgrave, from *Grave-Dirt and Selected Strawberries* (Toronto, The Macmillan Company of Canada Ltd., 1973). Reprinted by permission of the author.

"Chief Jammisit's Dance" by Jacinto Caamaño, translated by Captain Harold Grenfell, R.N., from "The Journal of Jacinto Caamaño," Part II, as published in *The British Columbia Historical Quarterly*, vol. II, no. 4, October, 1938. Reprinted by permission of the Provincial Archives of British Columbia.

"From *George, Vancouver: a discovery poem*" by George Bowering, from *George, Vancouver: a discovery poem* (Toronto, Weed/Flower Press, 1970). Reprinted in *Selected Poems: Particular Accidents* (Vancouver, Talonbooks, 1980). Reprinted by permission of the author.

"A Walk at Cape Mudge" by George Vancouver, from *A Voyage of Discovery to the North Pacific Ocean and Round the World*, vol. I (1798).

"Indian Graveyard, Vancouver Island" by Robin Skelton, from *Collected Shorter Poems* (Victoria, Sono Nis Press, 1981). Reprinted by permission of the publisher.

"Massacre at Nootka Sound" by John R. Jewitt, from *The Adventures and Sufferings of John R. Jewitt, Captive Among the Nootka, 1803–1805* edited by Derek G. Smith (Toronto, The Macmillan Company of Canada Ltd., 1974. Carleton Library).

"The Myth of the Man Who Changed His Face," "The Myth of the Wolves and the Corpse," and "Matq, or the Fire Myth" by Charles Hill-Tout, from *The Salish People*, vol. 3, 1978, published by Talon Books Ltd., 201—1019 E. Cordova St., Vancouver, B.C., Canada V6A 1M8, (604) 253-5261. Reprinted by permission of the publisher.

"Source" by Robin Skelton, from *Collected Shorter Poems* (Victoria, Sono Nis Press, 1981). Reprinted by permission of the publisher.

"Alexander Mackenzie Reaches the Pacific" by Roy Daniells, from *Alexander Mackenzie and the North West* (Toronto, Oxford University Press, 1972).

"Fraser's River" by Charles Lillard, from *Drunk on Wood and Other Poems* (Victoria, Sono Nis Press, 1973). Reprinted by permission of the publisher.

"The Perils of the Fraser Canyon" by Simon Fraser, from *The Letters and Journals of Simon Fraser* edited by W. Kaye Lamb (Toronto, The Macmillan Company of Canada Ltd., 1960). Reprinted by permission of the editor.

"Skating Down Trout" by Kevin Roberts, from *Heritage* (Madeira Park, B.C., Harbour Publishing, 1981). Reprinted by permission of the publisher.

"First Winter on the Columbia" by David Thompson, from *David Thompson's Travels in Western North America 1784–1812* edited by Victor G. Hopwood (Toronto, Macmillan of Canada   A Division of Cage Publishing Limited, 1971). Reprinted by permission of the publisher.

"Lake" by Dale Zieroth, from *Clearing: Poems from a Journey* (Toronto: House of Anansi Press, 1973). Reprinted by permission of the publisher.

"The Headwaters of the Columbia" by Paul Kane, from *Wanderings of an Artist* (Edmonton, Hurtig Publishers, 1968).

"Day after day the sun" by Patrick Lane, *Poems, New and Selected* (Toronto, Oxford University Press, 1978). Reprinted by permission of the author.

"Fort Victoria—Fur Traders and Indians" by Paul Kane, from *Wanderings of an Artist* (Edmonton, Hurtig Publishers, 1968).

"In the Gulf" by Robin Skelton, from *Collected Shorter Poems* (Victoria, Sono Nis Press, 1981). Reprinted by permission of the publisher.

"A Reminiscence of 1850" by Dr. John Sebastian Helmcken from a *Victoria Colonist* article, 1887. Reprinted in *The Reminiscences of Doctor John Sebastian Helmcken* edited by Dorothy Blakey Smith (Vancouver, University of British Columbia Press, 1975).

"On the Old Trail" by Bruce Hutchison, from *The Fraser* © 1950 by Bruce Hutchison. Used by permission of Clarke, Irwin & Company Limited.

"Old Cariboo Wagon Road North" by Eric Ivan Berg, from *The Malahat Review*, no. 45, University of Victoria.

"From *Hope: The Colours of Time. A Drama for Voices*" by Michael Mercer, from an unpublished radio play. Reprinted by permission of the author.

"The Black Canyon of the Ominica" by William Francis Butler, from *The Wild North Land* (Edmonton, Hurtig Publishers, 1968).

"The Birth of Vancouver" by Margaret Ormsby, from *British Columbia: A History* (Toronto, Macmillan of Canada A Division of Gage Publishing Limited, 1971). Reprinted by permission of the publisher.

"November Walk near False Creek Mouth" by Earle Birney, from *The Collected Poems of Earle Birney*, vol. II, used by permission of The Canadian Publishers, McClelland and Stewart Limited, Toronto.

"Touring B.C." by Dale Zieroth, from *Mid-River* (Toronto: House of Anansi Press, 1981). Reprinted by permission of the publisher.

"Ebb Tide" by Marjorie Pickthall, from *The Complete Poems of Marjorie Pickthall* (Toronto, McClelland and Stewart Limited, 1927).

"Salt Water and Tideflats" by Roderick Haig-Brown, from *Measure of the Year* (Toronto, Collins Publishers, 1968). Reprinted by permission of the publisher.

"On the Cape Scott Trail" by Tom Wayman. Reprinted by permission of the author; originally published in *For And Against The Moon: Blues, Yells And Chuckles* by the Macmillan Company of Canada Ltd., 1974.

"Mike" by M. Wylie Blanchet, from *The Curve of Time*. Reprinted by permission of Gray's Publishing Ltd., Sidney, B.C. (1980 edition.)

"Petroglyphs" and "Blue Heron" by Ken Cathers, from *The Malahat Review*, no. 45, University of Victoria. Reprinted by permission of the author.

"The Old Men of Telegraph Creek" by Edward Hoagland, from *Notes from the Century Before*. Copyright © 1969 by Edward Hoagland. Reprinted by permission of Random House, Inc.

"The Forest Jungle" by Emily Carr, from *Hundreds and Thousands: The Journals of Emily Carr* © 1966 by Clarke, Irwin & Company Limited. Used by permission.

"Target Practice at Findlay Creek" by Dale Zieroth, from *Clearing: Poems from a Journey* (Toronto: House of Anansi Press, 1973). Reprinted by permission of the publisher.

"Sailing to the Logging Camps" by M. Allerdale Grainger, from *Woodsmen of the West* (New Canadian Library, 1964), used by permission of The Canadian Publishers, McClelland and Stewart Limited, Toronto.

"Swan Song" by Gary Geddes. Copyright Gary Geddes. Reprinted by permission of the author.

"The Last Spar-Tree on Elphinstone Mountain" by Peter Trower, from *Ragged Horizons*, used by permission of The Canadian Publishers, McClelland and Stewart Limited, Toronto.

"A Summer Journey" by Emily Carr, from *Hundreds and Thousands: The Journals of Emily Carr* © 1966 by Clarke, Irwin & Company Limited. Used by permission.

"Encounter with an Archangel" by George Woodcock, from *The Rejection of Politics* (Toronto, New Press, 1972). Reprinted by permission of the author.

"Prospector" and "Wild Horses" by Patrick Lane, from *Poems, New and Selected* (Toronto, Oxford University Press, 1978). Reprinted by permission of the author.

"The Mountains; The Valley" by Peter Trower, from *Ragged Horizons*, used by permission of The Canadian Publishers, McClelland and Stewart Limited, Toronto.

"Canadian Pacific Camp" by Daphne Marlatt, from *Steveston Recollected* (Provincial Archives of British Columbia, 1975). Reprinted by permission of the author.

"What Do I Remember of the Evacuation?" by Joy Kogawa, from *A Choice of Dreams* (Toronto, McClelland and Stewart Limited, 1976). Reprinted by permission of the author.

"Fog" by Ethel Wilson, from *Mrs. Golightly and Other Stories* (Toronto, The Macmillan Company of Canada Ltd., 1961). Reprinted by permission of the University of British Columbia.

"Social Credit Elected in B.C." by Lionel Kearns, from *Practicing Up to be Human* (Toronto, Coach House Press, 1978). Reprinted by permission of the author.

"They Are Burning" by Fred Wah, from *Selected Poems*, 1980, published by Talon Books Ltd., 201—1019 E. Cordova St., Vancouver, B.C., Canada V6A 1M8, (604) 253-5261. Reprinted by permission of the publisher.

"The Medicine Cross" by Hugh Brody, from *Maps and Dreams* (Vancouver, Douglas & McIntyre, 1980).

"From 'Some Objects of Wood and Stone'" by Margaret Atwood, section from "Some Objects of Wood and Stone" © Margaret Atwood 1966 from *The Circle Game* (Toronto: House of Anansi Press, 1967). Reprinted by permission of the publisher.

"The Cariboo Horses" by Al Purdy, from *The Cariboo Horses*, used by permission of The Canadian Publishers, McClelland and Stewart Limited, Toronto.

"From Flores" by Ethel Wilson, from *Mrs. Golightly and Other Stories* (Toronto, The Macmillan Company of Canada Ltd., 1961). Reprinted by permission of the University of British Columbia.

"A Drowning at François Lake" by Andrew Wreggitt, from *Riding to Nicola Country* (Madeira Park, B.C., Harbour Publishing, 1981). Reprinted by permission of the publisher.

"Mist on the River" by Hubert Evans, reprinted with permission from *Mist on the River* by Hubert Evans. Published by McClelland and Stewart Limited (New Canadian Library Series). Copyright Copp Clark Co. Limited, 1954.

"Ito Fujika, The Trapper" by Howard O'Hagan, from *The Woman Who Got On at Jasper Station and Other Stories*, 1977, published by Talon Books Ltd., 201—1019 E. Cordova St., Vancouver, B.C., Canada V6A 1M8, (604) 253-5261. Reprinted by permission of the publisher.

"Nausikaa, Vancouver Island" by Theresa Kishkan, from *The Malahat Review*, no. 45, University of Victoria. Reprinted in *Ikons of the Hunt* (Victoria, Sono Nis Press, 1978). Reprinted by permission of the author.

"Bushed" by Earle Birney, from *The Collected Poems of Earle Birney*, vol. 1, used by permission of The Canadian Publishers, McClelland and Stewart Limited, Toronto.

"At Sechelt" and "Seashelter" by Dorothy Livesay, from *Collected Poems: The Two Seasons* by Dorothy Livesay. Reprinted by permission of McGraw-Hill Ryerson Limited.

"Ted's Wife" by Audrey Thomas, from *Real Mothers*, 1981, published by Talon Books Ltd., 201—1019 E. Cordova St., Vancouver, B.C., Canada V6A 1M8, (604) 253-5261. Reprinted by permission of the publisher.

"Finches Feeding" by P. K. Page, reprinted from *Evening Dance of the Grey Flies* by permission of the author.

"By the River" by Jack Hodgins, from *Spit Delaney's Island* (Toronto, Macmillan of Canada   A Division of Gage Publishing Limited, 1977). Reprinted by permission of the publisher.

"Christ Walks in This Infernal District Too" by Malcolm Lowry, from *Selected Poems of Malcolm Lowry*, copyright © 1962 by Margerie Lowry. Reprinted by permission of City Lights Books, San Francisco.

"Blue River; Clearwater" by Tom Wayman. Reprinted by permission of the author; originally published in *For And Against The Moon: Blues, Yells And Chuckles* by the Macmillan Company of Canada Ltd., 1974.

"Autumn" by Rona Murray, from *Journey* (Victoria, Sono Nis Press, 1981). Reprinted by permission of the publisher.

"Hagar's Escape" by Margaret Laurence, from *The Stone Angel* (New Canadian Library, 1964), used by permission of The Canadian Publishers, McClelland and Stewart Limited, Toronto.

"November Day on Howe Sound" by George Woodcock, from *The Mountain Road* (Fredericton, Fiddlehead Poetry Books, 1980). Reprinted by permission of the author.

"Closeted" by David Watmough, first published in *Waves* magazine, vol. 10, no. 4, Spring 1982. Reprinted by permission of the author.

"Lardeau/Summer, 1964" by Fred Wah, from *Selected Poems*, 1979, published by Talon Books Ltd., 201—1019 E. Cordova St., Vancouver, B.C., Canada V6A 1M8, (604) 253-5261. Reprinted by permission of the publisher.

George Woodcock

I owe special thanks to the Silins family, and to Catherine Young and Bo Curtis (who, among other things, did the flying for several of the aerial photographs in this book). I also thank Colin Jackson, Arvo and Debbie Koppel, Ian Greene, John and Gill Tucker, Tom and Andrea Duchastel, Frances Cochran, Pat Morrow, Karen Paynter, Linda Morrow, Sharon Lazare and David Usher, Margie Jamieson and Art Twomey, Damian Regan, Gilles Lepage, and all the other people who hosted, guided, or otherwise assisted me in my travels through British Columbia.

Immeasurable thanks I owe my wife, Linda, who inspired a great many of the images and contributed greatly to the final editing of the photography.

J. A. Kraulis

Introduction

British Columbia is the frontier—sea and mountain—of a vast land, the shore of the westernmost of Canada's three oceans. As Earle Birney said in his great poem about Vancouver, "November Walk near False Creek Mouth," its people live, in relation to the rest of their country

> in the last of warmth
> and the fading of brightness
> on the sliding edge of the beating sea.

It is not only the sun that finishes its Canadian journey on the shores of British Columbia, dipping down into the great sea that has Japan as its farther shore. There are many people whose earthly travels have led them here and who, having arrived, never wish to live anywhere else than in this land which the nineteenth-century Liberal leader Edward Blake described, not without horror, as "a sea of mountains," the succession of vast ranges that continue in gigantic parallels six hundred kilometres from the Continental Divide—which is also the province's eastern boundary—until the last of them dips its fjord-bitten feet into the islanded waters off the Pacific coast.

I have compiled this anthology and write its introduction as one of these adoptive British Columbians who end as passionate local patriots. I was born in Winnipeg, and for the first half of my life never went west of it for the simple reason that my parents took me back to their English home when I was a small child, and I did not decide to return to the land of my birth until 1949. When I did, it was to British Columbia that I came, principally with the idea that if I were going to settle in Canada I might as well see the whole sweep of the country before making up my mind where to settle. And so, almost as far towards the sunset as one could get in Canada, beside a blue and island-studded harbour at Sooke on the west coast of Vancouver Island, I put down my first roots in the country.

There were years of adjustment, fitting in to a new way of life among loggers and fishermen and decayed remittance men, enduring the isolation that was so much more the lot of Canadian writers in the early 1950s than it is today, and going through some sharp skirmishes with poverty at a time when such writers were neither greatly paid nor even greatly noticed. But all the time I was exploring, bit by bit, the great land beyond the mountains, dipping into its history and its long Indian past before history, living myself into its unpeopled landscapes, its open cities, the visual delights of its breathtaking combinations of mountains and water—the big rivers, the many lakes, the intricate coastal seaways. It was the subject of my first travel book, *Ravens and Prophets*.

Yet two years after I came, I was still undecided whether I would stay. Then I won a fellowship that took me for a year in Europe and California; it enabled me to see in reflection that first foray into Canadian life, and by the year's end I had finally decided where I wanted to live the rest of my life and came back to British Columbia. I settled in Vancouver, which I have found the perfect writer's haven; near to the white peaks and the salt water; a real city yet not big or impersonal enough to be a metropolis; far enough from the great centres for a writer to work in peace, nurtured by his environment, yet at the knot of a network of air routes that take him in a few hours to Paris or Tokyo, to Lima or Rome, to Athens or Sydney. For British Columbia belongs as much to the long curve of the Pacific Rim as it does to the North American continent, and its cultural and historical links run over the pole to England and across the Pacific to China and Japan and down the coast to San Francisco as certainly as they do across the Rockies to Ontario and Quebec. In this sense, to live in Vancouver is to live in a world city, but a world city like no other because of the wilderness which begins the other side of the mountains that protect its harbour.

On the routes out of Vancouver I have travelled far and often, but I have been drawn back always to this place that has become the centre of my life. I have written my books here, some of them about British Columbia, but most of them on other themes and places, for a writer's home sustains but does not limit him. And during my three decades here I have seen the birth of local movements in the arts, and especially in painting and writing. Many of the writers who have contributed to that renaissance appear in these pages.

But before we come to their writings, let me paint in the background by speaking about the land and its people. British Columbia is in many ways a unique fragment of the earth, if one can use the word "fragment" appropriately to describe a land that is larger than France, Chile, or Sweden, in fact larger than most member countries of the United Nations. Its 950,000 square kilometres (or 366,000 square miles if you are attached to the older ways of measurement) contain an unexampled variety of terrains: the successive ranges of high mountains paralleling each other from the Rockies to the Cascades; the desert lands of the dry interior contrasting with the lush rain forests of the coast and the rich pastoral country of the lower Fraser valley; and scattered offshore the pattern of large islands and archipelagos that protect from Pacific storms the intricate network of channels and probing inlets in which the main cities of the province—Vancouver and Victoria—are sheltered. British Columbia has greater extremes of climate than any other province in Canada, from the temperatures far below zero experienced in the tiny backwoods settlements on the Yukon border to the mild winters of the Lower Mainland and the offshore islands, where some years the snow never falls and the first spring flowers appear not long after the last roses have faded.

The province's contrasts run in other ways. In Vancouver it boasts Canada's third largest city, a place that combines a setting of spectacular beauty with a notable and sophisticated cultural life. But in the little-travelled areas of its northern interior, around the headwaters of the Nass and the Stikine and the Nahanni, it also possesses much of Canada's unspoilt wilderness country, the last refuge of many threatened species of animals and birds, the country where the famous outlaw Simon Gun-an-Noot hid undetected for thirteen years.

British Columbia is the home of ancient Indian tribes, and when Captain Cook and the early Spaniards arrived at the end of the eighteenth century they found among the peoples of the coast the most sophisticated native American culture north of the valley of Mexico. Yet British Columbia was then, and still remains, a thinly populated land, with even today a good deal less than three million inhabitants—not even three per square kilometre. Half of these live in and around the two main cities. Get out of the towns, and British Columbia still seems an almost empty land where the forests and the mountains and the great lakes cupped in their folds and the vast rivers cutting through their walls are dominant, filling the eye, filling the space.

These great natural features, the forest, the mountains and the sea, provide the means for the primary industries out of which British Columbia's prosperity has grown. But they themselves are mainly uninhabitable, and apart from a small amount of dryland plateau like the Cariboo and Chilcotin region, all they have left for British Columbians to live in are the narrow valleys and the river deltas and the offshore islands. These are the only areas that are fertile or flat enough to be cultivable, though some of the small farming areas, like the fruit-growing valley of the Okanagan and the dairy country of the Lower Mainland, are among the richest parts of the province. Many British Columbians live scattered in small logging or mining towns and even smaller farming and ranching villages that have sprung up wherever a cultivator can gain a toehold or a hundred cattle can graze or a prospector can find something to tear from the surface or mine from the interior of the earth.

Perhaps the tendency to live separated from each other in steep valleys and pockets of farm land separated by mountain barriers is one of the reasons why there are so many varied types of people to be encountered in British Columbia, though the history of the province, with its gold rushes and other migrations, has a great deal to do with it. The Indian cowboys of the Cariboo have little in common with the God-intoxicated Russian Doukhobors in the Kootenays; the Chinese, who came to work on the railways and stayed to become a major element in Vancouver's population, come from an entirely different culture from the Sikhs of India who dominate much of the timber industry; it would be hard to find a greater contrast than exists between the remnants of English gentility that survive in parts of Vancouver Island and the tough loggers and miners with their traditions of labour militancy inherited from the Wobbly agitators who moved through the province early in the century. If these people have anything in common it is a strongly developed individualism that the mountain barriers between them have perhaps exaggerated. They have a paradoxical collective image of themselves as loners in a world of loners. The traditions of Man against the Wilderness were developed in early days among the first Europeans to reach the province: the prospectors and hand loggers, the settlers in remote valleys and the fishermen risking their lives single-handed in small gill-netters. These traditions linger among their descendants, even when they have become city men, and are even acquired by those who came over the mountains only a few years ago. Indeed, the prevalent individualism, and the fractionable kind of society it produces, are enhanced by the sheer variety of minority cultures that have been transplanted here from Europe and Asia or have survived and come alive again from the past, like those of the native Indians.

This British Columbian individualism goes far beyond differences in lifestyles. As surveys and polls repeatedly show, the province's inhabitants are more distrustful of established authority than are other Canadians. They are the most politically volatile people in the country, the despair of nationally organized mass parties, always inclined to put their support behind populist local leaders, like John Oliver and Duff Patullo, like W. A. C. Bennett and Dave Barrett, who seem to reflect their own sense of difference from the rest of the country.

The sheer magnitude of the province's natural features impresses the land upon the minds of British Columbians, but their sense of involvement in the natural environment—which emerges in their writings—is deepened by the dependency of so many of them on the raw materials it produces to support the basic industries. This has given the province an economy plagued by booms and depressions; it has also saved the landscape from the worst effects of manufacturing industry, while the mountains and forests that provide work and a daily living also offer an endless variety of challenges to those who in their leisure time wish to pit their endurance against the land's demands or merely to enjoy its easily accessible beauties, the beauties of a region where so many vistas end in a snow peak.

Such a contact between man and land assumes many aspects—the economic, the athletic, the poetic. Out of it comes experience and understanding, enjoyment and celebration. And it is to the celebration of British Columbia that this book is devoted, a celebration that is both visual and verbal.

The visual element is provided by the work of one of Canada's finest contemporary photographers, Janis Kraulis, who offers a wonderful collection of images of the province in all its moods and aspects: the extremities of its seasons and settings, the intimacies where people and land relate to each other. These photographs project the face of the province as a sensitive observer looks into it at this moment in time. Yet that very moment, the images tell us, extends into the past that leaves around us the relics which tell how rapidly the land has passed from the Late Stone Age which Captain Cook encountered in Nootka Sound two centuries ago into the Nuclear Age.

In no way are these photographs meant to serve as direct illustrations of anything that appears in the text. When Janis Kraulis and I met to discuss the book, we agreed to go our separate ways, and to accept as fortunate but perhaps natural any correspondences that might emerge between the photographs and the writing. I suspect a better unity has resulted from this strategy, since both of us were going directly to source—he to the images the land presented and I to the human reactions to it—and we end by offering each other—as well as our readers—the discoveries we have made. Such free offering is in the true spirit of celebration.

People have been writing about British Columbia ever since the first European explorers came by sea and land. They were the first literate men in the country, but even before them other men were expressing their contact with the land in myths and stories passed from mouth to ear during the long centuries when the Indian peoples—the Haida and the Kwakiutl, the Tsimshian and the Nootka and the Salish—developed their splendid traditions of ritual and art. Some of these stories find their place in my selection.

The writing I offer demonstrates the richness and variety literature in British Columbia has acquired over the province's two centuries in history. The earliest pieces are narratives of experience: what travellers by sea and land encountered and saw; what the less fortunate, like Maquinna's captive John R. Jewitt, endured. None of these writers uses the arts of invention; the virtue of their accounts lies in descriptive directness, a transparency of prose that preserves experience like a mammoth in ice. Sometimes—with Fraser, Thompson, Vancouver—I have let great travellers speak the history they made. Elsewhere, if the classic accounts seemed too familiar, I have proceeded less directly, telling of Cook's arrival at Nootka Sound, for example, through the narrative of the marine John Ledyard, a minor actor but a shrewd observer, and letting a twentieth-century poet, Roy Daniells, narrate the story of Mackenzie's descent of the Bella Coola Valley to the saltwater edge of the Pacific. Other modern writers have used the factual narratives of the early travellers, but when poets like George Bowering and Charles Lillard give us their versions of the feats of Vancouver and Fraser in this volume, they are obviously not merely retelling a past moment in history. They are taking history into the world of the imagination and transforming it into literary art.

Two of the most interesting writers in this collection were also artists of another kind. When the painter Paul Kane travelled with the fur traders across Canada in the 1840s to observe the Indian life of the Pacific coast, and when his great successor Emily Carr travelled around British Columbia almost a century later in search of paintable scenes, they left vivid accounts of their adventures. Their writings show them trying to grapple verbally as well as visually with a country where travel was hard but which it was just as difficult—because of its very scale and strangeness—to fit into artistic form, particularly if one's training had been in the traditions of long-settled countries. Writers shared such problems in coping imaginatively with the land, and very little poetry showing a real empathy with the environment was written before Earle Birney's mountain verses began to appear in the late 1930s and early 1940s, dates which are not very far from Emily Carr's.

Thus British Columbia went through the usual literary evolution of a pioneer society growing to maturity. At first, when the sheer practical problems of gaining a foothold in the wilderness were uppermost, narrative and descriptive writing which rendered experience rather literally was the dominant and most successful mode, just as most of the better early visual art tended to be topographical and informational. Even a novel about logging like Allerdale Grainger's *Woodsmen of the West*, appearing as late as 1908, had this descriptive and didactic quality.

Only after men and women had been living in British Columbia for a generation or two, and had come to accept the land and feel accepted by it, did the other, imaginative approach become important. A recognizably local voice began to speak of the land in tones that emerged from a true sense of place and of the meaning of a past that all at once we started to see as history. Then writers began to emerge in growing numbers, both native-born British Columbians and those who came from other parts of Canada and from other countries to live between the mountains and the ocean, or—sometimes—merely to see and depart and then write about what they had seen.

My selection shows the variety of forms in which writers have projected their experience of British Columbia and their imaginative interpretation of it. There are chapters from novels; part of a radio play; fragments of history and of travel narrative; short stories and much verse, for British Columbia has been especially attractive to poets. The great number and variety of British Columbian writers is represented by the fifty and more included here, but the richness and range of their work are only suggested. A number of excellent writers who have worked in British Columbia are not here, because what they have written has not fitted the intent of this collection, essentially concerned with writing that celebrates the land and man as its inhabitant.

The two parts of the book reflect my sense of the two currents of writing that exist in British Columbia. One is writing that links us to our past, our history, because it either describes or in some way reflects particular historic events, like the arrival of explorers or the coming of gold miners or the completion of the transcontinental railway, or, alternatively, gives us the sense of a continuity of existence that stems back to the primal encounter with the land, as many of the poems do.

The second current is the writing that emerges in a settled society like that of modern British Columbia in which many traditions have mingled. There is more of a social element in such writing, more concern for manners and mores, though it does not exclude the individual experience, the privileged insight. We are made aware of the small societies that combine to create the mosaic of British Columbian life: the villages of hunting and fishing Indians and of visionary Doukhobors; the Chinese and Japanese who form such a large part of the coastal population and notably affect its lifestyle; the occupational fraternities of loggers and miners and fishermen; the remotenesses outside society where hunters and prospectors follow their special obsessions; the lost peaceful villages on the edge of the wilderness that history has walked over and left to the old; the dreaming, summer-obsessed lotus land of the Gulf Islands with its Edenic serpents; the violence and beauty of the cities on the edge of the ocean, as they are evoked in Birney's monumental poem, "November Walk near False Creek Mouth," and in Ethel Wilson's moving and terrible story, "Fog."

It is all there—the darkness and the light, the endlessly varied beauty of the settings, the hardness of the land, and the energy it has provoked in men and women who have sought, perhaps not to conquer it, which is well nigh impossible, but to come to terms with it, to understand it not only with their reasons but also with their imaginations. Such imaginative understanding is what we mean by celebration.

George Woodcock

Flowering dogwoods along Stamp River, Stamp Falls Provincial Park.

Rocky headland, northern end of Vancouver Island.

At Owen Point along the West Coast Trail in Pacific Rim National Park.

Above timberline on Nub Peak, Mount Assiniboine Provincial Park.

Rainbow and Columbia River Valley south from Parson.

Alpine larch in autumn at Floe Lake, Kootenay National Park.

Tidal zone at Camper Creek, Pacific Rim National Park.

Moss above timberline on Mount Cautley, with Mount Assiniboine in the distance,
Mount Assiniboine Provincial Park.

Backpacking above Heckman Pass in Tweedsmuir Provincial Park.

Aerial view of the icefields around Mount Garibaldi.

Wedgemount Lake above morning clouds, Garibaldi Provincial Park.

Aspen forest above the Kiskatinaw River, south of the Peace River near Rolla.

Harvested hay and field near Canoe Creek in the canyon of the Fraser River.

Wildflowers below Thunder Lake in Manning Provincial Park.

Oak tree in Galiano Bluffs Park, Galiano Island.

PART ONE
Time in Its Place

Totem and carved facade, Thunderbird Park, Victoria.

From *Out of the Silence*
Bill Reid

At most there were probably no more than a hundred thousand people, scattered along a thousand miles of coastline—ten thousand miles more likely—if bays and promontories and islands were measured. Isolated in clusters of a few hundred each, miles from their nearest neighbours, cut off by dense jungles, by stormy seas for most of the year, by five separate language groups, and hundreds of distinct dialects, and by suspicions and animosities that often separated them more than the elements.

What can a few people do, except cling to a marginal existence?

And yet—one of these clusters was Tanu. It wasn't even a single political entity, but two villages separated by only a few yards.

It knew no law beyond custom, no history beyond legend, no political unit larger than the family, no government beyond an informal meeting of family heads, plus the tacit acceptance of the superiority of the ranking chief.

At the height of its influence, it had less than a thousand people, living in about twenty-five houses.

But if the wooden structures of Tanu had survived the hundred years of north coast weather since the last of its survivors left, its ruins would rival man's greatest achievements. Tanu may have been the crowning gem of West Coast material culture. Some old memories still recall its artists and builders as the best, and old photographs show something of its glory. But it was only one of dozens of proud citadels—Kaisun, Kiusta, Squonquai, Skidegate, Massett, Kitwancool, Kispiox, Gitsixukla, Kitwanga, Kincolith, Kasaan, Klukwan, Bella Bella, Bella Coola, Koskimo, Quatsino, Nootka, and many more.

In each village were great houses some seventy feet by fifty feet of clear roof span, with gracefully fluted posts and beams. In the houses there was wealth—not gold or precious stones—but treasures that only great traditions, talent, and sometimes genius, with unlimited time and devotion, can create.

There were treasures in profusion—thousands of masks, painted and carved chests, rattles, dishes, utensils of all kinds, ceremonial regalia—all carefully stored or proudly displayed during the great feasts and winter ceremonies.

The people of the Northwest coast were rich, their sea even richer; they were enormously energetic, and they centred their society around what was to them the essence of life: what we now call "art".

Old people can still tell "How it was" when, by boat, they rounded a point of land and entered a sheltered bay to find a village of large houses and totem poles facing the sea.

Like heraldic crests, these poles told of the mythological beginnings of the great families, at a time before time, when animals and mythic beasts and men lived as equals, and all that was to be was established by the play of raven and eagle, bear and wolf, frog and beaver, thunderbird and whale.

The poles were many things. The house pole told of the lineage of the chief who presided within. The memorial pole commemorated some great event. The grave pole contained the body and displayed the crest of a leading noble.

In many of the great houses, massive figures—illuminated by firelight—supported the roof beams.

Each pole contained the essential spirit of the individual or family it commemorated, as well as the spirit of the artist who made it, and, by an extension, the living essence of the whole people. While the people lived, the poles lived, and long after their culture died, the poles continued to radiate a terrible vitality that only decay and destruction could end.

Even trapped in the stairwells of museums, truncated and dismembered in storage sheds, or lying in shattered fragments in now vanished villages they once glorified, the contained power—born of magic origins and the genius of their creators—still survives. All things must die, and great art must be a living thing, or it is not art at all.

These monuments were the work of master carvers and apprentices who brought to final perfection an art style whose origins lay deep in the past and partly in Asia.

It was an austere, sophisticated art. Its prevailing mood was classical control, yet it characterized even the simplest objects of daily life. These sea-going hunters took the entire environment as art form.

That effort is now wholly past. Even memory of it fades.

Already the forest has reclaimed the tiny clearings men once maintained along the twisting walls of this stormy coast.

Only a handful of poles now stand, or more frequently lie, in the damp, lush forests.

Like the fallen trees they lie beside, they have become the life-blood of younger trees growing from their trunks.

In a scene subdued by a magnificent moss covering and by silence, they return to the forest that gave them birth.

With Captain Cook in Nootka Sound

John Ledyard

On the 7th of March we fell in with the coast of America...
a little below Cape Blanco, and tracing it northerly until the
28th we entered an inlet in 49°N. From the 7th to the 28th
we had the ruggedest weather we had yet experienced. The
weather was cold, the gales of wind were successive and strong,
and sometimes very violent. Our ships complained. We were
short of water and had an unknown coast to explore. And the
very day we purposed to reconnoitre for a harbour, the wind
veered to the N.E. and forced us off the coast a full week. We
entered this inlet about 4 o'clock in the afternoon. The
extremes of the opening at the entrance were about 2 miles
distant and we had the prospect of a snug harbour. It was a
matter of doubt with many of us whether we should find any
inhabitants here, but we had scarcely entered the inlet before
we saw that hardy, that intriped, that glorious creature man
approaching us from the shore. As we advanced into the inlet
we found it still more favorable, and perceived several small
islands between the two shores. Night approaching we came to
an anchor between one of those islands and the eastern shore
about a quarter of a mile from each. In the evening we were
visited by several canoes full of the natives; they came abreast
our ship within two rods of us and there staid the whole night,
without offering to approach nearer or to withdraw farther
from us, neither would they converse with us. At the approach
of day they departed in the same reserve and silence.

On the 30th we sent our boats to examine a small cove in
the opposite island, which answering our wishes we moved
with both ships into it and moored within a few yards of the
surrounding beach.

This inlet proving to be a sound was called George's Sound
[Nootka Sound]. It lies in lat. 49.33. N. and in 233.16. E. long.
and as it afforded excellent timber we furnished ourselves with
a new mizen-mast, spare yards and other spars, besides wood.
It also afforded us excellent water, a variety of good fish and
the shores with some excellent plants. The country round this
sound is generally high and mountainous, though further to
the northward and eastward it appears more open and level. It
is intirely covered with woods, such as maple, ash, birch, oak,
hemlock, but mostly with tall well grown pine. We also found
currant bushes, wild rasberry and juniper bushes, and little
crabed apple-trees, but could not learn whether they bore any
fruit, neither is it probable they do. We saw no plantations or
any appearance that exhibited any knowledge of the
cultivation of the earth, all seemed to remain in a state of
nature; but as our observations did not extend three miles into

the country they are imperfect. Neither did we explore the
sound higher up than three leagues, as that satisfied us that it
was of no great extent beyond. The light in which this country
will appear most to advantage respects the variety of its
animals, and the richness of their furr. They have foxes, sables,
hares, marmosets, ermines, weazles, bears, wolves, deer,
moose, dogs, otters, beavers, and a species of weazle called the
glutton; the skin of this animal is sold at Kamchatka, a
Russian factory on the Asiatic coast for sixty rubles, which is
near 12 guineas, and had it been sold in China it would have
been worth 30 guineas. We purchased while here about 1500
beaver, besides other skins, but took none but the best, having
no thoughts at that time of using them to any other advantage
than converting them to the purposes of cloathing, but it
afterwards happened that skins which did not cost the
purchaser sixpence sterling sold in China for 100 dollars.
Neither did we purchase a quarter part of the beaver and other
furrskins we might have done, and most certainly should have
done had we known of meeting the opportunity of disposing of
them to such an astonishing profit.

On the 1st of April we were visited by a number of natives
in their boats, which resemble our batteaux: They are about
20 feet in length, contracted at each end, and about 3 feet
broad in the middle, and 2 feet and a half deep from end to
end: They are made from large pine-trees, and we suppose
burnt out....

I had no sooner beheld these Americans than I set them
down for the same kind of people that inhabit the opposite
side of the continent. They are rather above the middle
stature, copper-coloured, and of an athletic make. They have
long black hair, which they generally wear in a club on the top
of the head, they fill it when dressed with oil, paint and the
downe of birds. They also paint their faces with red, blue and
white colour, but from whence they had them or how they
were prepared they would not inform us, nor could we tell.
Their cloathing generally consists of skins, but they have two
other sorts of garments, the one is made of the inner rind of
some sort of bark twisted and united together like the woof of
our coarse cloths, the other very strongly resembles the New-
Zealand Togo, and is also principally made with the hair of
their dogs, which are mostly white, and of the domestic kind:
Upon this garment is displayed very naturally the manner of
their catching the whale—we saw nothing so well done by a
savage in our travels. Their garments of all kinds are worn
mantle-wise, and the borders of them are fringed or
terminated with some particular kind of ornament like it:
Their richest skins when converted to garments are edged with
a great curiosity. This is nothing less than the very species of
wampum so well known on the opposite side of the continent:
It is identically the same and this wampum was not only found
among all the aborigenes we saw on this side the continent,

but even exists unmutilated on the opposite coasts of North-Asia. We saw them make use of no coverings to their feet or legs, and it was seldom they covered their heads: When they did it was with a kind of basket covering made after the manner and form of the Chinese and Chinese-Tartar hats. Their language is very guttural, and if it was possible to reduce it to our orthography would very much abound with consonants.

In their manners they resemble the other aborigenes of North-America, they are bold and ferocious, sly and reserved, not easily provoked but revengeful; we saw no signs of religion or worship among them, and if they sacrifice it is to the God of liberty.

When a party was sent to procure some grass for our cattle they would not suffer them to take a blade of it without payment, nor had we a mast or yard without an acknowledgment. They intimated to us that the country all round further than we could see was theirs. Water and wood they charged us nothing for. Capt. Cook would not credit this fact when he first heard it and went in person to be assured of it, and persisting in a more peremptory tone in his demands, one of the Indians took him by the arm and thrust him from him, pointing the way for him to go about his business. Cook was struck with astonishment, and turning to his people with a smile mixed with admiration exclaimed, "This is an American indeed!" and instantly offered this brave man what he thought proper to take; after which the Indian took him and his men to his dwelling and offered them such as he had to eat. This characteristic of theirs and having found but one instance of theft among them set these people high in Cook's opinion. The houses we saw near this cove appeared to be only temporary residences from whence it was supposed that in winter they retired into the interior forests, and in summer lived any where that best answered the purposes of fishing and hunting.

The food we saw them use consisted solely of dried fish and blubber oil, the best by far that any man among us had ever seen: this they put into skins. We purchased great quantities of it, and situated as we were with respect to butter or suet, it was a very good succedaneum to either, and was constantly used to fry with; besides it furnished our lamps, and answered many other purposes useful and necessary. Like all uncivilized men they are hospitable, and the first boat that visited us in the Cove brought us what no doubt they thought the greatest possible regalia, and offered it to us to eat; this was a human arm roasted. I have heard it remarked that human flesh is the most delicious, and therefore tasted a bit, and so did many others without swallowing the meat or the juices, but either my conscience or my taste rendered it very odious to me.

We intimated to our hosts that what we had tasted was bad, and expressed as well as we could our disapprobation of eating it on account of its being part of a man like ourselves. They seemed to be sensible by the contortions of our faces that our feelings were disgusted, and apparently paddled off with equal dissatisfaction and disappointment themselves. We were complimented once before in the same stile, at our first discovery of Sandwich-Islands. . . .

These people are possessed of a variety of impliments calculated for war, hunting, fishing and other purposes, some of which are remarkably analogous to ancient models, particularly the lance, which is every way similar to that used in ancient tournaments and feats of chivalry. They have also a kind of armour that covers the body from the breast downward to the knees; this consists of moose-skin, covered externally with slips of wood sewed to the leather transversely, and made short or long as best suits the part of the body it covers. They have also good bows and arrows, and stone hatchets; also a variety of snares both for fowl and quadrupedes. Their fishing gear is highly curious. I can give no adequate description of the variety and singularity of these matters: They have near a dozen different kinds of fish-hooks, and all made of wood, but was an European to see any of them without any previous information of their design, he would as soon conclude they were intended to catch men as fish. They have a harpoon made from a mushel shell only, and yet they have so disposed of it as to subdue the great leviathan, and tow the unweildy monster to their shores. . . .

We found a few copper bracelets and three or four rough wrought knives with coarse wooden hafts among the natives at this place, but could not learn from the appearance of either of those articles or from any information they could give us how they became possessed of them, but it was generally thought they came from a great distance and not unlikely from Hudson's-Bay. Commerce is defusive and nothing will impede its progress among the uninformed part of mankind, but an intervention of too remote a communication by water, and as this cannot be the case with regard to the inhabitants of a continent, it seems intirely conclusive to suppose no part of America is without some sort of commercial intercourse, immediate or remote.

On the 26th of April we towed out of the sound in a calm, about sun down we were favored with a breeze that gave us a tolerable offing, but before 12 at night the wind veered from N.N.W. and E.S.E. and was succeeded by a sudden and impetuous gale that threw us into the utmost confusion from its unexpected approach and our unprepared situation to receive it. This gale continued with very little intermission until the 1st of May, when it abated and we had fair weather. We parted company with our consort the Discovery the first night and concluded from our own distresses some irreparable misfortune had attended her. We lay to on that account the greatest part of the time, and she adopting the same plan occasioned our meeting again two days before the gale entirely subsided. This gale was very severe, and was the means of opening a defective place in the Resolution's bottom, which was of an alarming nature. We did not meet with an opportunity of repairing it untill some time after, when we found that the complaint originated from a hole eat through the bottom of the ship as far as the sheathing by the rats, and the sheathing being old gave way when the ship strained; we were surprized to find the apperture stoped up by some old shakings of yarns and oakum, that by some accident was washed into it.

We continued our course, after this the coast tending about N.W. until the 10th of May being then in Lat. 59°. 33 N. and Long. 217. 23 E. without any particular occurrence.

Pacific Door
Earle Birney

Through or over the deathless feud
of the cobra sea and the mongoose wind
you must fare to reach us.
Through hiss and throttle come,
by a limbo of motion humbled,
under cliffs of cloud
and over the shark's blue home.
Across the undulations of this slate
long pain and sweating courage chalked
such names as glimmer yet.
Drake's crewmen scribbled here their paradise
and dying Bering, lost in fog,
turned north to mark us off from Asia still.
Here cool Cook traced in sudden blood his final bay
and scurvied traders trailed the wakes of yesterday
until the otter rocks were bare
and all the tribal feathers plucked.
Here Spaniards and Vancouver's boatmen scrawled
the problem that is ours and yours,
that there is no clear Strait of Anian
to lead us easy back to Europe,
that men are isled in ocean or in ice
and only joined by long endeavour to be joined.
Come then on the waves of desire that well forever
and think no more than you must
of the simple inhuman truth of this emptiness,
that down deep below the lowest pulsing primal cell
tar-dark and still
lie the bleak and forever capacious tombs of the sea.

Three Indian Tales
Franz Boas
(Translated by Dietrich Bertz)

K·ōmō′k·oa, Rich One
(Bella Bella)

Four young men went out in their boat to hunt seals. They stayed out over night and dropped anchor at the foot of a mountain. The anchor-stone fell straight onto the roof of K·ōmō′k·oa's house, whereupon he sent his slave, the Shark, to find out who was there. Shark climbed up along the anchor rope and made a great noise in order to frighten the people away. The four men were kept awake by the noise, so they caught the Shark, cut off his fins and threw him back into the water. He wept, swam back to his master and cried, "There are four men up there who have thus mutilated me!" K·ōmō′k·oa said that they were going to get them down when they were fast asleep. And he did what he had said. Soon one of the men woke up and noticed at once that he was in an unknown country. He thought that he was dreaming and bit his hand in order to wake up. Then he roused the others and they discovered that they were right in front of K·ōmō′k·oa's house. He gave orders for them to be invited in and sat down beside them and said, "You shall stay with me for four days and become my brothers." Then he invited all the people for a great feast. But an old woman, Mouse, warned the young men not to eat of the food, else they would never reach the upper world again. And she told them to beware of the sea monster Hā′nak·atsē. So two of the men went out and coated their canoe with a magic substance so that Hā′nak·atsē would be unable to devour it. K·ōmō′k·oa asked his guests, "Don't you have any mountain goat fat?" They gave him a little, which he divided into four parts and threw into the four corners of his house which filled up with mountain goat fat at once. Then the noise of the arriving guests could be heard. All the fish came and also chief Yāēqoē′ok·oa who makes the tides. The house filled with water and a huge whirlpool formed which nearly capsized the canoe. The door of K·ōmō′k·oa's room opened and closed like jaws and slurped up all the water. Every time their boat came close to the door, the men flung poison into the water and thus escaped safely. This door was the monster Hā′nak·atsē. At long last the men fell asleep and when they woke up again, they found themselves back at the surface of the water. K·ōmō′k·oa had ordered four Killer Whales to bring them back, who filled their canoe with seals. They thought that they had been with him for only four days, but in reality it had been four years. Their anchor-stone and anchor-rope were covered all over with seaweed. They brought it on shore with them and this is how all the seaweed originates.

K·asā′na
(Bella Coola)

Once upon a time there was a man called K·asā′na who consisted of only half a body. He had only one leg, one arm, half a trunk, and half a head. He had his house in Kiltē′itl and always caught many mountain goats. He carved himself a wife from a tree-stump, made a hat for her and called her K·ulɛ′ms. He carved her in a squatting position and arranged her arms so that it appeared as if she were weaving a blanket. Then he placed her in front of a loom and put a blanket in her hands. He intended to deceive the people and make them believe that he had a wife. In K·inā′at, near Tsainahat, not far from TǪōnik (Bella Bella), there lived a chief in those days who had two daughters. He sent them across the mountain to Kiltē′itl, having said to them, "K·asā′na has no wife, he will marry you." They obeyed and reached K·asā′na's house just when he was out hunting. So they peeped in through a knot-hole in the wall to see if anyone was inside and to their surprise saw the woman sitting at her loom. What amazed them even more was that she made no movement at all. They went into the house, the younger sister fearfully hiding behind the older girl. When they now saw that the woman took no notice of them at all, they nudged her, and when she paid no attention to this either, they grasped her by the chin and noticed that she was made of wood. They tore off her hat and pushed her over, then hid. When K·asā′na came home and found the woman toppled over, he grew angry and beat her, shouting, "If you can't sit still I have no use for you." At this one of the girls couldn't help laughing. K·asā′na found them and took both of them for his wives. Some time afterwards they both had children and so the women wished to return home. K·asā′na was willing to go with them, so they all embarked in his canoe, journeyed to K·inā′at, and on the way the children played flutes.

The Frog Woman
(Haida)

Once upon a time there were ten young men who went out to fish for salmon. Nine of them went ashore to fish while the tenth remained as guard in the canoe. While sitting there he looked down into the water in order to pass the time, when his hat, which was painted with cormorant designs, fell repeatedly into the water. He grew angry, cursed the water, and beat it with his hat. After some time his nine friends returned laden with many salmon and they roasted them. All at once they saw a great Frog hopping towards the fire. They cursed it and flicked it away with a stick. But in a short while they saw it coming back, so they threw it into the fire. They were amazed when it didn't burn up but only became red-hot. At last it

burst and scattered the burning logs. The men heaped them up again, but the Frog soon burst once more and again scattered the logs. This happened a third and a fourth time. By then the salmon had been roasted; they ate them and returned home. While paddling along the shore they saw a completely red man running along the beach. This was Frog. He called to them but they only mocked him. So the Frog Man grew angry at last and called, "You shall all die one after the other once you've reached yonder headland! Only one of you shall stay alive to recount your fate at home, then he shall also die." The young men kept on mocking but when they reached the headland one of them dropped dead and everything happened as foretold by Frog. Only the steersman reached land and he had scarcely told what had befallen them when he also fell down dead. The people were very sad and cursed Frog. The following day they observed the glow of a huge fire on the mountains. It appeared to come closer day by day. But still they continued to curse Frog, calling, "Why don't you burn our village?" On the sixth day the glow could be seen on the sea, the water began to boil and soon the village was ablaze and all the villagers lost their lives.

While all this was happening, a girl who had just reached womanhood was secluded in a small hut as demanded by custom. When the fire approached, she dug a pit and hid in it. The fire consumed the whole village and also her hut, but she remained unhurt. Some time afterwards Frog visited the village in the shape of an old woman wearing a huge hat painted all over with frogs. She called herself Tlkyānk·'ostā′n k'uns (Frog Woman). She was very, very old and supported herself on a stick. When she saw what she had done she cried sadly. She extended her finger and moved it about in a circle, then smelled it. She repeated this motion and then walked straight up to the girl's hiding-place, calling, "Come out, I have scented you!" When the girl came out, she told her that she was Frog, that the young men had thrown her into the fire, and that she had destroyed the village and killed all its inhabitants in revenge. She took pity on the girl and led her into the forest.

On the Rocks in Queen Charlotte Sound

George Vancouver

By this expedition, the continental shore was traced to the westernmost land in sight. We had now only to proceed along it, as soon as the wind and weather would permit our moving. This, however, a thick fog and a calm, prevented, until Sunday afternoon, when a light breeze between S.W. and west, enabled us, by sun-set, to advance about 2 leagues to the westward of point Boyles, which, by compass, bore from us S.85 W.; an island, previously considered to lie in mid-channel, but now discovered to be divided into four or more islets, S.38 E.; the more distant part of the opposite shore south, 4 or 5 leagues off; and the nearest taken by us to an island, W.S.W. about a league. These positions are not, however, to be received as correct, because the fog, still continuing, alternately obscured place after place, in the southern quarters, so as to render it impracticable, either to acquire the true position, or even to gain a distant view of those shores. The northern, or continental side, was not in the like manner, obscured; its nearest part bore by compass north about half a league from us; and its western extremity N.78 W. Between this point and a cluster of islands, bearing west, a channel appeared to lead along the coast of the main land, in which were some small islets and rocks; south of the cluster, the haze and fog rendered it impossible to determine of what that region principally consisted, though the imperfect view we obtained, gave it the appearance of being much broken. In this situation, we had 60 and 70 fathoms, muddy bottom; but, as we had sufficient space to pass the night in under sail, I preferred so doing, that we might be the more ready to pursue the above-mentioned channel in the morning.

The wind continuing light in the S.W. quarter, we plied until day-break, when the breeze was succeeded by a calm and a very thick fog that obscured every surrounding object until noon, without our being able to gain soundings; so that we were left to the mercy of the currents, in a situation that could not fail to occasion the most anxious solicitude. The fog had no sooner dispersed, than we found ourselves in the channel for which I had intended to steer, interspersed with numerous rocky inlets and rocks, extending from the above cluster of islands towards the shore of the continent. The region to the S.W. still remained obscured by the fog and haze; at intervals, however, something of it might be discerned, serving only to shew there was no great probability of our finding a less intricate passage to navigate, than that immediately before us along the continental shore; which must either be now traced by the ship, or by the boats on a future occasion. This made me determine on the former mode, although there was reason to apprehend it would engage our utmost attention, even in fair weather, to preserve us from latent dangers. The dispersion of the fog was attended by a light breeze from the N.N.W., and as we stood to windward, we suddenly grounded on a bed of sunken rocks about four in the afternoon. A signal indicating our situation was immediately made to the Chatham, she instantly anchored in 50 fathoms water, about a cable and a half distant from us, and we immediately received all her boats to our assistance. The stream anchor was carried out, and an attempt made to heave the ship off, but to no effect. The tide fell very rapidly; and the force with which the ship had grounded, had occasioned her sewing considerably forward. On heaving the anchor came home, so that we had no resource left but that of getting down our topmasts, yards, &c. &c. shoaring up the vessel with spars and spare topmasts, and lightening her as much as possible, by starting the water, throwing overboard our fuel and part of the ballast we had taken on board in the spring. Soon after the ship was aground, the tide took her on the starboard quarter; and as she was afloat abaft it caused her to take a sudden swing, and made her heel so very considerably on the starboard side, which was from the rocks, that her situation, for a few seconds, was alarming in the highest degree. The shoars were got over with all possible dispatch, but notwithstanding this, by the time it was low water, the starboard main chains were within three inches of the surface of the sea. Happily, at this time, there was not the smallest swell or agitation, although we were in the immediate vicinity of the ocean. This must ever be regarded as a very providential circumstance, and was highly favorable to our very irksome and unpleasant situation, which under the persuasion of the tide falling as low as had been lately observed in our several boat expeditions, nothing short of immediate and inevitable destruction presented itself, until towards the latter part of the ebb tide, when more than one half of the ship was supported by such a sufficient body of water, as, in a great measure, to relieve us from the painful anxiety that so distressing a circumstance necessarily occasioned. When the tide was at the lowest, about nine at night, the ship's fore foot was only in about $3^1/_2$ feet water, whilst her stern was in 4 fathoms.

In this melancholy situation, we remained, expecting relief from the returning flood, which to our inexpressible joy was at length announced by the floating of the shoars, a happy indication of the ship righting. Our exertions to lighten her were, however, unabated, until about two in the morning; when the ship becoming nearly upright, we hove on the stern cable, and, without any particular efforts, or much strain, had the undescribable satisfaction of feeling her again afloat, without having received the least apparent injury. We brought up in 35 fathoms water, about a quarter of a mile from the bed of rocks from whence we had so providentially escaped. After about three hours rest, all hands were employed in the re-equipment of the ship. The main top-gallant top-rope unluckily broke, and by this accident, John Turner, a seaman, had his arm unfortunately fractured. By noon, the hold was re-stowed, and the ship, in every respect, ready again to proceed.

A light breeze springing up from the S.W. about one o'clock, we were again under sail, and knowing of no safer channel, we directed our course through that before us, along the continental shore. This was a narrow passage, and as we advanced, became more intricate by an increased number of rocky islets and rocks, as well beneath, as above the surface of the water; the former being ascertained by the surf breaking with some violence upon them. This dangerous navigation seemed to continue as far as discernible towards the ocean, between the shore of the continent and the land forming the opposite side of the channel, which appeared to be an extensive range of islands.

Having so recently been preserved from the dangers of a most perilous situation, the scene before us, in presenting a prospect of many such snares, was extremely discouraging. We had, however, not the least hope of finding a less difficult way for the execution of the adventurous service in which we were engaged; nor any alternative but to proceed with all the possible circumspection and caution that the nature of our situation would permit, through a channel not more than half a mile wide, bounded on one side by islands, rocks, and breakers, which in some places appeared almost to meet the continental shore on the other. However intricate, this apparently was the only navigable channel in the neighbour-hood. About five in the afternoon we had fortunately escaped through its narrowest part; the wind now became light and baffling; the ebb tide sat us towards the ocean, where we now had a view of the distant horizon, although intercepted by the same rocky region that surrounded us in every direction. About six o'clock some of its hidden dangers arrested the progress of the Chatham. We instantly anchored in 70 fathoms water, and sent our boats to her assistance. Thus, before we had recovered from the fatiguing exertions and anxious solicitude of one distressing night, the endurance of a similar calamity was our portion for the next.

I had less reason at first to hope for the preservation of the Chatham under the circumstances of her disaster, than I had the preceding night for that of the Discovery; as the oceanic swell was here very perceptible, and caused a considerable surf on the shore. On the return of our small boat, I became acquainted that, in consequence of its having fallen calm, she had been driven by the tide on a ledge of sunken rocks, but had the consolation of hearing, that although she had frequently struck when lifted by the surge, it had not been violently; that no damage had yet been sustained; and that her

present very uncomfortable situation could not be of long duration, as it was nearly half ebb when she grounded.

Our present anchorage bore by compass from the rocks, on which the Discovery had struck, though intercepted by various others, S.42 E. 5 miles, and from the ledge of rocks on which the Chatham was then lying, S.61 E. 3 miles distant. Our estimated latitude was 51°2′, longitude 232°25′. Since the commencement of the month of august, the foggy weather had totally precluded our making any celestial observations; the situation therefore of the islands, coasts, rocks, &c. westward from Deep Sea bluff, could only be ascertained by an estimated protraction, which may be liable to errors we had no means to detect; hence this portion of intricate navigation is not to be implicitly depended upon in this particular, as exhibited by the chart; but the continued direction of the continental shore, (the nearest part now bearing by compass N.E. at the distance of about half a league) was positively ascertained to this station: and I trust, its latitude and longitude will not be found to deviate many miles from the truth.

The rocks between our present anchorage and the ocean having the appearance of being almost impenetrable, Mr. Whidbey was dispatched to discover the most safe channel for us to pursue. The day-light just served him to execute his commission; and on his return at night he informed me, that there were three passages; one nearly through the center of the rocks; another about midway between the continental shore, and a very broken country to the southward of us; and a third between the nearest cluster of rocks and the continent. This for a small distance seemed to be clear; but further to the north-westward a labyrinth of rocks appeared to stretch from the continent towards land, forming like two islands. These rocks nearly joined to the north-easternmost about 9 miles from us, bearing by compass N.50 W., the westernmost at about the same distance, N.64 W.

The nearest cluster of rocks, whose southern part was almost in a line with the easternmost island, not quite a league from us, we were to pass to the south of; between them and other rocks and rocky islets, to the westward and S.W., forming a channel about two miles wide, in which no visible obstruction had been discovered by Mr. Whidbey. These rocks and rocky islets presented an appearance of being as nearly connected with the southern broken shore, as those further north did with the continent, giving us little to expect but a very intricate and hazardous navigation.

An extremely thick fog ushering in the morning of the 8th, precluded our seeing or knowing any thing of the Chatham's situation; and obliged us to remain in the most painful state of suspense until about nine in the forenoon, when the fog in some measure dispersing, we had the satisfaction of seeing our consort approaching us under sail; and having a light southerly breeze, with the ebb tide in our favor, we immediately weighed in order to proceed together through the channel before mentioned between the rocks.

On the return of the boats, lieutenant Baker, who had been with our people assisting the Chatham during the night, informed me that latterly she had struck so hard, as intirely to disable both the spare topmasts, which had been used for shoars; but that about half past one they succeeded in heaving her off, without the appearance of her having sustained any very material damage. Our sails were scarcely set when the wind became variable; and soon after mid-day partial fogs and a clear atmosphere succeeded each other in every direction. These by one o'clock obliged us to anchor again in 55 fathoms water, as did the Chatham about 2 miles to the northward of our former station, and within a quarter of a mile of the continental shore. Here we were detained until nine the following morning, when with a light eastwardly breeze, and clear weather, we directed our course as before stated. On passing near the rocks on the eastern side of the channel, we had soundings at the depth of 28 fathoms, rocky bottom; but immediately afterwards gained no ground with 60 and 70 fathoms of line. As it was my intention to seek a channel between the two islands, the Chatham's signal was made to lead. The wind being light we advanced slowly, passing some very dangerous rocks, whose situation was only to be known by the breakers upon them at low tide, lying about 2 miles to the S.E. of the north-easternmost island.

Though clear immediately overhead, the horizon was encumbered with partial fogs in every direction. This rendered the view of surrounding objects not less limited than undefined, and prevented such observations being made, as were necessary for ascertaining our positive situation. About noon we were becalmed between these islands, whose shores were about two miles and a half asunder; soundings were obtained at the depth of 70 fathoms, rocky bottom. They lie from each other about north and south; the southernmost is about a league in circuit, with a small island lying off its eastern extremity. The northernmost, instead of being one island, as had been supposed, was now found to comprehend eight or nine small islets, lying in a direction about N.50 W. and occupying in that line an extent of four miles; their breadth about half, or perhaps three quarters of a mile. With the assistance of the boats a-head, we passed through this channel about one o'clock. At this time a light breeze springing up from the north-westward, we stood towards the southern shore; it was not, however, as was usual with the north-westerly winds, attended with clear and pleasant weather, but with a remarkably thick fog; and having no soundings we were obliged to ply to windward under an easy sail until about five o'clock, when we gained bottom and anchored in 55 fathoms water. The fog soon after cleared

away, and discovered our situation to be near the southern shore, before a small opening at the distance of about a mile. This by compass bore S.7 W.; a channel that appeared to stretch to the S.E. through the range of islands to the southward of that we had navigated, bore S.80 E. and seemed tolerably clear of those dangers and impediments with which we had lately contended. The southernmost of the islands we had passed at noon bore by compass N.7 E. at the distance of about a league, and the north-westernmost of the islets, N.8 W. distant about 2 leagues; a low point of land forming the south point of an opening on the continental shore N.14 W. a high distant mountain being the northernmost land in sight N.30 W. and the westernmost land on the southern shore S.55 W. Between these latter directions the oceanic horizon seemed perfectly clear and uninterrupted.

We now appeared to have reached the part of the coast that had been visited and named by several of the traders from Europe and India. The Experiment, commanded by Mr. S. Wedgborough, in august, honored the inlet through which we had lately passed, with the name of "QUEEN CHARLOTTE'S SOUND"; the opening on the continental shore was discovered, and called "SMITH'S INLET", by Mr. James Hanna, the same year; the high distant mountain that appeared to be separated from the main land, formed part of a cluster named by Mr. Duncan "CALVERT'S ISLANDS"; and the channel between them and the mainland, was by Mr. Hanna called "FITZHUGH'S SOUND." These being the names given, so far as I could learn, by the first discoverers of this part of the coast, will be continued by me, and adopted in my charts and journal.

Lure
Susan Musgrave

Earth place
Water place

Deep
Red
Overhanging mountain

Old fish-slaughter at
Root-Baking Place.

Half-fish
Land-locked salmon

Drift pile
Green
Gravelly river.

Cracked rocks in the
Old fish-cache.

Earth place
Other place

The fish die
The water is too deep.

Blood
Dark
Falling-Away Mountain

Fish-eye feeds the
White bird

Lay bones around his heart.

Chief Jammisit's Dance

Jacinto Caamano
(Translated by Harold Grenfell)

He [Jammisit], together with his nearest relatives, arrived in one of two canoes lashed alongside each other. Jammisit's head appeared from behind a screen formed of brilliantly white deerskin; on it according as the action demanded or his own particular fancy dictated, he would place various masks or heads of the different animals that he proposed to imitate; the deerskin serving as a curtain by which he was entirely hidden when he wished, unseen, to put on or change one of these masks or faces. They remained alongside thus for some time, singing and continuing their antics, until Jammisit with great eagerness explained that he had come to conduct me to his village . . .

[*Caamano agrees and as he gets into his cutter the canoes race to Jammisit's village to make preparations.*]

By the time we in the cutter reached the strand, there were already six lusty natives carrying a very clean deerskin awaiting me on the beach. These at once dashed into the water up to the waist alongside our boat, making signs to me to sit on the skin to be carried ashore on their shoulders. . . .

The moment that I placed myself on the deerskin these six fellows hoisted my 150 lb. carcass on to their shoulders and carried me at a run across the shingle and up the pretty steep slope leading from it to the village, whither they brought me at a surprising speed. To pass through the narrow doorway of the chief's house, over which was painted a huge mask, it was necessary to make a litter or hammock of the deerskin. Two of the strongest of the Indians did this, with the other four assisting as best they could, while I was shrinking myself into as small a compass as possible (though my bearers were careful enough) to avoid being bumped against the door posts. Once inside, I tried to get to my feet, but this they would not allow before bringing me to the place prepared for my seat, which was to the right of the entrance. The seat was formed of a case or chest, raised higher than those for the others, fitted for only one person, and covered with a new mat; while a similar one was spread before it. The seats for my officers, ranged on either hand of mine, were made in a similar manner; those for my men, were formed of mats spread on the floor. . . . By this time, the whole native company, amounting to about eighty people of both sexes, was arranged on the floor. Jammisit, his three wives, and grown family, were in front. Myself, with all my officers and men, were on the right, and only women were allowed behind us. On the left were the remainder from Jammisit's village, and those from that of Gitejon. In this situation, then, Jammisit began to emit piercing howls in a pitiful key; after which, throwing back his head as if about to

faint, he sat down, clutching at the collar laces of his cloak, as if wishing to throw it off. Several of his family nearby, who were watching to give him any help that might be necessary, when they noticed this, gathered around him forming a screen so that he might not be seen changing his garments in which some of the others were assisting him.

So soon as he had put on those in which he was to show himself, they would break up and sit down out of his way, leaving only a couple of his nearest relations standing by ready to help him as he might require. When he was ready, these also left him and the actor arose.

On his head was a large well-imitated representation of a seagull's head, made of wood and coloured blue and pink, with eyes fashioned out of polished tin; while from behind his back stuck out a wooden frame covered in blue cloth, and decked out with quantities of eagles' feathers and bits of whale bone, to complete the representation of the bird. His cloak was now of white calico, bearing a blue flowered pattern, trimmed with a brown edging. Round his waist hung a deerskin apron falling to below the knee, whose fringe or flounce was made from narrow strips of the same leather, every one being split into two tails, each of which carried half the hoof of a deer. Over this kilt or apron he wore another, shorter one, of bluejean ornamented with numerous metal buttons arranged symmetrically, and two rows of antelope hide pendants or tassels, each finished off with an eagle's claw. On his legs were deer skin leggings, tied behind with four laces, ornamented with painted masks and trimmed with strips of hide bearing claws. Clad in this weird rattling rig, he then began to leap and cut capers, reminding one of a rope dancer trying his rope. He also waved his arms, keeping them low down. . . . After two or three preliminary attempts, he started a song. This was at once taken up by every one inside the house, man or woman, and produced a terrific volume of sound, to whose measure he then began to dance, while a specially chosen Indian beat the time on a large drum.

[*Jammisit dances until he appears exhausted, retires behind a hide screen, and later emerges "with a half-length wooden doll on his head."*]

Two Indians at some distance behind him, who endeavoured to conceal their actions, then proceeded—by means of long fishing rods—to open and close the eyes of the doll, and raise its hands, in time to another tune that was struck up, while the dancer himself imitated the movements of the doll's face, which was sufficiently frightful in appearance, being coloured black and red, and furnished with an owl's beak and nostrils. For this scene, he wore a bear skin cloak, with the remainder of his costume as before. So soon as the music ceased, his attendants again hid him from sight. Before long, however, he again appeared, this time wearing a heavy wooden mask on his head, of which the snout, or upper jaw, was moveable.

From *George, Vancouver: a discovery poem*

George Bowering

The soft air of the inland sea
& heavy spray in the dark spruce
offer no grail, it was no grail
he was after, he was not
sailing with that kind of purity.

He stopt to dine on the silver plates
of the Spanish, Quadra saw no
Celt there, but Vancouver, the reformed
Dutchman, a young sailor
with an appetite.

        As the sea
for its archipelago, wooded islands,
barks with yards wet in the rain,
appetite awakened early, for the
whole world. He sailed
seven days against the tide
thru drifting weed, sputum
of land birds.

        Totem poles
falling in the rain, like Spaniards
in the south, never seen by
land eyes, carry no sail,
the coal underneath, no human bones,
Asiatic footsteps melted into the
Japanese current, gone home, as
Vancouver, to die early,
to be passed over in favour
of another man, another voyager,
but always re-encountered
in the names, Japanese & lonely.

    . . . .

That far south
this far north
there is no winter.

The current we rested on
moved us without wind.

They say
the Strait of Anian
leads to Scotland snow.

A cold
dream.

Here the rains
nourish maidens' bellies
such as Huklyt never felt,

& flowers, here
where no weed grows,
what we will call

epigaea repens
for fancy,
lately called science.

    . . . .

If we could invite the fog
of the Japanese current
& sail the map in their heads
we may be in Hudson's Bay
tomorrow.

        But the rocks,
        white snow fields,
        the wet trees,
        there are empires
        to discover as to map

But that is conjecture
& there are orders
I take & give.

The sea
does the same.

    . . . .

Let us say
This is as far as I, George,
have travelled.

the line
obscured still, the coast
I mean, toucht, sighted,
mapt to some extent,
the islands
noted.

Now on this side, east,
it is that much,
water, pines, the Spanish
& their names, the savages
on the edge of the water.

I have seen some
of what lies in the mind,
the fancy of the British king
gone like fish odour
into the life-giving fog of that coast.

A Walk at Cape Mudge

George Vancouver

In this route we passed through the assemblage of islands and rocks lying at some distance before the entrance into Desolation sound; some of which presented an appearance infinitely more grateful than that of the interior country. These were mostly of a moderate height from the sea, tolerably well wooded, and the shores not wholly composed of rugged rocks, afforded some small bays bounded by sandy beaches. The wind continued light from the northern quarter, and the weather being serene and pleasant, made a most agreeable change. Numberless whales enjoying the season, were playing about the ship in every direction; as were also several seals; the latter had been seen in great abundance during our residence in Desolation sound, and in all the remote excursions of our boats, but they were so extremely watchful and shy, that not one could be taken. These animals seem to have had the exclusive possession of the gloomy region we had just quitted; but the scene now before us was more congenial to our minds, not only from the different aspect of the shores, but from the attention of the friendly Indians, who as we were crossing the gulph, visited us in several canoes, with young birds, mostly sea fowl, fish, and some berries, to barter for our trinkets and other commodities. Soon after mid-day we anchored about half a mile to the northward of point Mudge at 37 fathoms water, on a bottom of black sand and mud. A very strong flood tide came from the northward, and although nearly convinced that our conjectures were right, the launch and cutter with lieutenant Puget and Mr. Whidbey, were immediately dispatched to examine the channel as to its communication with Johnstone's straits; that in the event of there being any obstructions where such rapid tides were running, we might have sufficient notice, and be prepared to avoid them.

From the village situated on point Mudge, we were visited by several of the natives, who brought fish and the wild fruits of their country, which they exchanged for our European articles, in a very fair and honest manner.

After dinner, accompanied by Mr. Menzies and some of the officers, I went on shore to return the visit of our friends, and to indulge our curiosity. On landing at the village, which is situated a little to the N.W. within the promontory, and nearly at the summit of a steep sandy cliff, we were received by a man who appeared to be the chief of the party. He approached us alone, seemingly with a degree of formality, though with the utmost confidence in his own security, whilst the rest of the society, apparently numerous, were arranged and seated in the most peaceful manner before their houses. I made him such presents as seemed not only to please him excessively, but to confirm him in the good opinion with which he was prepossessed; and he immediately conducted us up to the village by a very narrow path winding diagonally up the cliff, estimated by us to be about a hundred feet in height, and within a few degrees of being perpendicular. Close to the edge of this precipice stood the village, the houses of which were built after the fashion of Nootka, though smaller, not exceeding ten or twelve feet in height, nearly close together in rows, separated by a narrow passage sufficiently wide only for one person. On the beach, at the foot of the cliff, were about seventy canoes of small dimensions, though amongst them were some that would carry at least fifteen persons with great convenience. On a computation, therefore, deduced from these and other circumstances, we were led to consider that this village, though occupying a very small space, could not contain less than three hundred persons. The spot where it was erected appeared to be well chosen to insure its protection; the steep loose sandy precipice secured it in front, and its rear was defended by a deep chasm in the rocks; beyond these was a thick and nearly impenetrable forest: so that the only means of access was by the narrow path we had ascended, which could easily be maintained against very superior numbers. Having gratified our curiosity, and, in return for the cordial attention of these friendly people, made our acknowledgments by presents of such trivial articles as we had about us, we took our leave of the village for the purpose of indulging ourselves before dark, with a refreshing walk, on a low margin of land extending from the more elevated woodland country, some distance along the water-side to the northward; a luxury we had not for some time experienced. In this excursion, which was extremely grateful and pleasant, we saw two sepulchres built of plank about five feet in height, seven in length, and four in breadth. These boards were curiously perforated at the ends and sides, and the tops covered with loose pieces of plank, as if for the purpose of admitting as great a circulation of air as possible to the human bones they enclosed, which were evidently the relics of many different bodies. A few of the Indians attended us in our walk, picking the berries from the trees as we passed, and with much civility presenting them to us on green leaves. The evening approaching obliged us to return on board, against a very strong ebb tide.

Indian Graveyard, Vancouver Island

Robin Skelton

for Rona Murray

The island is a ghost.
Through greys of rain
it humps its black whale;
fathoms of belief
uncountable as years
accept its flank,
and pull the spinning
emptiness of grief
through deep to darker deep;
here, daubed and clad
with every symbolism,
heads roped high
to outstare sunlight
with their flies, the dead
were bound in trees:
years back, men came this way
to look things over,
curious; they found
no human corpses;
not a thought remained
of all the rotting gauds,
but on the ground
and unexplained, dead birds,
whole hosts of birds.

Massacre at Nootka Sound

John R. Jewitt

In this manner, with a fair wind and easy weather from the 28th of December, the period of our passing Cape Horn, we pursued our voyage to the northward until the 12th of March, 1803, when we made Woody Point in Nootka Sound, on the North-West coast of America. We immediately stood up the Sound for Nootka, where Captain Salter had determined to stop, in order to supply the ship with wood and water before proceeding up the coast to trade. But in order to avoid the risk of any molestation or interruption to his men from the Indians while thus employed, he proceeded with the ship about five miles to the northward of the village, which is situated on Friendly Cove, and sent out his chief mate with several of the crew in the boat to find a good place for anchoring her. After sounding for some time, they returned with information that they had discovered a secure place for anchorage, on the western side of an inlet or small bay, at about half a mile from the coast, near a small island which protected it from the sea, and where there was plenty of wood and excellent water. The ship accordingly came to anchor in this place, at twelve o'clock at night, in twelve fathom water, muddy bottom, and so near the shore that to prevent the ship from winding we secured her by a hawser to the trees.

On the morning of the next day, the 13th, several of the natives came on board in a canoe from the village of Nootka, with their king, called Maquina, who appeared much pleased on seeing us, and with great seeming cordiality welcomed Captain Salter and his officers to his country. As I had never before beheld a savage of any nation, it may readily be supposed that the novelty of their appearance, so different from any people that I had hitherto seen, excited in me strong feelings of surprise and curiosity. I was, however, particularly struck with the looks of their king, who was a man of a dignified aspect, about six feet in height and extremely straight and well proportioned; his features were in general good, and his face was rendered remarkable by a large Roman nose, a very uncommon form of feature among these people; his complexion was of a dark copper hue, though his face, legs, and arms were, on this occasion, so covered with red paint, that their natural colour could scarcely be perceived; his eyebrows were painted black in two broad stripes like a new moon, and his long black hair, which shone with oil, was fastened in a bunch on the top of his head and strewed or powdered all over with white down, which gave him a most curious and extraordinary appearance. He was dressed in a large mantle or cloak of the black sea-otter skin, which reached to his knees, and was fastened around his middle by a broad belt of the cloth of the country, wrought or painted with figures of several colours; this dress was by no means unbecoming, but, on the contrary, had an air of savage magnificence. His men were habited in mantles of the same cloth, which is made from the bark of a tree, and has some resemblance to straw matting; these are nearly square, and have two holes in the upper part large enough to admit the arms; they reach as low as the knees, and are fastened round their bodies with a belt about four inches broad of the same cloth.

From his having frequently visited the English and American ships that traded to the coast, Maquina had learned the signification of a number of English words, and in general could make himself pretty well understood by us in our own language. He was always the first to go on board such ships as came to Nootka, which he was much pleased in visiting, even when he had no trade to offer, as he always received some small present, and was in general extremely well treated by the commanders. He remained on board of us for some time, during which the captain took him into the cabin and treated him with a glass of rum—these people being very fond of distilled spirits—and some biscuit and molasses, which they prefer to any kind of food that we can offer them.

As there are seldom many furs to be purchased at this place, and it was not fully the season, Captain Salter had put in here not so much with an expectation of trading, as to procure an ample stock of wood and water for the supply of the ship on the coast, thinking it more prudent to take it on board at Nootka, from the generally friendly disposition of the people, than to endanger the safety of his men in sending them on shore for that purpose among the more ferocious natives of the north.

With this view, we immediately set about getting our water-casks in readiness, and the next and two succeeding days, part of the crew were sent on shore to cut pine timber, and assist the carpenter in making it into yards and spars for the ship, while those on board were employed in refitting the rigging, repairing the sails, etc., when we proceeded to take in our wood and water as expeditiously as possible, during which time I kept myself busily employed in repairing the muskets, making knives, tomaxes, etc., and doing such ironwork as was wanted for the ship.

Meantime more or less of the natives came on board of us daily, bringing with them fresh salmon, with which they supplied us in great plenty, receiving in return some trifling articles. Captain Salter was always very particular, before admitting these people on board, to see that they had no arms about them, by obliging them indiscriminately to throw off their garments, so that he felt perfectly secure from any attack.

On the 15th the king came on board with several of his chiefs; he was dressed as before in his magnificent otter-skin robe, having his face highly painted, and his hair tossed with the white down, which looked like snow. His chiefs were dressed in mantles of the country cloth of its natural colour, which is a pale yellow; these were ornamented with a broad border, painted or wrought in figures of several colours, representing men's heads, various animals, etc., and secured around them by a belt like that of the king, from which it was distinguished only by being narrower: the dress of the common people is of the same fashion, and differs from that of the chiefs in being of a coarser texture, and painted red, of one uniform colour.

Captain Salter invited Maquina and his chiefs to dine with him, and it was curious to see how these people (when they eat) seat themselves (in their country fashion, upon our chairs) with their feet under them crossed like Turks. They cannot endure the taste of salt, and the only thing they would eat with us was the ship bread, which they were very fond of, especially when dipped in molasses; they had also a great liking for tea and coffee when well sweetened. As iron weapons and tools of almost every kind are in much request among them, whenever they came on board they were always very attentive to me, crowding around me at the forge, as if to see in what manner I did my work, and in this way became quite familiar, a circumstance, as will be seen in the end, of great importance to me. The salmon which they brought us furnished a most delicious treat to men who for a long time had lived wholly on salt provisions, excepting such few sea fish as we had the good fortune occasionally to take. We indeed feasted most luxuriously, and flattered ourselves that we should not want while on the coast for plenty of fresh provisions, little imagining the fate that awaited us, and that this dainty food was to prove the unfortunate lure to our destruction!

On the 19th the king came again on board, and was invited by the captain to dine with him. He had much conversation with Captain Salter, and informed him that there were plenty of wild ducks and geese near Friendly Cove, on which the captain made him a present of a double-barrelled fowling-piece, with which he appeared to be greatly pleased, and soon after went on shore.

On the 20th we were nearly ready for our departure having taken in what wood and water we were in want of.

The next day Maquina came on board with nine pair of wild ducks, as a present; at the same time he brought with him the gun, one of the locks of which he had broken, telling the captain that it was *peshak*, that is, bad. Captain Salter was very much offended at this observation, and, considering it as a mark of contempt for his present, he called the king a liar, adding other opprobrious terms, and, taking the gun from him, tossed it indignantly into the cabin, and, calling me to him, said, "John, this fellow has broken this beautiful fowling-piece, see if you can mend it." On examining it, I told him that it could be done. As I have already observed, Maquina knew a number of English words, and unfortunately understood but too well the meaning of the reproachful terms that the captain addressed to him. He said not a word in reply, but his countenance sufficiently expressed the rage he felt, though he exerted himself to suppress it, and I observed him, while the captain was speaking, repeatedly put his hand to his throat, and rub it upon his bosom, which he afterwards told me was to keep down his heart, which was rising into his throat and choking him. He soon after went on shore with his men evidently much discomposed.

On the morning of the 22nd the natives came off to us as usual with salmon, and remained on board; when about noon Maquina came alongside, with a considerable number of his chiefs and men in their canoes, who, after going through the customary examination, were admitted into the ship. He had a whistle in his hand, and over his face a very ugly mask of wood, representing the head of some wild beast, appeared to be remarkably good-humoured and gay, and whilst his people sang and capered about the deck, entertaining us with a variety of antic trick and gestures, he blew his whistle to a kind of tune which seemed to regulate their motions. As Captain Salter was walking on the quarter-deck, amusing himself with their dancing, the king came up to him and inquired when he intended to go to sea? He answered, "To-morrow." Maquina then said, "You love salmon—much in Friendly Cove, why not go there and catch some?" The captain thought that it would be very desirable to have a good supply of these fish for the voyage, and, on consulting with Mr. Delouisa, it was agreed to send part of the crew on shore after dinner with the seine, in order to procure a quantity. Maquina and his chiefs stayed and dined on board, and after dinner the chief mate went off with nine men in the jolly-boat and yawl, to fish at Friendly Cove, having set the steward on shore at our watering place, to wash the captain's clothes.

Shortly after the departure of the boats, I went down to my vice-bench in the steerage, where I was employed in cleaning muskets. I had not been there more than an hour, when I heard the men hoisting in the longboat, which, in a few minutes after, was succeeded by a great bustle and confusion on deck. I immediately ran up the steerage stairs, but scarcely was my head above deck, when I was caught by the hair by one of the savages, and lifted from my feet; fortunately for me, my hair being short, and the ribbon with which it was tied slipping, I fell from his hold into the steerage. As I was falling he struck at me with an axe, which cut a deep gash in my forehead, and penetrated the skull, but in consequence of his losing his hold I luckily escaped the full force of the blow, which otherwise would have cleft my head in two. I fell, stunned and senseless, upon the floor; how long I continued in this situation I know not, but on recovering my senses, the

first thing that I did was to try to get up, but so weak was I, from the loss of blood, that I fainted and fell. I was, however, soon recalled to my recollection by three loud shouts or yells from the savages, which convinced me that they had got possession of the ship. It is impossible for me to describe my feelings at this terrific sound. Some faint idea may be formed of them by those who have known what is it to half waken from a hideous dream and still think it real. Never, no, never shall I lose from my mind the impression of that dreadful moment. I expected every instant to share the wretched fate of my unfortunate companions, and when I heard the song of triumph, by which these infernal yells was succeeded, my blood ran cold in my veins.

Having at length sufficiently recovered my senses to look around me, after wiping the blood from my eyes, I saw that the hatch of the steerage was shut. This was done, as I afterwards discovered, by order of Maquina, who, on seeing the savage strike at me with the axe, told him not to hurt me, for that I was the armourer, and would be useful to them in repairing their arms; while at the same time, to prevent any of his men from injuring me, he had the hatch closed. But to me this circumstance wore a very different appearance, for I thought that these barbarians had only prolonged my life in order to deprive me of it by the most cruel tortures.

I remained in this horrid state of suspense for a very long time, when at length the hatch was opened, and Maquina, calling me by name, ordered me to come up. I groped my way up as well as I was able, being almost blinded with the blood that flowed from my wound, and so weak as with difficulty to walk. The king, on perceiving my situation, ordered one of his men to bring a pot of water to wash the blood from my face, which having done, I was able to see distinctly with one of my eyes, but the other was so swollen from my wound, that it was closed. But what a terrific spectacle met my eyes: six naked savages, standing in a circle around me, covered with the blood of my murdered comrades, with their daggers uplifted in their hands, prepared to strike. I now thought my last moment had come, and recommended my soul to my Maker.

The king, who, as I have already observed, knew enough of English to make himself understood, entered the circle, and, placing himself before me, addressed me nearly in the following words: "John—I speak—you no say no; You say no — daggers come!" He then asked me if I would be his slave during my life—if I would fight for him in his battles, if I would repair his muskets and make daggers and knives for him—with several other questions, to all of which I was careful to answer, yes. He then told me that he would spare my life, and ordered me to kiss his hands and feet to show my submission to him, which I did. In the meantime his people were very clamorous to have me put to death, so that there should be none of us left to tell our story to our countrymen, and prevent them from coming to trade with them; but the king in the most determined manner opposed their wishes, and to his favour am I wholly indebted for my being yet among the living.

As I was busy at work at the time of the attack, I was without my coat, and what with the coldness of the weather, my feebleness from loss of blood, the pain of my wound, and the extreme agitation and terror that I still felt, I shook like a leaf, which the king observing, went into the cabin, and, bringing up a greatcoat that belonged to the captain, threw it over my shoulders, telling me to drink some rum from a bottle which he handed me, at the same time giving me to understand that it would be good for me, and keep me from trembling as I did. I took a draught of it, after which, taking me by the hand, he led me to the quarter-deck, where the most horrid sight presented itself that ever my eyes witnessed. The heads of our unfortunate captain and his crew, to the number of twenty-five, were all arranged in a line, and Maquina, ordering one of his people to bring a head, asked me whose it was: I answered, the captain's. In like manner the others were showed me, and I told him the names, excepting a few that were so horribly mangled that I was not able to recognise them.

I now discovered that all our unfortunate crew had been massacred, and learned that, after getting possession of the ship, the savages had broke open the arm-chest and magazine, and, supplying themselves with ammunition and arms, sent a party on shore to attack our men, who had gone thither to fish, and, being joined by numbers from the village, without difficulty overpowered and murdered them, and, cutting off their heads, brought them on board, after throwing their bodies into the sea. On looking upon the deck, I saw it entirely covered with the blood of my poor comrades, whose throats had been cut with their own jack-knives, the savages having seized the opportunity, while they were busy in hoisting in the boat, to grapple with them, and overpower them by their numbers; in the scuffle the captain was thrown overboard, and despatched by those in the canoes, who immediately cut off his head. What I felt on this occasion, may be more readily conceived than expressed.

After I had answered his questions, Maquina took my silk handkerchief from my neck and bound it around my head, placing over the wound a leaf of tobacco, of which we had a quantity on board. This was done at my desire, as I had often found, from personal experience, the benefit of this application to cuts.

Maquina then ordered me to get the ship under weigh for Friendly Cove. This I did by cutting the cables, and sending some of the natives aloft to loose the sails, which they performed in a very bungling manner. But they succeeded so far in loosing the jib and top-sails, that, with the advantage of fair wind, I succeeded in getting the ship into the Cove, where, by order of the king, I ran her ashore on a sandy beach.

The Myth of the Man Who Changed His Face
(A Cowichan Indian story)
Charles Hill-Tout

There was once a young man who fell in love with a maiden, but she repulsed him, telling him he was not handsome enough for her. This grieved and hurt him, and he went to his grandmother to learn how he might improve his looks. The old woman instructs him in this wise. "Take some deer fat and red paint and go into the forest and follow the trail to the prairie beyond. In the centre of this prairie you will see a column of smoke rising. Go towards this and you will presently come to a lodge. This is the house of the Face-maker; he will give you a new face for your old one if you ask him." The young man set out to seek the home of the Face-maker, and after many days' travel arrived at the edge of the prairie his grandmother had spoken of. It was about mid-day. He sees the smoke in the distance and makes towards it. When he gets close to the spot, he perceives that the smoke is coming out of a small hole in the ground. He looks down the hole and his body casts a shadow below. Within the underground house was a man, who when he saw the shadow cried out: "Hep, hep, hep!" He thought it was a cloud passing over. The youth looks down a second time and again darkens the interior. "That's a strange cloud," thinks the man, and looks upward and perceives his visitor. "Hullo! is that you?" he calls out. "Come down." The youth begins to climb down. The floor seemed far below him, but as soon as his feet were inside, the floor came up to meet him. The old man now asks him what he has brought. Said he, "I have this fat." "What else have you got?" "I have also this red paint." "All right," said the old man, "give them to me and choose your face."

The youth looked round the place at all the faces but found none to his liking. Said he, "I don't like any of these I see; haven't you some more?" The old man then opened a chest and offered its contents to his visitor. Said he, "I don't like any of these either." The old man opened the last chest, in which he kept his best faces, saying as he did so, "How will these suit you?" The young man saw amongst them a face that pleased him, and said, "I will take this one." The Face-maker now removed the youth's own head and replaced it with the one he had chosen. When this was accomplished he instructed the youth thus: "When you return to your own country, be careful to keep away from yonder mountain. A witch woman lives there, who devours everyone she gets within her clutches. No one ever escapes her if they go near her abode. Her name is Zoholats; be careful of her."

Now the young man was a great runner, and he despised the advice of the Face-maker and went near the mountain trusting to his fleetness of foot to save him if the witch sought to seize him. As he passed he heard a voice say, "Come back to me, my husband." He looked behind and saw a monstrous woman as tall as a tree coming after him. He took to his heels, but in a few strides she caught up with him and seized him by his belt, his feet dangling on one side and his head on the other. Thus she carried him to her dwelling. Now she kept as slave a handsome young woman, whom she had caught, and as she entered she said to her, "Tcietqen, look at my new husband; isn't he a fine young man?" The youth sought every opportunity to escape but found none. Every night he slept between her huge breasts, and if he tried to steal away she awoke in an instant and grasped and placed him in his place again. She kissed and fondled him for a while and then after her manner swallowed him whole. Now it was his turn to be avenged, and he took her heart in his hands, and squeezed it till she cried and rolled in agony.

Not knowing the cause of her pain, she sent for all the animals to come and try and heal her. She asks of them: "Which of you is the best doctor?" Blue-jay, who was a *seuwa*, claimed the distinction. He sang his medicine-song over her, but as she got no better he remarked to the others, "I don't think we can cure her; I think she will die." Smokwa the Crane said, "Here, let me try what I can do. All of you beat time to my song with your sticks." "All right," said Crow, the spokesman of the crowd. The Crane then put his long bill into the stomach of the witch, which, the young man perceiving, he caught hold of and firmly held. The Crane tried to withdraw his bill and struggled with all his might. Presently the youth let go, and the Crane fell back with such force that he turned a complete somersault. He knocked all the breath out of his body and lay on the ground a moment to recover. Said first one and then another, "How was it Crane could not pull out his bill? It can't be just a sickness. I believe there is somebody inside of her." All this time the witch is crying and rolling with the pain, and presently she expires. The slave woman now says to the people, "Cut her open, there is a man inside of her." They cut her open, and the young man comes forth alive.

The woman now takes possession of all the witch's property, which was immense. With the help of the young man she makes a raft and places all the property upon it, and together they float down the river to the salt water, where the father of the young man lived. The latter had been missed and all his friends had wondered where he had gone, and were now much astonished to see him return with a handsome young wife and a raft full of property. When the maiden whom he had formerly wooed saw him, and how handsome he had grown, she desired now to become his wife. But he rejects her in the same manner as she had rejected him, and tells her she is not handsome enough for him. She learns now how he had got his handsome face, and determines to go and get hers changed. She accordingly set out and in due time arrived at the Face-maker's home and requested him to change her face. He did so, but gave her a head with a frightful countenance, so that she became hideous in the extreme. Thus was she punished for the rejection of her lover.

Source
Robin Skelton

Somewhere back of my days
there is a river

shovelling stones
down slopes of sliding rock,

licking and lashing
the red stems of alder,

turning over and over
its every thought

in a perpetual
solitary passion.

High in the hills it is:
none has been there

for centuries perhaps
or perhaps ever,

yet I know it
back of all my days,

shining, shivering,
rushing steel and silver,

waiting for my star
to lead me on

to see it, feel it
for the first, last time,

and climb up through the trees
into the cavern.

Alexander Mackenzie Reaches the Pacific

Roy Daniells

Next day they went through a pass, walking on hard, drifted snow, directed by local Indians who told them that the river flowing into salt water, which they were seeking, was not far off. A storm of hail, snow and rain drove them for shelter to leeward of a huge rock. The hunters now brought in a small caribou but at this altitude and in this exposed position only a few crowberry bushes, not yet in blossom, and some stunted willows could be seen. Shivering they plodded on and in due course found wood, roasted their meat and were able to shave and change their clothes beside the comfort of a fire.

Ahead of them was a peak in the Coast Range, now known as Stupendous Mountain, from Mackenzie's own phrase: 'Before us appeared a stupendous mountain, whose snow-clad summit was lost in the clouds; between it and our immediate course flowed the river to which we were going.' Into the valley, which opened to their view as they went on, they began to descend, by a series of precipices covered with pine, spruce, hemlock, birch and other trees, their great size testifying to the rainfall. As they came down to the floor of the valley, cedars and alders appeared, larger than any Mackenzie had ever seen. He was in a quite different climate now and the berries on the bushes were ripe.

As darkness fell, their guides having gone ahead, they were obliged to feel their way through the dense woods but Mackenzie was determined to push on toward a village they had seen from above. At last they reached it and were soon being entertained, with fine hospitality, in a great house, raised on posts and reached by a broad timber cut with steps. Mats were placed before Mackenzie and Mackay and each was given a roasted salmon. The men received half a salmon each. To avoid inconvenience to his hosts, Mackenzie decided to sleep with his men outside. A fire was lit for them and boards placed for them to lie on. Two large dishes of creamed salmon roes flavoured with fruit and herbs were produced. Amid this warmth of hospitality, Mackenzie relaxed. 'I never enjoyed a more sound and refreshing rest, though I had a board for my bed, and a billet for my pillow.' The Indians were Bella Coolas.

In the morning, he was shown a weir which had been built into the river to lead the salmon into traps. It was ingeniously constructed and a great deal of labour had gone into laying down the alternate rows of logs and layers of gravel of which it was composed. The salmon and all that concerned taking them were regarded with great reverence. With meat the natives would have nothing to do, saying that the salmon would smell it and abandon them. Mackenzie's men had some

caribou meat with them. A dog who swallowed a bit of the bone was beaten till he disgorged it. Another bone was thrown into the river, only to be retrieved by a native, who dived in, brought it out and burned it, then washed his hands to remove all taint. . . .

At noon Mackenzie took an observation which gave 52° 28′11″ North latitude. Since the voyage began he had taken dozens of observations for latitude or longitude, often under very difficult conditions. Sometimes the terrain itself had defeated him, when he could establish no horizon, and once he had forgotten to wind his chronometer.

At one o'clock they embarked with their small baggage in two canoes, accompanied by seven of the natives, whose skill in handling their craft surpassed even that of the voyageurs themselves.

After two and a half hours they landed and came on foot to a village where, after a tumultuous reception, they were led to a house, larger and better built than anything they had yet seen. Here they were fed on roasted salmon and, as a great delicacy, cakes made of the dried inner rind of the hemlock tree which their hosts soaked in water, shredded and sprinkled with sweet oil.

The habits and customs of these Bella Coolas aroused Mackenzie's interest; he recognized that he was in the midst of a culture quite unknown to Canadian fur traders. The salmon were running and two Indians, out fishing, came in with their large canoe filled; some of the fish weighed as much as forty pounds. Unfortunately, Mackenzie had no one with him who could speak the language of the Bella Coolas, but many things can be understood through signs and it was clear that not even his kettle could be dipped in the river for fear of disturbing the fish, who 'dislike the smell of iron.'

Some of the dwellings, sheathed with boards and bark, were over a hundred feet long and forty feet in breadth. Each could contain several hearths; for partitions cedar planks were employed. The smoke found its way out through holes near the ridge pole and light came in the same way.

Painted figures on cedar panels and poles carved with animal crests or totems met Mackenzie's eye. Admiring the skill of these red and black formalized shapes and 'hieroglyphics', he assumed they had a religious significance.

Though they had an abundant and assured food supply, from their position on a salmon river, and although, in building, weaving and carving, they seemed to show civilized skill unknown to the hunting peoples, yet in some matters these coast Indians were merely barbarous. One of the chief's sons was dying of malignant ulcers and Mackenzie was asked to give him some medicine. The native doctors were blowing on him, whistling, poking his stomach, putting their fingers into his mouth and spouting water through their lips into his face. They ended by carrying him into the woods, lighting a fire, and scarifying and cauterizing his ulcer so that Mackenzie, unable to bear the sight, had to leave.

In this village there were many signs of trade with white men. Spear points, arrow heads and personal ornaments were often of brass or copper. There was bar iron to make axes. There were poniards and daggers, some with Spanish coins inlaid in their handles.

When Mackenzie produced his sextant to take an altitude, he was warned not to do so and finally understood that the salmon would be frightened and might leave the river. As one would expect, he managed, nevertheless, to determine his latitude as 52° 25′ 52″. It was clear, also, that he was approaching salt water. By signs he was told that, about ten winters ago, the chief and forty of his people had taken the great cedar canoe—painted black, decorated with white figures of fish and inlaid on the gunwales with sea-otter teeth—and had paddled off toward the midday sun. They had seen two large vessels filled with men like Mackenzie, who received them kindly. These ships were quite likely Captain Cook's *Resolution* and *Discovery*.

Cook had lost his life in the Hawaiian Islands in a dispute over a theft. A similar situation, common to many explorations, now confronted Mackenzie. As his party was about to leave the village, one of their axes was missing. Mackenzie appealed to the chief, who would not understand him. He then sat on a stone, with his gun, and made it appear that he would stay there till the axe returned. The village went into an uproar and it seemed possible the party would be attacked. The axe, however, appeared from under the chief's canoe and they left soon afterwards in a large craft with four of the village Indians. Mackenzie's comment on the lost axe is illuminating. 'Though this instrument was not in itself of sufficient value to justify a dispute with these people, I apprehended that the suffering them to keep it, after we had declared its loss, might have occasioned the loss of every thing we carried with us, and of our lives also. My people were dissatisfied with me at the moment; but I thought myself right then, and I think now, that the circumstances in which we were involved, justified the measure which I adopted.'

They went down the rapid current, stopping at some settlements and being obliged to shoot a cascade, and in the evening reached a village near the mouth of the river on the south bank. They ate the remains of their last meal, as no fish could be got from the natives in this place, and they slept in an empty house.

Next morning, 20 July, after some trouble about guides, they got off at an early hour and, about eight o'clock, reached salt water from the Pacific. They saw great numbers of 'sea-otters', perhaps seals, which eluded their bullets by the speed with which they dived. They saw gulls and porpoises.

Mackenzie was now in the same quandary he had been, for slightly different reasons, when he had reached the Arctic. Then he was a little unsure of his position, for lack of navigational instruments; now he was better equipped but, among these mountains and clouds, he might have difficulty in seeing the horizon and in finding a clear sky when he wanted it. In the Arctic, he had been in an estuary, not the open sea, but reasoned that no end would be served by his going further. Here he was at the end of a fiord, now known as North Bentinck Arm, and, considering the uncertainty of his relation with the local Indians and his dwindling stock of food, he knew he must begin the return journey with the least possible delay.

A young Indian, brother to the chief's son they had left so desperately ill, had accompanied the party down to this point. He was now eager to return: the swell was high, the wind boisterous, the canoe leaking. Mackenzie agreed that he should go and promised that he would himself return to the village in three nights.

Mackenzie's anxiety at this time was well founded. 'I had flattered myself with the hope of getting a distance of the moon and stars, but the cloudy weather continually disappointed me, and I began to fear that I should fail in this important object; particularly as our provisions were at a very low ebb, and we had as yet no reason to expect any assistance from the natives. Our stock was, at this time, reduced to twenty pounds weight of pemmican, fifteen pounds of rice, and six pounds of flour, among ten half-starved men, in a leaky vessel and on a barbarous coast.'

The barbarity which he had begun to sense was in part attributable, it is said, to the practices of white traders who came, in their ships, to secure beaver, sealskin and, particularly, sea-otter to be sold in China. Whereas the fur traders from Hudson's Bay or Canada were well aware of their utter dependence on co-operation from the Indians and made every effort to secure their goodwill, the captains of vessels on the Pacific were often little better than pirates and mixed fraud and violence with barter, careless of the future and concerned only to make a killing. The natives responded in kind and there were drownings and bloodshed.

Next day, 21 July, they met three canoes with fifteen men in them. They were Bella Bellas, who neighboured the Bella Coolas, though their language was different. One of them, with an insolent air, said that a large canoe, with white men in it, had recently been in that bay. A white man, Macubah, had fired on him and his friends, and another, Bensins, had struck him on the back with the flat of his sword. The names sound like Vancouver and Menzies—a naturalist who was with him. Vancouver's log shows he was in this fiord (Dean Channel) the previous month but records only his efforts to get in touch with the natives by every possible means, though in vain, because of their timidity. Mackenzie, knowing nothing of all this but with a strong distaste for the objectionable Bella Bella, concluded, 'I do not doubt but he well deserved the treatment which he described. He also produced several European articles, which could not have been long in his possession. From his conduct and appearance, I wished very much to be rid of him.' The man, however, forced himself into their canoe and asked to be taken to a narrow channel on the opposite shore, which he pointed to, saying it led to his village. They landed at the mouth of the channel, now known as Elcho Harbour, near some sheds which looked from a distance as though they might have been built by Europeans. It was only a ruined village but beside it a great rock stood up, which had clearly been used as a refuge or strongpoint and on the top of this Mackenzie camped. The natives, having harassed the party somewhat, went off near sunset with several stolen articles. Then another canoe arrived carrying seven men, with a sea-otter skin and a beautifully white skin, probably of a mountain goat. Mackenzie tried to barter for the former and for a seal they had just killed but without success. A scanty supper was eaten round a fire and throughout the cool, moonlight night the party kept a double watch in case of danger.

Mackenzie's precautions were not unwarranted. The Bella Bella had been culturally influenced by the Kwakiutl, a coastal people whose secret societies, elaborate masks and dramatic ceremonies are well known. A cultural trait among leading men of the Bella Bella was an aggressive arrogance. Mackenzie, ignorant of all these facts, must nevertheless have sensed the situation and decided to take a bold and wary attitude toward those who harassed him.

Soon after eight in the morning, Mackenzie made five observations to determine his longitude. Two canoes now arrived and some pieces of seal's flesh were obtained at a high price. At this point Mackay happened to light a piece of touch-wood with a burning glass, amazing the newcomers, who offered him the best of their otter skins for it. Two more canoes appeared and the young Indian who had come with them from upriver entreated Mackenzie to leave. They would soon gather to shoot their arrows and hurl their spears, he said. He was extremely anxious and foamed at the mouth. Mackenzie's own men, panic-stricken, asked if he intended to sacrifice them all. He replied that he had to complete his observations but that they should load the canoe, for instant departure. His task was almost done and he wished to leave a sign for any who might follow him or come in by sea. 'I now mixed up some vermilion in melted grease, and inscribed, in large characters, on the South-East face of the rock on which we had slept last night, this brief memorial—"Alexander Mackenzie, from Canada, by land, the twenty-second of July, one thousand seven hundred and ninety-three".'

The observations were still unfinished but, as a precaution against attack, they paddled three miles to reach a small cove on a point in what is now Dean Channel, where they could only be approached from one direction and could most readily defend themselves.

They were in one of the many long arms of the Pacific which, on this slowly sinking coast, reproduce all the features of a Norwegian fiord. The water was very deep, though the sounding line Mackenzie had hoped to plumb it with had just been stolen. The shores were of solid rock, rising from three to five hundred feet above high water mark. In odd pockets of soil grew cedar, spruce, birch and other trees, far larger than similar species in the mountains. Down the precipices threaded streams of clear and intensely cold water.

The local Indians followed, in two canoes, and tried to lure the young chief away. Mackenzie prevented this, for fear he might come to some harm or return alone to his father's village. It is extremely revealing to find that, in this difficult situation, none of the men would take any responsibility for the young chief's safekeeping. Mackenzie was obliged, in the midst of his other preoccupations, to keep watch over any attempt to escape. It is clear, however, that apart from removing him, when they first arrived, from one of the village canoes, Mackenzie used no force. Nor did he use threats. As usual, he was balancing all the elements of the situation against one another. 'I thought it much better to incur his displeasure, than to suffer him to expose himself to any untoward accident.'

In the afternoon, Mackenzie took five more altitudes, and observed the 'emersion' of Jupiter's first and third satellites. He reckoned his longitude as 128° 2' 0" West of Greenwich. 'I had now determined my situation, which is the most fortunate circumstance of my long, painful, and perilous journey, as a few cloudy days would have prevented me from ascertaining the final longitude of it.' As soon as this was done, they left, the men being very anxious to escape from the neighbourhood of these Indians. The tide was running out strongly but, by keeping close to the rock and working hard at their paddles, they made good progress.

Myth of the Wolves and the Corpse
(A Chehalis Indian story)
Charles Hill-Tout

Once a man and his wife lived together by themselves. The wife became ill, and shortly after died. The husband is very sorry, and grieves much over her death. He puts the corpse of his wife away in the branch of a tree. The night following he went to the place and lay down alongside the corpse. Now, during the night four wolves came along and discovered the bodies in the tree. Three of the wolves were males, the other was a female. Each of the male wolves tried in turn to jump up and seize the corpses, as they thought they were, but all three failed to reach them. Then the female wolf tried, and she succeeded in getting into the tree at the first spring. She felt both of the bodies, and found one was bound up like a corpse and the other was not. The bound one she threw down to the others, saying that that was their share and she would have the other for herself and they were not to touch it. When she got down she said to them, "You pack that one and I'll pack this." So they took the two bodies home to their *skumel*. Now the man had held his breath and pretended to be dead in the tree, but as he was being carried by the wolf-woman he had to open his lungs occasionally and breathe. The wolf-woman perceived this and knew that he was not dead. When they got home the three wolf-men ate the corpse of the wife, but the wolf-woman put the husband upon a shelf. When night fell and they had gone to bed, she took him down and put him on her own bed and lay with him. The next morning when the wolf-men arose they saw their sister was lying with a man. They say nothing, but go out hunting deer, but fail to find any because the man, who was a great hunter, had got up and gone out hunting too and had driven all the deer in the neighbourhood into a secluded gulch and hidden them there. The wolf-men came home day after day without any game. One day when they were almost starved the man went out and killed all the deer and made the meat into four packages. By his mystery power he made these so small that he could easily carry them all at once. He took them home. Now in the wolf village there were four *skumel*. So he bids his wolf-wife to take a pack to each of the four houses and throw the meat down to the inmates. She does so and when the packs are untied the meat nearly fills the houses. The whole village then feasts on the deer meat.

After this the man went away towards the shore, which was a long way off. When he got there he calls upon a whale to come up upon the beach. The whale comes up and opens his mouth wide, and the man enters it and cuts off a large quantity of the blubber. This he makes into a small pack by his mystery power and leaves it on the beach. He then goes home and bids his wife go and fetch it, telling her that he had found the whale on the beach and taken some of its fat. He instructs her to share the fat among the people, and say to them that if they liked that kind of food they might accompany him to the shore and get some more for themselves. They like the whale blubber so much that they one and all accompany him. Not a single person is left behind. When they get to the shore the man cuts a hole in the side of the whale, and tells the wolf-people to go in and help themselves. When everybody has passed in he gives the whale a kick and off it goes spouting and groaning into deep water. Thus the man revenged himself upon the wolf-people for eating his wife's corpse, and thus it is the whale spouts and groans to this day. It is caused by the wolves inside it.

Fraser's River
Charles Lillard

Sometimes the noise we don't hear
is Simon Fraser on his river.

He passed quietly, quick
as a skeeter-bug on the pond
passes the dog's nose;
his story was waiting
at saltwater, he had no time
to talk, this man
hurrying into myth,
things were real to him
and he despised those horizons
giving in,
like this river that couldn't
kill him.
And before he reached the end
the return faced him,
Grin at the rapids,
they'll pass
like noise following wind,
or the first yawn
awakening sleep.

Back at the headwaters
the door was still there
to open, to close;
after a bath and a shave
everyone recognized him
except the river
withering south,
now only a reflection of a voyage
going home to tidewater
while we noon behind this island.

The Perils of the Fraser Canyon

Simon Fraser

[On the 19 June, 1808, on his exploration of the Fraser River, Simon Fraser reached the junction of the Fraser and the Thompson rivers, just north of the present site of Lytton. The next morning, the 20th, he set out on the most difficult and dangerous part of his journey.]

June 20. . . . About 10 A.M. we embarked. Now all our people were in canoes. Our three new guides, the great chief, a little fellow from whom we received much attention, and some others embarked to keep us company. Aided by heavy rapids and a strong current, we, in a short time, came to a portage. Here the canoes and baggage were carried up a steep hill; the ascent was dangerous—stones and fragments of rocks were continually giving way from our feet and rolling off in succession; from this cause one of our men was much hurt, and a kettle bouncing into the river was lost. The Indians informed us that some years since, at this place, several of their people, having lost their balance from the steps giving way, rolled down to the river and perished, and we saw many graves covered with small stones all over the place. . . .

Two Indians from our last encampment overtook us with a piece of Iron which we had forgotten there. We considered this as an extraordinary degree of honesty and attention, particularly in this part of the world. After we had encamped, the chief with his friends went away.

June 21. Early in the morning the men made a trip with two of the canoes and part of the things which they carried more than a mile and returned for the rest. I sent Mr. Quesnel to take charge of the baggage in the absence of the men. About this time Indians appeared on the opposite bank. Our guides harangued them from our side, and all were singing and dancing.

After breakfast the men renewed their work, and Mr. Stuart and I remained in the tent writing. Soon after we were alarmed by the loud bawling of our guides, whom upon looking out we observed running full speed towards where we were, making signs that our people were lost in the rapids. As we could not account for this misfortune we immediately ran over to the baggage where we found Mr. Quesnel all alone. We inquired of him about the men, and at the same time we discovered that three of the canoes were missing, but he had seen none of them nor did he know where they were. On casting our view across the river, we remarked one of the canoes and some of the men a shore there. From this incident we had reason to believe that the others were either a head or perished, and with increased anxiety we directed our speed to the lower end of the rapids.

At the distance of four miles or so, we found one of our men, La Chapelle, who had carried two loads of his own share that far; he could give us no account of the others, but supposed they were following him with their proportions. We still continued; at last growing fatigued and seeing no appearance of the canoes of which we were in search, we considered it advisable to return and keep along the bank of the river.

We had not proceeded far when we observed one of our men D'Alaire walking slow with a stick in his hand from the bank, and on coming up to him we discovered that he was so wet, so weak, and so exhausted that he could scarcely speak. However after leaning a little while upon his stick and drawing breath, he informed us that unfortunately he and the others finding the carrying place too long and the canoes too heavy, took it upon themselves to venture down by water—that the canoe in which he was happened to be the last in setting out.

"In the first cascade," continued he, "our canoe filled and upset. The foreman and steersman got on the outside, but I, who was in the centre, remained a long while underneath upon the bars. The canoe still drifting was thrown into smooth current, and the other two men, finding an opportunity sprang from their situation into the water and swam ashore. The impulse occasioned by their fall in leaping off raised one side of the canoe above the surface, and I having still my recollection, though I had swallowed a quantity of water, seized the critical moment to disentangle myself, and I gained but not without a struggle the top of the canoe. By this time I found myself again in the middle of the stream. Here I continued astride, humouring the tide as well as I could with my body to preserve my balance, and although I scarcely had time to look about me, I had the satisfaction to observe the other two canoes a shore near an eddy, and their crews safe among the rocks. In the second or third cascade (for I cannot remember which) the canoe from a great height plunged into the deep eddy at the foot, and striking with violence against the bottom splitted into two. Here I lost my recollection, which however, I soon recovered and was surprised to find myself on a smooth easy current with only one half of the canoe in my arms. In this condition I continued through several cascades, untill the stream fortunately conducted me into an eddy at the foot of a high and steep rock. Here my strength being exhausted I lost my hold; a large wave washed me from off the wreck among the rocks, and another still larger hoisted me clear on shore, where I remained, as you will readily believe, some time motionless; at length recovering a little of my strength I crawled up among the rocks, but still in danger, and found myself once more safe on firm ground, just as you see."

Here he finished his melancholy tale, and pointed to the place of his landing, which we went to see, and we were lost in astonishment not only at his escape from the waves, but also at his courage and perseverence in effecting a passage up through a place which appeared to us a precipice. Continuing our course along the bank we found that he had drifted three miles among rapids, cascades, whirlpools, &c. all inconceivably dangerous.

Mr. Quesnel being extremely anxious and concerned left his charge and joined us. Two men only remained on shore carrying the baggage, and these were equally ignorant with ourselves of the fate of the others. Some time after upon advancing towards the camp, we picked up all the men on our side of the river. The men that had landed on the other side, joined us in the evening. They informed us that the Indians assisted to extricate them from their difficulties. Indeed the natives shewed us every possible attention in the midst of our misfortunes on this trying occasion.

Being all safe we had the happiness of encamping together as usual with our baggage. However we lost one of our canoes, and another we found too heavy to be carried such a distance. Our guides asked permission to go and sleep at the Indian Village, which was below the rapids; this was granted on condition that they should return in the morning. . . .

June 22. Our guides returned as they had promised. Four men were employed in bringing down the canoes by water. They made several portages in course of this undertaking. The rest of the men carried the baggage by land. When this troublesome and fatiguing business was over, we crossed over to the village, where we were received with loud acclamations and generously entertained. . . .

I sent two men to visit the rapids; but the Indians, knowing our indiscretion yesterday, and dreading a like attempt, voluntarily transported our canoes over land to a little river beyond the rapids. We encamped some distance from the village. The Chief went before to inform the Indians of the next village of our approach. He promised to accompany us untill we should have passed all the dangerous places—and the Little Fellow assured us that he would not leave us untill our return.

The Indians having invited us into the village, Mr. Quesnel and some of the men went; the Indians sang and danced and were very civil. They gave the men three dogs. At this time we depended wholly upon the natives for provisions, and they generously furnished us with the best they could procure; but that best was commonly wretched if not disgusting.

June 23. Rained this morning. One of the men was sick. We perceived that one way or other our men were getting out of order. They preferred walking to going by water in wooden canoes, particularly after their late sufferings in the rapids. Therefore I embarked in the bow of a canoe myself and went down several rapids.

We met some Indians and waited for the arrival of our people, who had gone by land. Walking was difficult, the country being extremely rough and uneven. Passed a carrying place; one of the men fell and broke his canoe almost to pieces. The natives from below came thus far with two canoes to assist us. They were probably sent by our friends who went a head. In one of the rapids, Mr. Stuart's canoe filled and was nearly lost.

Soon after we came to a camp of the natives where we landed for the night. The number of the Indians here may amount to 170. They call themselves Nailgemugh. We met with a hearty welcome from them; they entertained us with singing, dancing, &c. . . .

The weather was generally very hot in the day time; but at night, being in the neighbourhood of eternal snows, it was commonly cold.

June 24. This morning trade two canoes for two calico bed gowns. Sent some men to visit the rapids, and set out at 8 A.M. After going a mile we came to a carrying place of 800 yards. Mr. Stuart had a mer[idian] alt[itude]. 126° 57′.

Continued—passed a small camp of Indians without stopping and came to a discharge with steep hills at both ends, where we experienced some difficulty in carrying the things. Ran down the canoes; but about the middle of the rapids two of them struck against one another, by which accident one of them lost a piece of its stern, and the steersman his paddle: the canoe in consequence took in much water.

After repairing the damages we continued, and in the evening arrived at an Indian village. The Natives flocked about us, and invited us to pass the night with them. Accepting their invitation we were led to a camp which was at some distance up the hill. The Indians of this encampment were upwards five hundred souls. . . . We were well treated, they gave us fresh salmon, hazle nuts, and some other nuts of an excellent quality. The small pox was in the camp, and several of the Natives were marked with it. We fired several shots to shew the Indians the use of our guns. Some of them, through fear, dropped down at the report.

June 25. . . . We embarked at 5 A.M. After going a considerable distance, our Indians ordered us a shore, and we made a portage. Here we were obliged to carry up among loose Stones on the face of a steep hill, over a narrow ridge between two precipices. Near the top where the ascent was perfectly perpendicular, one of the Indians climbed to the summit, and with a long pole drew us up, one after another. This took three hours. Then we continued our course up and down, among hills and rocks, and along the steep declivities of mountains, where hanging rocks, and projecting cliffs at the edge of the bank made the passage so small as to render it difficult even for one person to pass sideways at times.

Many of the natives from the last camp, having accompanied us, were of the greatest service to us on these intricate and dangerous occasions. In places where we were obliged to hand our guns from one to another, and where the greatest precaution was required to pass even singly, the Indians went through boldly with loads. About 5 P.M. we encamped at a rapid....

June 26. This morning all hands were employed the same as yesterday. We had to pass over huge rocks, in which we were assisted by the Indians. Soon after met Mr. Stuart and the man. They reported that the navigation was absolutely impracticable....

As for the road by land, we scarcely could make our way in some parts even with our guns. I have been for a long period among the Rocky Mountains, but have never seen any thing equal to this country, for I cannot find words to describe our situation at times. We had to pass where no human being should venture. Yet in those places there is a regular footpath impressed, or rather indented, by frequent travelling upon the very rocks. And besides this, steps which are formed like a ladder, or the shrouds of a ship, by poles hanging to one another and crossed at certain distances with twigs and withes, suspended from the top to the foot of precipices, and fastened at both ends to stones and trees, furnished a safe and convenient passage to the Natives—but we, who had not the advantages of their experience, were often in imminent danger, when obliged to follow their example....

The Hacamaugh promised us canoes for the next day. But the canoes being above the rapids, some of the young men went for them. It being impossible to bring them by land, or to get them down by water, they were turned adrift and left to the mercy of the current. As there were many shoals and rocks the canoes were in the greatest danger of being broken to pieces before they got to the end of the rapids.

June 27. . . . We set out at 6 A.M. accompanied as usual by many of the natives, who assisted in carrying part of our baggage. The route we had to follow was as bad as yesterday. At 9 we came to the canoes that were sent adrift. One of them we found broken and the other much damaged. We lost some time in repairing them. Some of the men with the things embarked, and the rest continued by land.

We came to a small camp of Indians consisting about 60 persons. The name of the place is Spazum [Spuzzum], and is the boundary line between the Hacamaugh and Ackinroe Nations. Here as usual we were hospitably entertained, with fresh Salmon boiled and roasted, green and dried berries, oil and onions.

Seeing tombs of a curious construction at the forks on the opposite side, I asked permission of the Chief to go and pay them a visit. This he readily granted, and he accompanied us himself. These Tombs are superior to any thing of the kind I ever saw among the savages. They are about fifteen feet long and of the form of a chest of drawers. Upon the boards and posts are carved beasts and birds, in a curious but rude manner, yet pretty well proportioned. These monuments must have cost the workmen much time and labour, as they were destitute of proper tools for the execution of such a performance. Around the tombs were deposited all the property of the deceased.

Ready for our departure, our guides observed that we had better pass the night here and that they would accompany us in the morning. Sensible, from experience, that a hint from these people is equal to a command, and that they would not follow, if we Declined, we remained.

June 28. We set out at 5, our things in canoes as yesterday, and we continued by land. After much trouble both by land and water for eight miles, we came to a carrying place, where we were obliged to leave our canoes, and to proceed on foot without our baggage. Some of the Ackinroe Nation, apprised by our approach, came to meet us with roasted Salmon, and we made an excellent meal....

Continued and crossed a small river on a wooden bridge. Here the main river tumbles from rock to rock between precipices with great violence. At 11 A.M. we arrived at the first village of the Ackinroe nation, where we were received with as much kindness as if we had been their lost relations. Neat mats were spread for our reception, and plenty of Salmon served in wooden dishes was placed before us. The number of people at this place was about 140.

This nation is different in language and manners from the other nations we had passed. They have rugs made from the wool of *Aspai*, or wild goat, and from Dog's hair, which are equally as good as those found in Canada. We observed that the dogs were lately shorn....

At 1 P.M. we renewed our march, the natives still carrying part of our baggage. At the first point we observed a remarkable cavern in a rock which upon visiting we found to be 50 feet deep by 35 wide. A little above it is an excellent house 46 by 23 feet, and constructed like American frame houses. The planks are 3 or 4 inches thick, each passing the adjoining one a couple of inches. The posts, which are very strong, and rudely carved, receive the beam across. The walls are 11 feet high, and covered with a slanting roof. On the opposite side of the river, there is a considerable village with houses similar to the one upon this side.

About 4 P.M. arrived to a camp containing about 150 souls. Here we had plenty of Salmon cooked by means of hot stones in wooden vessels.

Here we understood that the river was navigable from this place to the sea....

Skating Down Trout

Kevin Roberts

for Pat Lane

In Winter on Lac La Hache
when cold snaps its fingers
quick
Indians skate down trout
over ice set two feet clear
till they scare up a big char
working it slowly
like sheep dogs
driving the dark-backed silver
glimmer closer into shore
turning back its runs
into deep water
the fish circling tighter
not knowing the shield
ice makes between
terror and shadows
impotent to touch it
in its element the trout
safe against all
but its own fears
forcing it shallower
closer to the clean cut skirr
of the skates
driven by forms
only the fish makes substance
until in panic
at the hiss and whirr
of the steel blades it runs
defeats itself
char jammed trembling
between the gravel bottom
and the frozen ice
beating delicate fins
till axe blows
open up the ice
deliver the fish
to its hunters

hanging limp by the gills
in the Indians hands.

First Winter on the Columbia

David Thompson

[In the early summer of 1807 David Thompson crossed the Rockies and reached the Columbia (which at first he thought was the Kootenay) near Golden on the 30th June. Reaching Lake Windermere on the 18th July he started to build a post there, but on the advice of the Kootenay Indians decided it would be indefensible against the hostile Piegans, and eventually picked a site for Kootenay House on Toby Creek, a tributary of the Columbia.]

We there built log houses, and strongly stockaded them on three sides, the other side resting on the steep bank of the river. The logs of the house, and the stockades, bastions, &c., were of a peculiar kind of a heavy resinous fir [larch], with a tough black bark. It was clean grown to about twenty feet, when it threw off a head of long rude branches, with a long narrow leaf for a fir, which was annually shed, and became from green to a red colour. The stockades were all ball-proof, as well as the logs of the houses.

At the latter end of autumn, and through the winter, there are plenty of red deer and the antelope, with a few mountain sheep. The goats with their long silky hair were difficult to hunt, from their feeding on the highest parts of the hills, and the natives relate that they are wicked, kicking down stones on them. But during the summer and early part of autumn very few deer were killed; we had very hard times and were obliged to eat several horses; we found the meat of the tame horse better than the wild horse; the fat was not so oily.

At length the salmon made their appearance, and for about three weeks we lived on them; at first they were in tolerable condition, although they had come upwards of twelve hundred miles from the sea, and several weighed twenty-five pounds. But as the spawning went on upon a gravel bank a short distance above us, they became poor and not eatable; we preferred horse meat.

As the place where they spawned had shoal swift clear water on it, we often looked at them. The female with her head cleared away the gravel, and made a hole to deposit her spawn in, of perhaps an inch or more in depth by a foot in length; which done, the male then passed over it several times, when both covered the hole well up with gravel. The Indians affirm, and there is every reason to believe them, that not a single salmon of the myriads that come up the river ever returns to the sea; their stomachs have nothing in them, probably from no food in fresh water; the shores of the river, after the spawning season, were covered with them, in a lean dying state, yet even in this state many of the Indians eat them. . . .

In my new dwelling I remained quiet, hunting the wild horses, fishing, and examining the country. Two canoes of goods arrived for trade, on horses, by the defiles of the Saskatchewan River. Half of these goods under the charge of Mr. Finan McDonald I sent to make a trading post at a considerable lake in McGillivray's [Kootenay] River; the season was late and no more could be done.

About the middle of November, two Piegans on foot crossed the mountains and came to the house, to see how it was situated. I showed the strength of the stockades and bastions, and told them, "I know you are come as spies and intend to destroy us, but many of you will die before you do so. Go back to your countrymen and tell them so"; which they did, and we remained quiet for the winter. I knew the danger of the place we were in, but could not help it.

As soon as the mountains were passable I sent off the clerk and men with the furs collected, among which were one hundred of the mountain goat skins with their long silky hair, of a foot in length of a white colour, tinged at the lower end with a very light shade of yellow. Some of the ignorant self-sufficient partners of the company ridiculed such an article for the London market; there they went and sold at first sight for a guinea a skin, and half as much for another lot, but there were no more. These same partners then wrote me to procure as many as possible. I returned for answer [that] the hunting of the goat was both dangerous and laborious, and for their ignorant ridicule I would send no more, and I kept my word.

I had now to prepare for a more serious visit from the Piegans, who had met in council, and it was determined to send forty men with a secondary chief to destroy the trading post and us with it. They came and pitched their tents close before the gate, which was well barred. I had six men with me, and ten guns, well loaded; the house was perforated with large augur holes, as well as the bastions. Thus they remained for three weeks without daring to attack us; we had a small stock of dried provisions which we made go as far as possible; they thought to make us suffer for want of water, as the bank we were on was about 20 feet high and very steep, but at night, by a strong cord, we quietly and gently let down two brass kettles, each of four gallons, and drew them up full, which was enough for us.

They were at a loss what to do, for Kootenae Appee, the war chief, had publicly told the chief of this party (which was formed against his advice) to remember he had men confided to his care, whom he must bring back, that he was sent to destroy the enemies, not to lose his men; finding us always on the watch, they did not think proper to risk their lives. When at the end of three weeks they suddenly decamped, I thought it a ruse de guerre. I afterwards learnt that some of them hunting saw some Kootenays who were also hunting. As what was being done was an act of aggression, something like an act

of war, they decamped to cross the mountains to join their own tribe while all was well with them.

The return of this party without success occasioned a strong sensation among the Piegans. The civil chief harangued them, and gave his advice to form a strong war party under Kootanee Appee, the war chief, and directly to crush the white men and the natives on the west side of the mountains, before they became well armed: "They have always been our slaves [prisoners] and now they will pretend to equal us. No, we must not suffer this, we must at once crush them. We know them to be desperate men, and we must destroy them, before they become too powerful for us."

The war chief coolly observed, "I shall lead to battle according to the will of the tribe, but we cannot smoke to the Great Spirit for success, as we usually do. It is now about ten winters since we made peace with them. They have tented and hunted with us, and because they have guns and iron-headed arrows, we must break our word of peace with them. We are now called upon to go to war with a people better armed than ourselves. Be it so; let the warriors get ready; in ten nights I will call on them." The old and intelligent men severely blamed the speech of the civil chief; they remarked, the "older he gets, the less sense."

On the ninth night the war chief made a short speech, to have each man to take full ten days of dried provisions, "for we shall soon leave the country of the bison, after which we must not fire a shot, or we shall be discovered." On the tenth night he made his final speech, and exhorting the warriors and their chiefs to have their arms in good order, and not forget dried provisions, he named a place: "There I shall be the morrow evening, and those who now march with me. There I shall wait for you five nights, and then march to cross the mountains."

At the end of this time about three hundred warriors under three chiefs assembled. They took their route across the mountains by the Stag River, and, by the defiles of another river of the same name, came on the Columbia, about twenty miles from me. As usual, by another pass of the mountains, they sent two men to see the strength of the house. I showed them all around the place, and they stayed that night. I plainly saw that a war party was again formed, to be better conducted than the last; and I prepared presents to avert it.

The next morning two Kootenay men arrived; their eyes glared on the Piegans like tigers; this was most fortunate; I told them to sit down and smoke, which they did. I then called the two Piegans out, and enquired of them which way they intended to return; they pointed to the northward. I told them to go to Kootanae Appee and his war party, who were only a day's journey from us, and delivering to them the presents I had made up [I said] to be off directly, as I could not protect them, "for you know you are on these lands as enemies"; the presents were six feet of tobacco to the chief, to be smoked among them, three feet with a fine pipe of red porphyry and an ornamented pipestem; eighteen inches to each of the three chiefs; and a small piece to each of themselves; and telling them they had no right in the Kootenay country, to haste away, for the Kootenay would soon be here, and they will fight for their trading post.

In all that regarded the Piegans, I chanced to be right. It was all guesswork. Intimately acquainted with the Indians, the country and the seasons, I argued and acted on probabilities; I was afterwards informed that the two Piegans went direct to the camp of the war party, delivered the presents and the message and sat down, upon which the war chief exclaimed: "What can we do with this man? Our women cannot mend a pair of shoes, but he sees them," alluding to my astro. observations. Then in a thoughtful mood he laid the pipe and stem with the several pieces of tobacco on the ground, and said: "What is to be done with these? If we proceed, nothing of what is before us can be accepted."

The eldest of the three chiefs, wistfully eyeing the tobacco,

of which they had none, at length . . . said, "You all know me, who I am and what I am; I have attacked tents, my knife could cut through them, and our enemies had no defence against us, and I am ready to do so again, but to go and fight against logs of wood that a ball cannot go through, and with people we cannot see and with whom we are at peace, is what I am averse to. I go no farther."

He then cut the end of the tobacco, filled the red pipe, fitted the stem, and handed it to Kootenae Appee, saying, "It was not you that brought us here, but the foolish Sakatow [civil chief] who himself never goes to war." They all smoked, took the tobacco, and returned, very much to the satisfaction of Kootenae Appee, my steady friend.

Thus by the mercy of good Providence I averted this danger; winter came in, the snow covered the mountains and placed us in safety. . . .

Although through the mercy of Providence we had hitherto escaped, yet I saw the danger of my situation. I therefore in the early part of the next spring took precautions to quit the place.

Matq, or the Fire Myth
(A story of the Thompson Indians)
Charles Hill-Tout

Long, long ago the Indians on Fraser River had no knowledge of fire. Beaver, who travelled about a good deal in the night prospecting the rivers, learnt from some source that away in the far north there lived a tribe who knew how to make fire. He determined to seek out this tribe and steal some of their fire and bring it back to the Stalo (i.e. Lower Fraser River) Indians. He told his brother Eagle to wait for him at a certain point on the Fraser while he went down the river to the coast to tell the people of the settlements along its banks that he was going to steal the fire for them in the far north. When he reached the coast he met a large tribe there. He begged from them the gift of a pair of clam shells in which to stow away the fire he should steal. They gave him the shells and he then returned to his brother, and the two set out together for the far north. "You go through the air," said Beaver to Eagle, "and I will travel by water." They continued their journey in this way for many days and nights, Beaver travelling by the Fraser. When they arrived near the village of the people who possessed the fire, Beaver called to his brother and told him his plan of action. "Tonight," he said, "I will build a dam across the water, and then burrow from the dam along under the ground until I come up under the house where the fire is kept. They will

spear me sooner or later, and take me to the village, but although they will spear me they will not be able to kill me. In the meantime I shall build myself a house in the river, and when they see it they will come out and spear me. When they have speared me they will take me to the house where the fire is kept to skin me. I shall put the clam shells inside my skin, and when the knife is nearly through to the shell beneath I shall open my eye and you will see a great flash of light in the sky. You must be close by, and when you see the flash you must fly over the house and attract their attention. They will leave me for a moment and run out to try and shoot you. When they are gone I shall seize the opportunity and open my clam shell and fill it with fire. I shall then clear away the soil from above the passage I have made from the river to the house, rush down it, and come out in the deep water of the river above the dam."

Eagle approved of the plan, and promised to do his share according to his brother's instructions. All that night Beaver worked at his dam and the passage. By morning all was ready. When one of the women went down to the stream to fetch her water next morning she found to her surprise a large lake where before was only a small stream. She dropped her pail and ran home, and told the people that a beaver was in the stream. Everybody rushed for his spear, and all made for the stream. Some one suggested breaking the dam and catching him in that way. This they did; and when the water was getting low Beaver came out of his house and swam about as if trying to get away. He played with them for a little while before he would permit them to spear him. Finally they speared him and carried him with great rejoicings to the house. Everybody now wanted his teeth, or his tail, or his claws. They presently set about skinning him, but as the point of the knife touched the shell hidden beneath the skin of his breast Beaver opened one eye. Now, the boy who was holding his leg saw the action, and told the others, who only laughed at him. Just at that moment Eagle, who had seen the signal, came soaring over the house, making a great noise, which diverted everybody's attention from Beaver. "An eagle! an eagle! Shoot it! Kill it!" shouted everybody, and all ran for their bows and arrows except the boy who was holding Beaver's leg.

This was the moment Beaver had planned for. Shaking himself free from the boy's hold, he took out his clam shells, quickly filled them with fire, and before the boy had recovered from his astonishment plunged head foremost down the passage hole and made for the river. The boy's cries speedily brought the people to him, and he told them what had happened. They now tried to dig out the hole down which Beaver had disappeared, but they no sooner tried than the water rushed up and stopped them. Beaver reached the stream safely, and from thence made his way to the Fraser, where he was joined by his brother Eagle. As they returned down the river Beaver threw fire on all the trees as they passed, but mostly on the cottonwood trees, and thus it was that the wood from these trees was the best for making fire with from that time onward. He continued to do this till he had reached the coast again and all his fire was gone.

After this he assumed a human form and taught the Indians how to make fire by means of the drill worked between the hands. He also taught them how to preserve the fire when once secured in the following manner. He procured a quantity of the inner bark of the cedar tree and made it into a long rope. This he then covered with the bark of some other trees which burnt less readily. When one end of this rope was lighted it would continue to smoulder for several days, according to the length of the rope. When the Indians were travelling and likely to be away from camp for several days they always carried one of these fire-ropes, called by themselves *patlakan*, coiled around their shoulders. After this great gift to them the Indians thought very highly of Beaver, and he was usually called by them "our head brother" because of his wisdom and goodness.

Lake
Dale Zieroth

In the morning, along the vacant shore,
when the water is still cool
and the trees bend down as if to drink,
there is a quietness like the deer who come for water
in the small round seconds of the dawn: the denials
are forgotten, the tough work of balance and
maintenance and hope has not yet begun.
It is a different place now, this view
that is a panorama, that is also
a reflection, these million leaves
opening like mouths to the sun and to the light
that rolls down the mountain, down
to the water in the urgent greeting that
turns the water blue and white and once more
familiar like the beautiful
brown hands of summer.

By evening, even the water does not flow
toward me: there is no order
outside the kind I need to impose and I
step back so easily into
a void at the end of the day where the
calm is waiting and I can
kneel down and let it touch my hands, let it
cool the palms and wash upwards over the shoulders
and the thin blind eyes. Now the lake
is company enough. Later I may turn,
leave the great dark face of the water
and take those first sweet steps
back to the earth.

The Headwaters of the Columbia
Paul Kane

Nov. 12th [1846]. Today we attained what is called the Height of Land. There is a small lake at this eminence called the Committee's Punch-bowl; this forms the head waters of one branch of the Columbia River on the west side of the mountains, and of the Athabasca on the east side. It is about three quarters of a mile in circumference, and is remarkable as giving rise to two such mighty rivers; the waters of the one emptying into the Pacific Ocean, and of the other into the Arctic Sea. We encamped on its margin, with difficulty protecting ourselves from the intense cold.

Nov. 13th. The lake being frozen over to some depth, we walked across it, and shortly after commenced the descent of the grand côte, having been seven days continually ascending. The descent was so steep, that it took us only one day to get down to nearly the same level as that of Jasper's House. The descent was a work of great difficulty on snow shoes, particularly for those carrying loads; their feet frequently slipped from under them, and the loads rolled down the hill. Some of the men, indeed, adopted the mode of rolling such loads as would not be injured down before them. On reaching the bottom, we found eight men waiting, whom M'Gillveray and the guide had sent on to assist us at Boat Encampment, and we all encamped together.

Nov. 14th. I remained at the camp fire finishing one of my sketches, the men having made a very early start in order to reach Boat Encampment, where they would get a fresh supply of provisions, ours being nearly exhausted. As soon as I had finished my sketch I followed them, and soon arrived at a river about seventy yards across, and with a very rapid current.

Having followed their track in the snow to the edge of the river, and seeing the strength of the current, I began to look for other tracks, under the impression that they might possibly have discovered a way to get round it. But I was soon undeceived by seeing in the snow on the other side of the path they had beaten down on the opposite bank; nothing, therefore, remained but for me to take off my snow shoes, and make the traverse. The water was up to my middle, running very rapidly, and filled with drift ice, some pieces of which struck me, and nearly forced me down the stream. I found on coming out of the water my capote and leggings frozen stiff. My difficulties, however, were only beginning, as I was soon obliged to cross again four times, when, my legs becoming completely benumbed, I dared not venture on the fifth, until I had restored the circulation by running up and down the beach. I had to cross twelve others in similar manner, being

seventeen in all, before I overtook the rest of the party at the encampment. The reason of these frequent crossings is, that the only pass across the mountains is the gorge formed by the Athabasca on one side, and the Columbia on the other; and the beds of these torrents can only be crossed in the spring before the thaws commence, or in the fall after the severe weather has set in. During the summer the melting of the mountain snow and ice renders them utterly impracticable.

Nov. 15th. It will be easily imagined with what regret we left a warm fire and comfortable encampment, to plunge at once into one of the deepest crossings we had yet encountered, covered like the preceding with running ice. Here, as in many other crossings, our only means of withstanding the force of the current was for all of us to go abreast shoulder to shoulder, in a line parallel with it, each man being supported by all below him. Mrs. Lane, although it was necessary to carry her in the arms of two powerful men across the river, acquitted herself in other ways as well as any of us. One of the greatest annoyances accompanying the use of snow shoes, is that of having to take them off on entering a river, and replacing them over the wet and frozen moccasins on coming out of it.

Before stopping to breakfast this morning, we crossed the river twenty-five times, and twelve times more before camping; having waded it thirty-seven times in all during the day.

The Columbia here makes long reaches, to and fro, through a valley, in some parts three miles wide, and backed with stupendous mountains, rearing their snowy tops above the clouds, and forming here and there immense glaciers, reflecting the rays of the sun with extreme brilliancy and prismatic beauty. The last part of the route lay through a slimy lake or swamp, frozen over, but not with sufficient solidity to bear us, so that we had to wade above our knees in a dense mass of snow, ice and mud, there being no such thing as a dry spot to afford a moment's respite from the scarcely endurable severity of the cold, under which I thought I must have sunk exhausted.

At length, however, we arrived at Boat Encampment, about 5 P.M., almost perishing with cold and hunger, having tasted nothing since what I have already termed breakfast, which consisted only of a small supply of soup made of pemmikon, this being the mode of making the most of a small quantity of it. On our arrival we found a good fire blazing, and some soup made from pork and corn, brought here from Fort Vancouver, boiling in the pot, which I attacked with so much avidity, that one of the men, fearing I might take too much in my present exhausted state, politely walked off with the bowl and its contents.

The men had been here waiting our arrival for thirty-nine days, and would have returned to Fort Vancouver the next day, had not the guide and M'Gillveray opportunely arrived in time to prevent them, as they thought we had either been cut off by the Indians, or that we had found it impossible to cross the mountains. In fact, they were clearing snow out of the boats preparatory to starting. Had our messengers not arrived in time, it would most likely have proved fatal to us all, as we could not have re-crossed the mountains without provisions. . . .

Nov. 16th. Our two boats were by this time ready; they were formed canoe fashion, with round bottoms of boards, clinker built. On leaving Boat Encampment the scene is exceedingly grand; immense mountains receding farther and farther in the distance on either side. Few who read this journal, surrounded by the comforts of civilized life, will be able to imagine the heartfelt satisfaction with which we exchanged the wearisome snow-shoe for the comfortable boats, and the painful anxiety of half-satisfied appetites for a well-stocked larder. True it was, that the innumerable rapids of the Columbia were filled with dangers of no ordinary character, and that it required the constant exercise of all our energy and skill to escape their perils, but we now had health and high spirits to help us. We no longer had to toil on in clothes frozen stiff from wading across torrents, half-famished, and with the consciousness ever before us, that whatever were our hardships and fatigue, rest was sure destruction in the cold solitudes of those dreary mountains.

About three hours after our departure we shot the celebrated "Dalle de Mort". It is about three miles long and is the most dangerous of all the rapids on the Columbia.

17th and 18th. We passed through the two lakes and were obliged to work day and night to avail ourselves of the calm weather, although the snow fell without ceasing.

19th. We again entered the current of the river, where the men were enabled to rest for a few hours.

Nov. 20th. About noon we ran through the Little Dalle, which, though short, is a series of dangerous whirlpools, which can only be passed with the greatest precaution, and arrived safe at Colville at 6 o'clock in the evening. . . .

Day after day the sun
Patrick Lane

Day after day the sun hurts these hills into summer
as the green returns to yellow in filaments as hard as stone.
Everywhere the old mortality sings.

Sagebrush breaks the bodies of the small.
Desiccated bits of fur huddle in the arroyos
as the land drifts away, melted by the wind.

Down by the drying lake a people curl on sand
having nothing more to do with beauty and desire
than to turn their bodies brown. The image of an image

they have forgotten the animal who lived in a hole.
Carrion-eater, digger of roots, worshipper of fear.
They burn as an eagle returns from the long weeks hunt

and tears from the bone the breast of a marmot
killed in the hills above Kalamalka.
Satiate she hunches on the dead tree's crest

while below her as she sleeps, magpies,
thin in the thorn trees, more ancient than hunger,
dance their dance of the sun.

Fort Victoria—
Fur Traders and Indians

Paul Kane

April 8th [1847]. I left Nasqually this morning with six Indians in a canoe, and continued paddling on the whole day and the following night, as the tide seemed favourable, not stopping till 2 P.M., when we reached Fort Victoria on Vancouver's Island, having travelled ninety miles without stopping. Fort Victoria stands upon the banks of an inlet in the island about seven miles long and a quarter of a mile wide, forming a safe and convenient harbour, deep enough for any sized vessel. Its Indian name is the Esquimelt, or, Place for gathering Camas, great quantities of that vegetable being found in the neighbourhood. On my arrival I was kindly welcomed by Mr. Finlayson, the gentleman in charge. He gave me a comfortable room, which I made my headquarters during the two months I was occupied in sketching excursions amongst the Indians of the neighbourhood and along the surrounding coasts.

The soil of this locality is good, and wheat is grown in considerable abundance. Clover grows plentifully, and is supposed to have sprung from accidental seeds which had fallen from the packages of goods brought from England; many of which are made up in hay.

The interior of the island has not been explored to any extent except by the Indians, who represent it as badly supplied with water in the summer, and the water obtained from a well dug at the fort was found to be too brackish for use. The appearance of the interior, when seen from the coast, is rocky and mountainous, evidently volcanic; the trees are large, principally oak and pine. The timbers of a vessel of some magnitude were being got out. The establishment is very large, and must eventually become the great depôt for the business of the Company. They had ten white men and forty Indians engaged in building new stores and warehouses. On the opposite side of the harbour, facing the fort, stands a village of Clal-lums Indians. They boast of being able to turn out 500 warriors, armed chiefly with bows and arrows. The lodges are built of cedar like the Chinook lodges, but much larger, some of them being sixty or seventy feet long.

The men wear no clothing in summer, and nothing but a blanket in winter, made either of dog's wool alone, or dog's hair and goosedown mixed, frayed cedar-bark, or wildgoose skin, like the Chinooks. They have a peculiar breed of small dogs with long hair of a brownish black and a clear white. These dogs are bred for clothing purposes. The hair is cut off with a knife and mixed with goosedown and a little white earth, with a view of curing the feathers. This is then beaten together with sticks, and twisted into threads by rubbing it down the thigh with the palm of the hand, in the same way that a shoemaker forms his waxend, after which it undergoes a second twisting on a distaff to increase its firmness. The cedar bark is frayed and twisted into threads in a similar manner. These threads are then woven into blankets by a very simple loom of their own contrivance. A single thread is wound over rollers at the top and bottom of a square frame, so as to form a continuous woof through which an alternate thread is carried by the hand, and pressed closely together by a sort of wooden comb; by turning the rollers every part of the woof is brought within reach of the weaver; by this means a bag is formed, open at each end, which being cut down makes a square blanket. The women wear only an apron of twisted cedar-bark shreds, tied round the waist and hanging down in front only, almost to the knees. They however, use the blankets more than the men do, but certainly not from any feeling of delicacy.

This tribe flatten the head, but their language varies very much from the Chinook; however, the same patois used on the Columbia is spoken by many of them, and I was thus enabled to communicate easily with them. I took a sketch of Clea-clach, their head chief, of whose inauguration I heard the following account from an eye-witness. On his father becoming too old to fulfil the duties of head chief, the son was called upon by the tribe to take his place; on which occasion he left [for] the mountains for the ostensible purpose of fasting and dreaming for thirty days and nights; these Indians, like all other tribes, placing great confidence in dreams, and believing that it is necessary to undergo a long fast whenever they are desirous of inducing one of any importance. At the end of the period assigned, the tribe prepared a great feast. After covering himself with a thick covering of grease and goosedown, he rushed into the midst of the village, seized a small dog, and began devouring it alive, this being a customary preliminary on such occasions. The tribe collected about him singing and dancing in the wildest manner, on which he approached those whom he most regarded and bit their bare shoulders or arms, which was considered by them as a high mark of distinction, more especially those from whom he took the piece clean out and swallowed it. Of the women he took no notice.

I have seen many men on the North-west coast of the Pacific who bore frightful marks of what they regarded as an honourable distinction; nor is this the only way in which their persons become disfigured. I have myself seen a young girl bleeding most profusely from gashes inflicted by her own hand over her arms and bosom with a sharp flint, on the occasion of losing a near relative. After some time spent in singing and dancing, Clea-clach retired with his people to the feast prepared inside a large lodge, which consisted principally of whale's blubber, in their opinion the greatest of all delicacies, although they have salmon, cod, sturgeon, and other excellent fish in great abundance.

All the tribes about here subsist almost entirely upon fish, which they obtain with so little trouble during all seasons of the year, that they are probably the laziest race of people in the world. Sturgeon are caught in considerable numbers, and here attain an enormous size, weighing from four to six hundred weight; this is done by means of a long pointed spear handle seventy to eighty feet in length, fitted into, but not actually fastened to, a barbed spear-head to which is attached a line, with which they feel along the bottom of the river where the sturgeon are found lying in the spawning season. Upon feeling the fish the barbed spear is driven in and the handle withdrawn. The fish is then gradually drawn in by the line, which being very long, allows the sturgeon to waste his great strength, so that he can with safety be taken into the canoe or towed ashore. Most of their fishing lines are formed of a long seaweed, which is often found 150 feet long, of equal thickness throughout the whole length, and about as thick as a black-lead pencil; while wet it is very strong. Their fish-hooks are made of pine-roots, made something in the shape of our ordinary hooks, but attached differently to the line; the barb is made of bone.

Clams are in great plenty, and are preyed on in great numbers by the crows, who seize them in their claws and fly up with them to some height, and then let them drop on the rocks, which of course smashes the shell to pieces. I have watched dozens of them at this singular employment. A small oyster of a fine flavour is found in the bays in great plenty. Seal, wild ducks and geese, are also in great numbers.

The Indians are extremely fond of herring-roe, which they collect in the following manner:—Cedar branches are sunk to the bottom of the river in shallow places by placing upon them a few heavy stones, taking care not to cover the green foliage, as the fish prefer spawning on anything green. The branches are all covered by the next morning with the spawn, which is washed off into their waterproof baskets, to the bottom of which it sinks; it is then squeezed by the hand into small balls and dried, and is very palatable.

The only other vegetable besides the camas and wappatoos that the Indians use, are the roots of fern roasted, which grow to a very large size.

Slavery in its most cruel form exists among the Indians of the whole coast, from California to Behring's Straits, the stronger tribes making slaves of all the others they can conquer. In the interior, where there is but little warfare, slavery does not exist. On the coast a custom prevails that authorises the seizure and enslavement, unless ransomed by his friends, of every Indian met at a distance from his tribe, although they may not be at war with each other. The master exercises the power of life and death over his slaves, whom he sacrifices at pleasure in gratification of any superstitious or other whim of the moment.

One morning while I was sketching, I saw upon the rocks the dead body of a young woman, thrown out to the vultures and crows, whom I had seen a few days previously walking about in perfect health. Mr. Finlayson, the gentleman in charge of Fort Victoria, accompanied me to the lodge she belonged to, where we found an Indian woman, her mistress, who made light of her death, and was doubtless the cause of it. She told us that a slave had no right to burial, and became perfectly furious when Mr. Finlayson told her that the slave was better than herself. "I," she exclaimed, "the daughter of a chief, no better than a dead slave!" and bridling up with all the dignity she could assume, she stalked out, and next morning she had up her lodge and was gone. I was also told by an eye-witness, of a chief, who having erected a colossal idol of wood, sacrificed five slaves to it, barbarously murdering them at its base, and asking in a boasting manner who amongst them could afford to kill so many slaves.

These Indians also flatten their heads, and are far more superstitious than any I have met with. They believe, for instance, that if they can procure the hair of an enemy and confine it with a frog in a hole, the head from which it came will suffer all the torments that the frog endures in its living grave. They are never seen to spit without carefully obliterating all traces of their saliva. This they do lest an enemy should find it, in which case they believe he would have the power of doing them some injury. They always spit on their blankets, if they happen to wear one at the time.

I was indebted to the superstitious fears which they attached to my pictures for the safety and ease with which I mingled amongst them. One of them gave me a great deal of annoyance by continually following and watching me wherever I went, for the purpose of warning the other Indians against my sketching them, telling them that it would expose them to all sorts of ill luck. I repeatedly requested him to desist, but in vain. At last I bethought myself of looking steadily at himself, paper and pencil in hand, as if in the act of taking his likeness; when he became greatly alarmed, and asked me what I was about. I replied, "I am taking a sketch of you." He earnestly begged of me to stop, and promised never to annoy me again.

These Indians have a great dance, which is called "The Medicine Mask Dance;" this is performed both before and after any important action of the tribe, such as fishing, gathering camas, or going on a war party, either for the purpose of gaining the goodwill of the Great Spirit in their undertaking, or else in honour of him for the success that has attended them. Six or eight of the principal men of the tribe, generally medicine-men, adorn themselves with masks cut out of some light wood with feathers, highly painted and ornamented, with the eyes and mouth ingeniously made to open and shut. In their hands they hold carved rattles, which are shaken in time to a monotonous song or humming noise (for there are no words to it) which is sung by the whole company as they slowly dance round and round in a circle. . . .

Their lodges are the largest buildings of any description that I have met with amongst Indians. They are divided in the interior into compartments, so as to accommodate eight or ten families, and are well built, considering that the boards are split from the logs with bone wedges; but they succeed in getting them out with great smoothness and regularity. I took a sketch one day while a party was engaged in gambling in the centre of the lodge. The game is called lehallum, and is played with ten small circular pieces of wood, one of which is marked black; these pieces are shuffled about rapidly by the player between two bundles of frayed cedar bark. His opponent suddenly stops his shuffling, and endeavours to guess in which bundle the black piece is concealed. They are so passionately fond of this game that they frequently pass two or three consecutive days and nights at it without ceasing.

Saw-se-a the head chief of the Cowitchins from the Gulf of Georgia, an inveterate gambler, was engaged at the game. He had come to the Esquimelt on a friendly visit. This chief was a great warrior in his younger days, and received an arrow through the cheek in one of his battles. He took many captives, whom he usually sold to the tribes further north, thus diminishing their chance of escaping back through a hostile country to their own people, the northern tribes making slaves only of those living south of them. He possessed much of what is considered wealth amongst the Indians, and it gradually accumulated from tributes which he exacted from his people. On his possessions reaching a certain amount it is customary to make a great feast, to which all contribute. The neighbouring chiefs with whom he is in amity are invited, and at the conclusion of the entertainment, he distributes all he has collected since the last feast, perhaps three or four years preceding, among his guests as presents. The amount of property thus collected and given away by a chief is sometimes very considerable. I have heard of one possessing as many as twelve bales of blankets, from twenty to thirty guns, with numberless pots, kettles and pans, knives and other articles of cutlery, and great quantities of beads, and other trinkets, as well as numerous beautiful Chinese boxes, which find their way here from the Sandwich Islands. The object in this giving his treasures away is to add to his own importance in the eyes of others, his own people often boasting of how much their chief has given away, and exhibiting with pride such things as they had received themselves from him.

In the Gulf
Robin Skelton

There is a great stone head
here on the island.

None on the island
sees it as a head

but as a boulder under
rain-soaked trees

where the tide rides high
in winter storms

and at the surge of Spring,
so some have scratched

initials on it,
and some other things,

not seeing how the great
blind eyeballs stare,

nor how the mouth is fastened
upon silence.

Forest fire, McLeod Lake north of Prince George.

Morning mist from above Trail.

Seven Veils Falls, Yoho National Park.

Breaking wave near Tlell on Graham Island in the Queen Charlottes.

Snow-covered boulders above Lake MacArthur, Yoho National Park.

Mount Odaray reflected in Lake O'Hara, Yoho National Park.

Sundown at Nels Bight, Cape Scott Provincial Park.

Lake Magog, Mount Assiniboine Provincial Park.

Sea caves at Owen Point, Pacific Rim National Park.

Swathed field and autumn colours at Bear Flat west of Fort St. John.

Irrigated field on the terraces above the Fraser River, south of Gang Ranch.

Sand dunes and dead trees between Experiment Bight and Guise Bay, Cape Scott Provincial Park.

Maple covered with moss and ferns, northern Vancouver Island.

Reeds in Lac Le Jeune, south of Kamloops.

Time exposure of star trails in winter, Mount Assiniboine Provincial Park.

Rainbow over Tatei Ridge, Mount Robson Provincial Park.

A Reminiscence of 1850

Dr. John Sebastian Helmcken

About March, 1850, I happened to spend a day in Victoria. The *Norman Morison* had arrived from England, bringing about eighty immigrants. The ship lay in Esquimalt harbor. The immigrants were busy ashore, scrubbing and washing their clothes, trunks and so forth, and I learned that soon after leaving England, the small pox broke out on board, but that for the past two months it had disappeared. The ship, men and four or five women were in quarantine. Nearly the whole of them were under engagement to the Hudson's Bay Co. at £25 per annum.

Upon my arrival, I was soon presented to Governor Blanshard, Chief Factor Douglas, Mr. Finlayson and some other gentleman, and turned over to the care of Dr. A. Benson, whom I had known in England—a well clothed man known by the soubriquet "Commodore." There he lived in "Bachelors' Hall," a gentleman good and kind as ever, but his garments! He had on a pair of "sea-boots" into one of which he had managed to put one leg with the pants on, the other with the pants outside, and other parts of his dress were equally conspicuous by their eccentricity. "Ah," said he, "you laugh, but if you were to remain here a few months you would of necessity become the same!" He had a coffee pot, and such a coffee pot! on the stove. The stove was square, made of sheet iron, bent in all directions by the heat, with a cast iron door, and it was fed with large billets of wood, of which plenty existed in the Hall. It looked mean and dilapidated, but it was soon found capital for roasting native oysters upon.

"Bachelors' Hall" was a portion of a large story and a half block building, having a common room in the centre, and two rooms on each side with a door opening into each. One was occupied by the Doctor, one by J. W. McKay, and a third by Capt. Nevin, the fourth being the "surgery." The latter was unique. It contained a gun case and a few shelves, with drugs in bottles or in paper in every direction. The tin lining of a "packing case" served for a counter; there was a 'cot' slung to the ceiling; to this room I was consigned. The remainder of the building (it occupied the site of the now Bank of British Columbia) belonged to the chaplain and lady, Mr. and Mrs. Staines, who kept a boarding school for young ladies therein—and a splendid teacher and preceptress she was.

Capt. Grant, of Sooke, arrived in the evening and domiciled in Capt. Nevin's room, and I turned into the hammock.

Every room had sporting weapons in it—muskets and rifles of great variety—swords, a saddle and bridle, tobacco and pipes, lots of dust, and the usual utensils, but not all supplied with the necessary articles. I slept well that night, and was awakened in the morning by the loud ringing of a bell, and a concert proceeding from a host of curs—these curs assembled under the bell at every meal, and looking up to it—howled, the howling being taken up by some dogs in the Indian village opposite.

Benson called out, "Get up quickly; that is the breakfast bell."

I did, and so did Captain Grant. Whilst dressing I heard the following dialogue:

"Dear, oh dear, where's the soap? Capt. Grant, have you my soap?"

"Aye, aye," was the response, "You shall have it directly."

"Why, what has become of my razor! Grant, have you my razor?"

"Yes, nearly finished, you can have it directly."

And he got it and shaved, then I heard:

"Where's my shirt? I shall be late for breakfast. Grant, have you taken my shirt?"

"I have, my dear fellow; I want to appear at table decent."

"This is too bad, Grant; it is the only clean shirt I have to put on!"

"Never mind, old fellow, put on your old one. It will be clean enough. Mine hasn't been washed for I don't know how long; more than a week, anyhow. You can get yours washed, and Benson, send mine, too, please."

However, we all got to breakfast and afterwards we returned and the following,

"Bless me, where's my tobacco? I left half a case of 'Cavendish' under the bed."

"Oh, yes," says Grant, "I took it, my good fellow, to pay my Indians with! *We'll* get some more soon!"

After having smoked a pipe of peace, for Grant was a splendid fellow and every inch an officer and a gentleman—he had been a captain in the "Scotch Greys"—Benson insisted upon showing me the "lions" of Victoria. He put on his sea-boots, with legs of pants inside—I had only my London-made thin soled—his were dirty; mine nicely polished—he was cute; I a greenhorn—so the doctor "practiced" a little on my verdancy.

Now the "lions" of Victoria then were the Fort and its contents. It had been built by Mr. Finlayson. The Fort was nearly a quadrangle, about one hundred yards long and wide, with bastions at two corners containing cannon. The whole was stockaded with cedar posts about six or eight inches in diameter, and about fifteen feet in length, which had been brought from near "Cedar Hill," hence its name (now called "Mount Douglas"). There were inside about a dozen large block story and a half buildings, say 60x40, roofed with long and wide strips of cedar bark. The buildings were for the storage of goods, Indian trading shop, and a large shop for general trade. It contained everything required. The mess-room, off from which lived Mr. Douglas and family, was at the corner (of now) Fort and Government streets. The "counting house" was near (now) Wharf street. Mr. Finlayson occupied this post and lived there with his family. A belfry stood in the middle of the yard and its bell tolled for meals, for deaths, for weddings, for church service, for fires, and sometimes for warnings. At meal time it was assisted by a chorus of curs. On Wharf street there existed a flagstaff and near it a well some eighty feet deep, but which contained but little water. The prevailing color of the paint was "Spanish brown," and "whitewash" was abundant. The Fort yard was muddy and the sidewalk to the stores consisted of two or three poles, along which Benson trudged, but off which my boots slipped every few steps! So my boots and my pants were not a little muddy, and the wretch Benson laughed at me, saying, "I told you so! you'll soon be like me, if you remain here." For all this exertion I saw nothing but "furs" and stores. Not very many of the former, as they had been already packed to be sent home by the returning *Norman Morison*, Captain Wishart being her commander.

As I could not very well get much muddier, we went outside the "fort" and there lay the *Beaver*, Capt. Dodd in command, so clean, so nice, so spruce, as well outside as in, with "boarding nettings" all round him, cannon on deck, muskets and cutlasses arranged in their proper places, beautiful cabins and good furniture, with a trading place for Indians, who, I was told, were only allowed a few at a time on board, when on trade. She had a large crew—active, robust, weatherbeaten, jolly good-tempered men—fat from not being overworked—some grey, some grizzled, some young; the former had once been similar to the latter in the "service." Outside the Fort there were no houses, save perhaps a block cabin or two. Forest more or less existed from "the ravine," Johnson street, to the north, and the harbor was surrounded with tall pines, and its bowers bedecked with shrubs, many of which were at this early period in blossom. Cultivated fields existed from Government street to the public schools; likewise across the bay, and I was informed the company exported the wheat to Sitka! There were barns up Fort street (this ran through the centre of the Fort) about the site of the Mechanics' Institute, and I think there I saw a few days ago a small shanty which existed then. It is covered with cedar bark. Benson next took me to Beacon Hill. The weather was lovely and warm, the sky bright, the mountains clear, and everything looked paradisiacal—and there we rested, looked at "Dutnall's fields," at the Beacon, which I thought in my ignorance a target; then walked along the beach to near the entrance of Victoria harbor. Benson said: "Now, I will go back by a 'short cut.'" The wretched man came to a swamp (Providence Pond, near Moffat's). Says he, "we cross somewhere about here; come on." He walked along a fallen tree, so did I, not very well, tho'; he jumped from hillock to hillock, so did I; we both jumped to a fallen tree again; it sunk and we both went knee-

deep into the water. He had "sea-boots" on; he looked at me and laughed, "I told you so; you will soon be like me. You are pretty well seasoned now, so come along for I have lost the track." So we followed through this swamp, got out somewhere, got to the Fort, I a wiser but not a sadder man. I had been introduced to "roughing it." My cockney boots and trousers were used up, but both of us were hungry.

After making ourselves decent, for I was told that Mr. Douglas was rather particular about this, the "bell and the dogs" told us it was time for dinner, and to it nothing loath we went. The mess room was more than thirty feet long, by say twenty wide, a large open fire-place at one end and large pieces of cordwood burning therein. A clock on the wall, a long table in the middle, covered with spotless linen, the knives and forks clean, decanters bright, containing wine and so forth. The chairs of wood (Windsor) but everything European. I suppose there must have been more than twenty people in the room, when Mr. Douglas made his appearance—a handsome specimen of nature's noblemen—tall, stout, broad-shouldered, muscular, with a grave bronzed face, but kindly withal. After the usual greetings, he took the head of the table, Mr. Finlayson the foot. Captain Dodd, Capt. Wishart, Capt. Grant and myself were guests. There were also present J. W. McKay, Charley Griffin, Capt. Sangster, and numerous others whom I do not recollect at this moment. Grace having been said by Mr. Douglas, (the chaplain did not dine at the mess, but all the other married officers did) on comes the soup, then the salmon, then the meats—venison on this occasion and ducks—then the pies and so forth, and down they go into their proper receptacle, each one ready and willing to receive them. Having done justice to the dinner and taken a glass "to the Queen," many of the junior members left, either to work or to smoke their pipes in their own quarters. We remained; the steward, a Kanaka, (the cook was also a Kanaka) brought on tobacco and long clay pipes of the kind called "alderman." Mr. Douglas took *his* pipe, which I noticed was beautifully colored, showing slow and careful smoking, (the clerks used to like to get hold of his colored pipes) and others took pipes either from the heap or their pockets. Everybody appeared to smoke calmly and deliberately.

During the dinner there was conversation, Mr. Douglas taking the lead. Capt. Wishart was asked to be careful of his men, as the gold fever was raging and the men deserting as often as they found an opportunity, giving great trouble and necessitating spies. California was spoken about, which led to someone asking where Solomon got his gold from, but no one could answer the conundrum. To change the conversation, perhaps, Mr. Douglas asked the Doctor why so many of the Hudson's Bay officers were bald? His answer was "*pro pelle cutem*—they had sent their furs home," at which some laughed, but Mr. Douglas gravely said, "perhaps, having given us the poetry of the thing, you will give the prose—the cause," which nonplussed the Doctor, as this was a conundrum too. By the *Norman Morison* files of newspapers and "The Four Reviews" of latest dates—that is to say nearly six months old—had come out and Mr. Douglas commenced about some Scotch battles fought long ago. This brought out Dodd, an Englishman, well read and well educated, who derided the breechless vagabonds, and ushered in the ten of diamonds—Johnny Cope got his share. Douglas and Dodd seemed to know how many men were engaged in each battle and all at once they tumbled into the battle of Waterloo, the one claiming that the Scotch did best, the other that the English did most execution, whilst a third claimed that both Scotch and English and Irish would have been beaten had it not been for Blucher and his host coming up just in the nick of time to save the lot. This question was not settled. "Old Tod" was chaffed for having fired a salute four years after the victory, *i.e.*, as soon as he heard of it. He was indignant and said it was less than three. His post had been somewhere near the North Pole. I was informed that no frivolous conversation was ever allowed at table, but that Mr. Douglas as a rule came primed with some intellectual or scientific subject, and thus he educated his clerks. All had to go to church every Sunday, the mess-room serving every purpose—baptisms, marriages, funerals, councils, dances, theatricals, or other amusements—and did not seem any the worse for it.

After dinner we went to see the Indian village. Benson just pointed out the bullet holes in the pickets and bastions made by hostile Indians. "But," said he, "don't be afraid, they are only dangerous when excited, and as a rule they don't get excited without cause given." He procured a canoe, of which I felt dubious, but he taught my tiny feet how to get into it, and so we arrived safely after what I then considered a dangerous passage. There must have been five or six hundred Indians. By far the greater number had a blanket only for clothing, but "King Freezy" had on a tall hat and a long coat and considered himself somebody, as indeed he was, and friendly to the whites. He had a most remarkably flattened head—indeed all the Indians had flattened heads—fearful foreheads, retreating backward. We saw babies undergoing the process, a pad and pressure being the instruments. They did not seem to suffer; perhaps it made them good. The cradles were hung on a flexible pole, stuck in the ground at an acute angle, so a slight touch on the pole put it into an up and down motion. In one house there were a number of people beating tom-toms and chanting. They had a sick child in the centre. The doctor was performing some incantations, such as sucking the child's skin and spitting upon it. The child had a devil, and I suggested he was standing alongside. Benson said no, he is the doctor, a man and a brother Medico. This was very interesting, but our time being precious, we looked at their "woolly dogs" and the dirt and filth and returned in our, what seemed to me then, very frail and treacherous conveyance. Bye-the-bye these "woolly dogs" seem to have become extinct. These Indians used to shear them and made a sort of blanket out of the wool. . . .

It being now supper time, we went to the mess room. The company was smaller, and after chatting around the fire and smoking of course, every one went his own way, but most to "the hall."

After adjourning to "Bachelors' Hall," a Frenchman came (all the men were French Canadians) and said to the Doctor, "Pierre has a bad stomach-ache." Doctor—"Bad stomach-ache, aye? Ah! eating too much. Ah, yes! Give him a tablespoonful of salts. Ah, yes! a tablespoonful of salts!" "Oh," said the man, "but he is very bad." Doctor—"Ah! hum, yes, very bad, eh! very bad! eh? Then give him two spoonfuls of salts! Oh, yes, that's the way to clean out the 'salt salmon.'"

There were a good many in Bachelors' Hall—all young men. After a while Capt. Grant began "to entertain the company." He showed how to use the sword. He stuck a candle on the back of a chair, and snuffed it therewith, but I am bound to confess he took off a good piece of the candle with it, and down it went. Again the candle was stuck up. Then he split it longitudinally and this time splendidly. He wanted to "cut" a button off Benson's coat (he had none too many) but Benson said—Oh! Oh! cut a button—no, no—split or spit one too! ho! ho! After a while he wanted to escort Her Majesty to Windsor Castle. All were to be cavalry. So down everybody went Kangaroo fashion. Grant being in command, took the lead, and so we hopped in this style round the room, and made considerable of a racket. . . . In the midst of which, some naughty school girl overhead . . . poured some water through a crack in the ceiling right down upon the cavalry! This put an end to the diversion, but only resulted in others, for some one wanted a song, and it came, for there were good singers among them. In the midst of this a spy brought word that some of the men had a canoe and were about to depart to the other side, so off McKay went. This broke up the party and away we went to bed, and so ended a day in Victoria.

I stand to-day upon the same spot, but oh! how changed. Of the twenty or thirty met before, but two or three answer to the call. Of the fields, naught remain. The forest has been removed and the bleak winds unhindered now rush in to what was before a genial, sheltered place. The *Beaver* remains, but . . . no more like the *Beaver* of former days than a coal barge is like a frigate. Mightier steamers float upon the harbor; the Indians, once half a thousand, have disappeared, homes occupy the fields; telegraph and telephone wires make the streets hideous; there is great hurry and scurry, but I doubt whether there is more happiness and content now than was enjoyed by the few but hospitable and kind-hearted Hudson's Bay Co. residents in 1850. Peace be with them—their works live after them.

(*Colonist*, Holiday Number, Dec. 1887)

On the Old Trail

Bruce Hutchison

What is left of the old Cariboo? Not much, but enough, perhaps, to tell us something of its spirit.

In the dusk of a bitter autumn day, in 1921, I found myself beside the gold creeks of the upper Fraser. I had come here on a fool's errand, to find some trace of the rush, some remnant of its adventure, a touch of the magic that had drawn men from the four corners of the earth. There were still reminders of the rush—the original road, a few decayed cabins, and now and then a grave with a rotting wooden cross at the roadside. But little flavour of the old days, no sense of great events, no feeling of history.

My horse, a hired animal with no stomach for such work, had turned lame. I was hungry, saddlesore, and soaked to the skin by the autumn's first sleet. Barkerville lay 30 miles ahead. I had begun to wonder where I could stop that night, and to remember with a new understanding the labours of other travellers on this road before me, when I saw a light gleaming through the trees. The horse broke into a trot and stopped before the door of a log house. By the oddest chance he had brought me to the one habitation where I could hear the story of the rush at first hand.

Harry Jones lived in that house. I suppose he was over seventy years old then but he looked under sixty—a lean, erect man with a fine weathered face, a plume of white hair and clear, quiet eyes. When he joined the rush of '62 he was a boy just over from Wales, a kind of mascot among the Argonauts. Half a dozen others of that company were still alive then but they were older than Jones and he alone remained beside the Cariboo Road.

He had left it once, after making a stake sufficient to keep him in luxury. He had gone back to Wales, had been a fellow townsman of a youth named Lloyd George, and by his own account had bought all the pleasures of London that gold nuggets could command. But the whole island of Britain, he said, was too small to hold a man who had stretched his muscles in the Cariboo. Jones came back to live beside the old road at Wing Dam on the bank of Lightning Creek. His stake was gone but he did not miss it.

By his fire that night, we could hear the chatter of the creek over gravel, dug and washed and sluiced by a thousand miners. Shivering on the creekbank in the spring of '61, some forgotten prospector looked up at a shattering thunderstorm and shouted to his fellows: "Well, boys, this is lightning!" Lightning Creek it remained, one of the richest and probably the most dangerous in the Cariboo.

Jones worked Lightning with the others. He remembered it as a quiet little river purling westward toward the Fraser. Now its banks were heaped up with the gravel litter of the miners' sluices and rockers. Its current swirled over a broken wing dam of logs thrust out to divert its water from the gold bars. Underneath it a rabbit warren of tunnels, laboriously shored up by wooden cribbing, was filling up with slum.

They never could get to the bottom of Lightning. At the edge of the river they dug down to bedrock and burrowed their tunnels under the stream, but always, just as the pay dirt was getting rich, oozing slum drove them back or trapped them like flies. Machinery had been brought in later, more tunnels bored, more gold exposed, but the slum oozed again.

Now Lightning was abandoned and Jones was left alone. He could sit by his window and watch the creek and think about the men who had worked with him here, and of the gold still lying deep down on the bedrock, more gold by far than the miners ever took out. The presence of that hoard, safe from prying hands, seemed to satisfy him.

Most of the night I plied him with questions. Cariboo Cameron, Barker, Stout, Deitz, Begbie and Douglas—he remembered them all as clearly as yesterday's weather, but he had little to say about them. To Jones they were companions of the trail, a few among the many who came and went and of no special note.

He finally told me, when I pressed him, how Cameron dug up the bodies of his baby daughter and wife, preserved them in an iron casket full of alcohol, packed them out to the coast on horses, shipped them by way of the Panama all the way to Ontario and buried them at home. This Jones mentioned as a passing incident and seemed surprised at my interest in it. Cameron, he said, had merely made good a promise to his wife. To pack two bodies in alcohol on the backs of horses, he allowed, was a formidable feat. But then, they'd packed pianos from the coast in the same way and even a huge English billiard table for Kelly's Hotel in Barkerville.

Jones knew Barkerville pretty well. A kind of wild town, he said. You had to pay the German hurdy-gurdy girls $10 for a dance and a lot more for larger favours. A respectable woman, he added quickly, was as safe on the Cariboo Road as in God's pocket. A man who looked at her would be run out of camp. But the German girls did all right, for there was plenty of money.

Why, one night Red Jack McMartin brought $44,000 in gold into the Shuniah saloon, setup drinks for everybody, paid for all the glasses in the place, broke them one by one against the wall, danced with hobnail boots on a case of champagne until it all leaked out, smashed a $3,000 mirror behind the bar with a last shower of nuggets, and ended in the street, penniless. McMartin never made another stake.

Billy Barker, who made the first big strike on Williams Creek, took out $600,000, spent it over the bar, got a job as a cook in a road camp, lived his last days in the old men's home in Victoria. Billy Deitz, who gave Williams Creek its name, ended the same way. Even Cameron, the millionaire, set up an estate back east, lost it, returned to the creek, and died a poor man at Barkerville. Jones had been wealthy too, but he had nothing now except the buried treasure of Lightning.

Of the whole story he gave me only such odd fragments and these unwillingly. I was young then or I would have known that to the man who was in it the rush was no adventure but a dull, hard livelihood of toiling, unremembered days. Like most human events, it became an adventure only when the historians put it on paper with an excitement unknown to the men who made it. Jones had no use for history books and magazine articles that tried to exaggerate the rush into an epic. They were wrong, he said, in most of their facts and in all their explanations.

A few years after this Jones met some of the historians face to face for the first time when, on their invitation, he unveiled a cairn in Barkerville and took the opportunity, in a few well-chosen words, to insult them. Their ceremony, he said, was bunk, their records were distorted, and they had put the cairn in the wrong place. His speech was attributed to his great age and was not reported.

If Jones had known that I would mention him in a book myself, I suppose he would have treated me differently that night. My intentions were then quite innocent. I had come only in the hope of re-discovering the old legends at first hand for myself and, of course, I was bound to fail, for the legends are an afterthought, the legendary figures old men who could give only the facts, never the contents. So I left Jones the next morning in his doorway, peering at Lightning Creek where the gold still lay thick on the bedrock.

It was nightfall again when I rode past the dark, unblinking eye called Jack of Clubs Lake, over the tailings of Lohee that spread for a mile across the valley, and down the last hill into Barkerville.

The town, a double row of shacks along a single street, lay cramped between Williams Creek and a naked hill. The creek had been churned up so long by the miners and so much gravel had flowed into it from the claims farther up the valley that even the log dikes could not keep it out of the town. Most of it seemed to be running down the street that night. Year after year the buildings had been propped higher out of the mud until they reeled on their stilts and seemed held together by two lines of crazy elevated sidewalks.

The stores with their false fronts, the cabins gaping windowless to the weather, had never been painted. They were the same colour as the welter of mud and gravel around them and they looked like some fungus growth in the niche of the hills. No, that was too fancy. They looked precisely like a movie set of two dimensions, such a town as a Hollywood director would build overnight for a western picture.

But Barkerville was real. Men had lived in these buildings, miners had walked these sidewalks, girls had danced in these empty barrooms, stagecoaches had clattered down this narrow street, bull teams had toiled through the mud, and in the opera house, with its queer tower, held up now by long props, strolling players had acted Shakespeare and taken their pay in nuggets.

Any ancient ruin has at least a myth about it, a patina, the scene of deeds and the feel of ghosts. Here was nothing but a huddle of shacks, a memorial of cardboard with no relic of life, no sign to stir the blood, or conjure visions. Having read the story of Cariboo and pictured Barkerville when it heaved with life, I was sorry now that I had come.

A few men still lived there, lacking energy to leave, the last dregs of the rush. Of the thousands who had swarmed in this curious nest there were ninety-one in the town and in all the country around it, according to the reliable census kept in the head of Fred Tregillus. None of these inhabitants could be seen out of doors that night, but a light or two flickered in the crooked street. I headed for the nearest one. It shone from the parlour of Kelly's Hotel, which had served the gold rush well and still welcomed the occasional visitor in its old style.

An ancient man with a Santa Claus beard was sitting by the fat belly of the drum stove when I came in. He looked at me suspiciously. His name was Bill Brown, he was one of the Argonauts, he lived alone in the hills, and he came to town for a bit of excitement now and then. But he would not talk with strangers. This turned out to be a big night for Barkerville, for three other outsiders drove in by automobile—too big a night for Bill Brown. At the sight of this mass invasion he shuffled out of the hotel without a word, mounted a horse almost as old as himself, and rode out of town.

Kelly's Hotel was a friendly, intimate sort of place. Its wooden walls were impregnated with the smell of rich cooking and old liquor, and the smell of good solid mahogany furniture and the smoke of wood fire. The bar (alas, unused under a barbarous prohibition law) still glistened in the lamplight. Nude Turkish ladies, of lavish bosom, smiled down at you with a fixed and sexless smile from heavy gilt frames. Upstairs the bedrooms were richly papered, the beds deep with feather mattresses, the washbasins and jugs of good English porcelain, all packed in by wagon from the coast.

Like every stopping place on the Cariboo Road in those days, Kelly's inundated you with food on heaped-up platters challenging you to deplete them. Also, it followed the fine old Cariboo custom of segregating the sexes at mealtimes. The men ate in the dining room, the women waited on them and then ate the leftovers in the kitchen. This was a man's country still.

How the desolate jumble of shacks and that sterile valley produced our dinner I have never been able to discover—a miracle performed over a stove like a locomotive by a grinning Chinese giant who had walked into Barkerville half a century before and never stopped cooking since. Somehow at Kelly's they had stood the siege and had kept alive a spark of Barkerville's old fire.

Thus warmed and fed, I set out for the Tregillus house, to which I had been directed. It lay at the end of the town, hard by the dike and below the level of the creek beside it. To reach it I had to navigate, by dead reckoning, the stilted sidewalk high above the mud of the street, together with many stairways, creaking bridges and single planks, all invisible in the darkness and slippery with rain.

It was a strange walk. An imaginative man would have felt the presence of spirits in a place so populous with memories. A nervous man would have imagined all sorts of things writhing in the blackness of these deserted stores, saloons and cabins. As I was neither imaginative nor nervous, I walked on concerned only with keeping upright, but the sound of the creek, of rain hammering on the roof, of water swirling down wooden gutters and gurgling through broken drains was like a sly whispering behind my back. I walked faster.

There were no spirits and no marauders—only four old men playing cards in a dismal room by the light of an old lamp (they played all winter with a few hours out for meals), and a young Chinese reading a newspaper on the counter of his store. A scrawled placard in the window announced that gold was bought here, and the idea of gold still circulating in Barkerville so intrigued me that I opened the door and went inside.

The Chinese—far too young to remember better days—was buying gold as it had been bought here since the sixties—a few tiny nuggets, a handful of dust painfully gathered by a couple of old men out of the tailings. On an antique scale the storekeeper weighed a nugget not much bigger than a pin's head and sold it to me for $3.55, but he had nothing else to offer, no realization that he was the end of a long line, the survivor of an ancient trade, the last gold buyer. So I walked on, as he explained the path, to the Tregillus house.

Fred Tregillus was a black-bearded Cornishman, short, powerful of limb and soft of speech—a hard-rock miner. He had come out from the old country when the placer mines were closing and he had remained in the belief that where gold can be found in the gravel it can be found somewhere in ore. He had spent most of his life looking for the mother lode of the Fraser and year by year he thought he was creeping up to it.

Meanwhile he had mastered geology out of books, and a great many other things as well. In that cabin against the dike there was a better knowledge of world history and current affairs than you would find in most of the houses of Vancouver. I have always contended that men in the wilderness know more about the news of the day than city folk who are close to it and lost in it. Tregillus is the prize exhibit in my case.

His household had been preserved intact from the old days. The furniture was English, substantial and Victorian. The chairs were protected by lace antimacassars. The tiny organ was pumped by foot pedals. While Mrs. Tregillus played this instrument, her husband, her children and I sang hymns, for it was a Sunday night.

The war had just ended in Europe, the world was hysterical, the era of flaming youth and perpetual prosperity had begun. It was hard to believe in such a time that such a house remained at the end of the Cariboo Road, where a Cornish miner, still searching for the ultimate treasure, spent his Sunday evenings singing hymns.

This at least was an unconscious touch of the original Cariboo, the first I had seen, innocent of any pretence. The Tregillus family around the creaky organ was the genuine article, the authentic breed, and quite unaware that they had become obsolete in this new and better world, that they lived in another century and on a worthless hope.

Next morning Tregillus showed me a little burrow in the rocks at the edge of the town, his latest assault on the mother lode, the work of many months, singlehanded. He said it looked promising and held up a sample of ore for my inspection. It meant nothing to me—a chunk of rock, in the hand of a deluded man who, under this calm, outer look, must have turned a little mad. Tregillus evidently saw what I thought, chuckled in the recesses of his beard, and said he would show me something of interest if I came back in a few years.

We met the Pack Rat that morning. His name was Joel Stevens, but it had been forgotten long ago. He was a bent gnome in rags, living amid the accumulation of unimaginable junk which he had crammed into his cabin—tin cans, old newspapers, rusty nails, gold pans, broken tools, anything he could lay his hands on. By now there was space left only for his bed and his stove and he had begun to heap up his miser's hoard outside. He seemed to value it as the miners had valued gold. Barkerville was always tolerant of idiosyncracy. The Pack Rat pursued his harmless dream in peace.

Near him lived two old ladies who had been born in Barkerville and had never travelled farther from it than Quesnel. They had gone there to see a railway train. Having seen it, they were glad to come home again. Barkerville, they said, was good enough for them, and one of these days it would get lively again. No one could believe such a prophecy on the empty street but, oddly enough, the old ladies were right.

Their snug little house, with potted plants in the windows, stood next to the opera house. We went inside this deserted building but there was little to see. When the rush subsided they had turned the opera house into the town firehall. The leather fire buckets and some axes still hung on the walls. It was here that Barkerville held its larger celebrations, and here that James Anderson, the civic poet, used to recite his latest verse, in Scottish doggerel. . . .

Anderson's Highland melancholy shows through all his verses, especially when he considers the price of goods in Barkerville:

> Your letter cam' by the express,
> Eight shillin's carriage, naethin' less!
> You maybe like to ken what pay
> Miners get here for ilka day?
> Jus' two poond sterling, sure as death—
> It should be four, between us baith—
> For gin ye coont the cost o' livin'
> There's naethin' left to gang an' come on.

There was more truth here than poetry. Potatoes retailed at $90 a sack, milk (frozen) at $1 a pound, boots $50, champagne 2 ounces of gold per pint, nails $1 a pound, and a stove $700. If you wanted a piano, and a good many people did, you paid $1 a pound to have it packed on mules.

Who cared? There was plenty of gold directly beneath the town. Not far from the opera house Tregillus showed me the entrance to Billy Barker's famous shaft, the first sunk into the clay on what was to be the town's main street. It was only a hole in the ground now, covered over with rotting planks like an abandoned well. But when it was dug the real wealth of Cariboo was uncovered for the first time. Results of surface workings on Williams Creek had been poor at the beginning and few men paused there. When Barker got down fifty feet on August 21, 1862, and came up with the richest pay dirt anybody had ever seen, the camp enjoyed a riot.

Bishop Hills, who had gone up from Victoria to serve the miners' spiritual needs, noted in his diary: "When lead struck on Barker's claim, about August 21st, all went on spree for several days, except one Englishman, well brought up." That Englishman was not Barker. The bars and a widow in Victoria got most of his share of the treasure.

After his shaft many others were sunk beside Williams Creek and tunnels from them were drifted under the creek bed. It was now so honeycombed with timber, the logs all preserved in the slum, that a dredge could not work under the old gravel. How much unfound gold still lay under the tailings of Bill Deitz's creek and far deeper in the gravel and in the blue clay against the bedrock? Tregillus shook his head. He was a hard-rock man.

Old Cariboo Wagon Road North
Eric Ivan Berg

for Pat Lane

This is a country of ghosts—
of the ghosts who've gone before us with
pick-axe, salt pork, rifle and pack train mule.
Wagonwheel ghosts still echo in the timber, the hubs of
winter still rasping away, ringing true to the ears of snow.

These early spirits drift away with the smelt fog.
It's low morning mists retreating in ranks far out
beyond the scrag pine tops as burnoff begins again.
Long dead men lie buried here in the sluice cricks
of the gold rush with the cold gold dust that they
sought now embedded in the marrow of their bones.

These giant men of yore-ago myth were born strongboned
and well willing to work the endless hours as slave
to the sluice shute, rocker pit and blowhole shaft.
They were wagonmasters, miners, outlaws, trappers and
    Chinamen
(who worked like devils to be treated like dogs) all of whom
carved open this big country and blasted this cliffhanging road.

Claimed by gold rush fever these old ghosts haunting us
died young with maddening losses in the muskeg sloughs littered
with broken pack trains, lost caches, blackfly bloodsuckers
and those gawdawful winters with their long underwear
frozen stiff into flatboard by the windchill at forty below!

Bearded hoarfrost ghosts of the old wagon road north
they linger on laughing at this country that killed them.
But now as mellow old farts they still go panning down beside
the new highway's sidewinding cricks. They're old fakers
always looking for paydirt and hooting their ire at those yahoo
Yankee tourists who throw garbage from speeding stationwagons.

From *Hope: The Colours of Time.*
A Drama for Voices
Michael Mercer

FIRST VOICE: This is the account of a place where history—or what we know as history—never really happened. The town is Hope, British Columbia, a place mid-way on the road to other places, and the time—if we can say such places have a time—is the month of June, 1911. In that month, the community of Hope was in the midst of a brief wave of gold fever, brought on by a strike on nearby Steamboat Mountain that was, for a short time at least, acclaimed the richest strike the world has ever known. In the flush of this momentary boom, the town was growing rapidly; new businesses and homes were under construction and property values were soaring.

To its residents—like the residents of many places in many times—the town of Hope thrived in a promising present that lay between an unknown future and an indistinguished past.

SECOND VOICE: This is the story of people who—but for a gravestone epitaph, or a line in a faded newspaper—might never have been.

. . .

[*Sound: A nighthawk's cry breaking the silence and moving as in flight.*]

SECOND VOICE: Creep down to the town: down through the wet and wind-hussed cedar, hemlock, jackpine, fir. Down to the edge of the forest where millesimal stars float like moon-spit, shredded and tangled, on the trembling, brimming pools of catkin marshes; where frogs and logs, swamp lanterns and newts, duckweed and toads curl floppy-wet and winking in the mud. A mountain chill barks foxfree in the darkness of an early June morning, slips up the banks of the Fraser and moves about the buildings of the town, rooting at the cracks of clapboard and doorframe, chimney and windowpane. Leaving dew where it moves up the mud length of Wallace Street: where the houses sleep more still than space, and in them space sleeps window-lidded with opalescence of muslin or cambric, muffle of broadcloth or canvas. It moves through the darkness into the meadows of witch-grass, bending blades with nose-drops of dew, and shining the green chinese windbells of the quaking aspen. Here on the edge of town, where even now new buildings rise, boxfloor and frame, it whispers about the raw white shinbone-and-femur forms, muting the fragrance of fresh-cut pine. In this river-born chill, the dreams of a river-born town germinate under the warmth of feather comforters and counterpanes: they grow in a head, in a bed, in a room in a building in a town; and take root finally in the friendly soil of an inward world far from the shriek of the lumbermill cat, that now cries on the steps of the Coquhalla Hotel.

[*Sound: A nighthawk's cry moving as in flight.*]

SECOND VOICE: Creep down to the town; down through the wet and wind-hussed cedar, hemlock, jackpine, fir. Down to the edge of the dreams where the chill and the night and the mud and the passion of cats cannot follow.

FIRST VOICE: To the east, the wagon-rutted length of Water Street becomes a mudpath, becomes a narrow passage through a screen of vine maple, becomes a cabin of ancient weathered shakes.

CHORUS 1 [*A.S. plaintive*]:
He dree. . .

CHORUS 2 [*A.S. indrawn breath*]:
Shhhhhh. . .

CHORUS 3 [*A.S. aspirant*]:
Hushhhhh. . .

[*Note: The above is repeated through next speech in B.G. and the desired effect is that of rhythmic breathing.*]

FIRST VOICE: Here in shadows black as coffee grounds, old deaf Daddy Yates, sworn enemy of magpies, hunches under the slush and slosh of water sounds where the Fraser River turns. It chimes from ear to ear beneath the old rock miner's face, and twists memory-mauled in lazy eddies where hair tufts from the porches of leather flesh.

CHORUS 1 [*A.S. plaintive*]:
He dreeee. . .

CHORUS 4 [*A.S.*]:
He dreams.

CHORUS 2 [*A.S. indrawn breath*]:
Shhhhh. . .

CHORUS 4 [*A.S.*]:
He dreams.

CHORUS 3 [*A.S. aspirant*]:
Hushhhh. . .

CHORUS 1:
Of rocks.

CHORUS 4:
Flat rocks.

CHORUS 1:
Hot flat rocks.

FIRST VOICE: Of flat rocks above the river.

CHORUS 4:
He dreams. . .

CHORUS 2 [*A.S. indrawn breath*]:
Shhhh . . .

CHORUS 3 [*A.S. aspirant*]:
Hushhhhh . . .

[*Note: Chorus 2 and 3 carry on through next two speeches in B.G.*]

FIRST VOICE: Above the river, flat rocks, stonetop hot in the noon, and spread with salal and serviceberries.

SECOND VOICE: Beneath them, Indians with skins dark as chewing tobacco troll on the river with lines of seaweed, smoked and knotted. On the bone fangs of their hooks they snag the bottom—leavings of his better days.

CHORUS 1: And up they come brown and eyeless on the ancient flood of him.

CHORUS 3 *repeats above coming in on word* brown and.
CHORUS 4 *repeats above coming in on word* they.
CHORUS 2 *repeats above, coming in on word* brown.

SECOND VOICE: About him he dreams again.

CHORUS 4:
Ten thousand men

SECOND VOICE: Bound for the goldfields of the Cariboo.

CHORUS 3:
Ten thousand men

CHORUS 4:
With river eyes

CHORUS 1:
that never stop moving

CHORUS 4:
with uncombed beards

CHORUS 1:
that wagged in laughter

CHORUS 3:
one thousand plumes of smoke

CHORUS 2:
curling into the sky like pillars in a temple

[*Music: Two or three bars of Jew's Harp hesitantly testing an intro.*]

CHORUS 1:
the smell of coffee

CHORUS 5:
saltpork

CHORUS 4:
lye soap

CHORUS 2:
cedar tobacco and sweat

[*Sound: Jew's Harp again picking up.*]

CHORUS 3:
the rattle of dice boxes

CHORUS 5:
jingle of coin

CHORUS 2:
squeak of moist corks

CHORUS 3:
bartenders with oiled heads, boiled shirts and brass studs all over them

[*Sound: Jew's Harp again picking up.*]

CHORUS 1:
Shining shining in the sun.

SECOND VOICE: And in the midst of it all, Daddy Yates, a man barely boy, dancing a jig with a jug in a ring of teethwhite goldcapped faces that stop up the spaces between the trees.

[*Music: Jew's Harp comes up again and plays short break and fades.*]

CHORUS 2 [*A.S. indrawn breath*]:
Shhhh . . .

CHORUS 3 [*A.S. aspirant*]:
Hushhhhh . . .

FIRST VOICE (*after pause*): Cold from the rush of passing years, the old body of Daddy Yates snuggles under the quilt for warmth, kills a magpie with a snore, and escapes yet again the ice blue vaulted mountain born hand of eternity.

[*Sound: Cry of nighthawk, as in flight.*]

The Black Canyon of the Ominica

William Francis Butler

About noon, on the 10th of May, we set out for the Ominica, with high hopes of finding the river still low enough to allow us to ascend it.

Ten miles above Toy's hut the Ominica enters the Peace River from the south-west. We reached its mouth on the morning of the 11th, and found it high and rapid. There was hard work in store for us, and the difficulties of passing the Great Cañon loomed ominously big. We pushed on, however, and that night reached a spot where the river issued from a large gap in a high wall of dark rock. Above, on the summit of this rock, pine-trees projected over the river. We were at the door of the Ominica Cañon. The warm weather of last week had done its work, and the water rushed from the gate of the cañon in a wild and impetuous torrent. We looked a moment at the grim gate which we had to storm on the morrow, and then put in to the north shore, where, under the broad and lofty pines, we made our beds for the night. . . .

Casting off from camp, on the morning of the 12th, we pushed right into the mouth of the cañon. At once our troubles began. The steep walls of smooth rock rose directly out of the water—sometimes washed by a torrent, at others beaten by a back-whirl and foaming eddy. In the centre ran a rush of water that nothing could stem. Poling, paddling, clinging with hands and nails to the rock; often beaten back and always edging up again, we crept slowly along under the overhanging cliff, which leaned out two hundred feet above us to hold upon its dizzy verge some clinging pine-tree. In the centre of the chasm, about half a mile from its mouth, a wild cataract of foam forbade our passage; but after a whole morning's labour we succeeded in bringing the canoe safely to the foot of this rapid, and moored her in a quiet eddy behind a sheltering rock. Here we unloaded, and, clambering up a cleft in the cañon wall two hundred feet above us, passed along the top of the cliff, and bore our loads to the upper or western end of the cañon, fully a mile from the boat. The day was hot and sweltering, and it was hard work. . . .

We pushed through the dense underwood, loaded down with all the paraphernalia of our travel, and even Cerf-vola carried his load of boots and moosemeat. When we had finished carrying our loads, it was time for dinner; and that over, we set to work at once for the stiffer labour of hauling the canoe up the rapid of the cañon; for, remember, there was no hope of lifting her, she was too heavy, and the rocky walls were far too steep to allow for it. Up along shore, through rapid and eddy we dragged our craft, for here the north side had along its base ledges of rock and bits of shore, and taking advantage of these, sometimes in the canoe and sometimes out of it in the water, we reached at length the last edge or cliff round which it was possible to proceed at the north shore.

For a long time we examined the spot, and the surrounding cañon. Jacques and I climbed up to the top above, and then down on hands and knees to a ledge from which we could look over into the chasm, and scan its ugly features. Beyond a doubt it was ugly—the rock on which we lay hollowed down beneath us until it roofed the shore of the cañon with a half cavern, against which a wild whirlpool boiled up now and again, sinking suddenly into stillness. Even if we could stretch a line from above the rock to where our canoe lay below it, she must have been knocked to atoms in the whirlpool in her passage beneath the cavern; but the distance was too great to stretch a line across. The next and only course was to make a bold crossing from below the rock, and gain the other shore, up which it was possible to drag our canoe. Once over, the thing would be easy for at least a couple of hundred yards more.

We climbed back to the canoe and imparted the result of our investigation to the other two men. From the level of the boat the proposed crossing looked very nasty. It was across a wild rush of water, in the centre of the cañon, and if we failed to make a small eddy at the farther shore we must drive full upon the precipice of rock where, below us, boiled and seethed the worst rapid in the cañon—a mass of wave, and foam, and maddened surge. Once out of the sheltering eddy in which we lay watching this wild scene, we would be in the midst of the rush close above the rapid. There was no time to get headway on the canoe. It would shoot from shelter into furious current, and then, if it missed yon little eddy, look out; and if you have any good angels away from home, pray that they may be praying for you—for down that white fall of water you must go broadside or stern on.

The more we looked at it, the less we liked it; but it was the sole means of passing the cañon, and retreat came not yet into our heads. We took our places—Kalder in the bow, Jacques at the stern, A___ and I in the middle; then we hugged the rock for the last time, and shoved out into the swirl of waters. There was no time to think; we rose and fell; we dipped our paddles in the rushing waves with those wild quick strokes which men use when life is in the blow; and then the canoe swung and rocked for a second, and with a wild yell of Indian war-whoop from Kalder, which rose above the rush of the water, we were in the eddy at the farther shore.

It was well done. On again up the cañon with line from rock to rock, bit by bit, until, as the sun began to slope low upon the forest, we reach the foot of the last fall—the stiffest we had yet breasted. Above it lies our camp upon the north shore; above it will be easy work—we will have passed the worst of the Ominica River.

Made bold by former victory we passed our line round the rock, and bent our shoulders to haul the canoe up the slant of water. Kalder with a long pole held the frail craft out from the rock. A____ and I were on the line, and Jacques was running up to assist us, when suddenly there came upon the rope a fierce strain; all at once the canoe seemed to have the strength of half a dozen runaway horses. It spun us round, we threw all our strength against it, and snap went the rope midway over the water; the boat had suddenly sheered, and all was over. We had a second line fastened to the bow; this was held by Kalder at the moment of the accident, but it was in loose coils about him, and of no service to stay the downward rush. Worse than all, the canoe, now going like an arrow down the rapid, tightened the tangled coils around Kalder's legs, and I saw with horror that he stood every chance of being dragged feet foremost from the smooth rock on which he stood, into the boiling torrent beneath.

Quicker than thought he realized his peril; he sprang from the treacherous folds, and dragged with all his strength the quick-running rope clear of his body; and then, like the Indian he was, threw all his weight to stay the canoe.

It was useless; his line snapped like ours had done, and away went the canoe down the surge of water—down the lip of the fall—away, away—bearing with her our sole means of travel through the trackless wilderness! We crouched together on the high rock, which commanded a long view down the Black Cañon, and gazed wistfully after our vanishing boat.

In one instant we were reduced to a most wretched state. Our canoe was gone; but that was not half our loss—our meat and tent had also gone with her; and we were left on the south shore of the river, while a deep, wide and rapid stream rolled between us and our camp, and we had no axe wherewith to cut trees for a raft—no line to lash them together. Night was coming on; we were without food, shipwrecked in the wilderness.

When the canoe had vanished, we took stock of all these things, and then determined on a course. It was to go back along the upper edge of the cañon to the entrance opposite our camping-place of the last night, there to make a raft from some logs that had been collected for a *cache* in the previous year, then to put together whatever line or piece of string we possessed, and, making a raft, endeavour to cross to the north shore, and thus gain our camp above the cañon.

It was a long piece of work, and we were already tired with the day's toil, but it was the sole means by which we could hope to get back to our camp and to food again. After that we would deliberate upon further movements.

When men come heavily to grief in any enterprise, the full gravity of the disaster does not break all at once upon their minds; nay, I have generally found that the first view of the situation is the ludicrous one. One is often inclined to laugh over some plight, which means anything but a laughing matter in reality.

We made our way to the mouth of the cañon, and again held a council. Jacques did not like the idea of the raft; he would go down through the Beaver swamps along the south shore, and, it might be, find the canoe stranded on some beach lower down. Anyhow he would search, and next morning he would come up again along the river and hail us across the water in our camp with tidings of his success; so we parted.

We at once set to work to make our raft. We upset the logs of the old *cache*, floated them in the water, and lashed them together as best we could, with all the bits of line we could fasten together; then we got three rough poles, took our places on the rickety raft, and put out into the turbid river. Our raft sank deep into the water; down, down we went; no bottom for the poles, which we used as paddles in the current. At last we reached the shore of a large island, and our raft was thrown violently amidst a pile of driftwood. We scrambled on shore, broke our way through drift and thicket to the upper end of the island, and found a wide channel of water separating us still from the north shore. Wading up to our middles across a shallow part of this channel, we finally reached the north shore and our camp of the previous night; from thence we worked through the forest, and just at dusk we struck our camp of the morning. Thus, after many vicissitudes and much toil, we had got safely back to our camp; and though the outlook was dreary enough—for three large rivers and seventy miles of trackless forest lay between us and the mining camp to which we were tending, while all hope of assistance seemed cut off from us—still, after a hearty supper, we lay down to sleep, ready to meet on the morrow whatever it might bring forth.

Early next morning the voice of little Jacques sounded from the other side. He had had a rough time of it; he had gone through slough and swamp and thicket, and finally he had found the canoe stranded on an island four miles below the cañon, half full of water, but otherwise not much the worse for her trip. "Let us make a raft and go down, and we would all pull her up again, and everything would yet be right." So, taking the axes and line with us, we set off once more for the mouth of the cañon, and built a big raft of dry logs, and pushed it out into the current.

Jacques was on the opposite shore, so we took him on our raft, and away we went down current at the rate of seven miles an hour. We reached the island where our castaway canoe lay, and once more found ourselves the owners of a boat. Then we poled up the cañon again, and, working hard, succeeded in landing the canoe safely behind the rock from which we had made our celebrated crossing on the previous day. The day was hot and fine, the leaves of the cotton-wood were green, the strawberries were in blossom, and in the morning a hummingbird had fluttered into the camp, carrying the glittering colours which he had gathered in the tropics. But these proofs of summer boded ill for us, for all around the glittering hills were sending down their foaming torrents to flood the Ominica.

On the night of the 13th the river, already high, rose nearly two feet. The morning of the 14th came, and, as soon as breakfast was over, we set out to make a last attempt to force the cañon. The programme was to be the same as that of two days ago; to cross above the rapid, and then with double-twisted line to drag the canoe up the fatal fall! We reached the canoe and took our places the same as before. This time, however, there was a vague feeling of uneasiness in every one's mind; it may have been because we went at the work coldly, unwarmed by previous exercise; but despite the former successful attempt, we felt the presage of disaster ere we left the sheltering rock. Once more the word was given, and we shot into the boiling flood. There was a moment's wild struggle, during which we worked with all the strength of despair. A second of suspense, and then we are borne backwards—slowly, faster, yet faster—until with a rush as of wings, and amid a roar of maddened water, we go downwards towards the cañon's wall.

"The rock! The rock!—keep her from the rock!" roared Jacques. We might as well have tried to stop an express train. We struck, but it was the high bow, and the blow split us to the centre; another foot and we must have been shivered to atoms. And now, ere there was time for thought, we were rushing, stern foremost, to the edge of the great rapid. There was no escape; we were as helpless as if we had been chained in that black cañon. "Put steerway on her!" shouted Jacques, and his paddle dipped a moment in the surge and spray. Another instant and we were in it; there was a plunge—a dash of water on every side of us; the waves hissed around and above us, seeming to say, "Now we have got you; for two days you have been edging along us, flanking us, and fooling us; but now it is our turn!"

The shock with which we struck the mass of breakers seemed but the prelude to total wreck, and the first sensation I experienced was one of surprise that the canoe was still under us. But after the first plunge she rose well, and amidst the surge and spray we could see the black walls of the cañon flitting by us as we glanced through the boiling flood. All this was but the work of a moment and lo! breathless and dripping, with canoe half filled, we lay safe in quiet eddies where, below the fall, the water rested after its strife.

Behind the rock we lay for a few minutes silent, while the flooded canoe rose and fell on the swell of the eddy.

If, after this escape, we felt loth to try the old road again, to venture a third time that crossing above the rapid, let no man hold our courage light.

We deliberated long upon what was best to be done. Retreat seemed inevitable; Kalder was strongly opposed to another attempt; the canoe was already broken, and with another such blow she must go to pieces. At last, and reluctantly, we determined to carry all our baggage back from the camp, to load up the boat, and, abandoning the Black Cañon and the Ominica altogether, seek through the Parsnip River an outlet towards the South. It was our only recourse, and it was a poor one. Wearily we dragged our baggage back to the canoe, and loaded her again. Then, casting out into the current, we ran swiftly down the remainder of the cañon, and shot from beneath the shadows of its sombre walls. As we emerged from the mouth into the broader river, the sheen of coloured blankets struck our sight on the south shore.

In the solitudes of the North one is surprised at the rapidity with which the eye perceives the first indication of human or animal existence, but the general absence of life in the wilderness makes its chance presence easily detected.

We put to shore. There was a camp close to the spot where we built our first raft on the night of the disaster; blankets, three fresh beavers, a bundle of traps, a bag of flour, and a pair of miner's boots. The last item engaged Jacques's attention. He looked at the soles, and at once declared them to belong to no less an individual than Pete Toy, the Cornish miner; but where, meantime, was Pete? A further inspection solved that question too. Pete was "portaging" his load from the upper to the lower end of the cañon—he evidently dreaded the flooded chasm too much to attempt its descent with a loaded canoe. In a little while appeared the missing Pete, carrying on his back a huge load. It was as we had anticipated—his canoe lay above the rapids, ours was below. Happy coincidence! We would exchange crafts; Pete would load his goods in our boat, we would once again carry our baggage to the upper end of the cañon, and there, taking his canoe, pursue our western way. It was indeed a most remarkable meeting to us. Here were we, after long days of useless struggle, after many dangers and hair-breadth escapes amid the whirlpools and rapids of the Black Chasm, about to abandon the Ominica River altogether, and to seek by another route, well known to be almost impassable at high water, a last chance of escape from the difficulties that beset us; and now, as moody and discouraged, we turned our faces to begin the hopeless task, our first glance was greeted, on emerging from the dismal prison, by a most unlooked-for means of solving all our difficulties. Little wonder if we were in high spirits, and if Pete, the Cornish miner, seemed a friend in need.

But before anything could be done to carry into effect this new arrangement, Pete insisted upon our having a royal feast. He had brought with him from the mining camp many luxuries; he had bacon, and beans, and dried apples, and sugar, and flour, and we poor toilers only moosemeat and frozen potatoes and sugarless tea in our lessening larders. So Pete set vigorously to work; he baked and fried, and cut and sliced, and talked all the time, and in less than half an hour laid out his feast upon the ground.... It was getting late when we broke up from the feast of Toy, and, loading once more all our movables on our backs, set out to stagger for the last time to the west end of the portage. There the canoe of the Cornish miner stood ready for our service; but the sun was by this time below the ridge of the Ominica Mountains, and we pitched our camp for the night beneath the spruce-trees of the southern shore.

At break of day the next morning we held our way to the west. It was a fresh, fair dawn, soft with the odours of earth and air; behind us lay the Black Cañon, conquered at last; and as its sullen road died away in distance, and before our canoe rose the snow-covered peaks of the Central Columbian range, now looming but a few miles distant, I drew a deep breath of satisfaction—the revulsion of long, anxious hours.

The Birth of Vancouver
Margaret Ormsby

Sunday, July 4, 1886, was a gala day at Port Moody. To welcome the arrival of the first passenger train from Montreal, excursion boats brought one thousand people from New Westminster, Nanaimo and Victoria. For those on board the *Yosemite*, which left Victoria very early in the morning, the day was especially full of interest: many of them had never seen the Gulf Islands or the Mainland before. The ladies promenaded the deck in costumes specially imported from London; the Victoria Brass Band "discoursed at intervals some of their choice musical selections"; members of an Italian Opera Company "were generous in their musical effusions, and some [passengers] were found so captivated as to engage in tripping the light fantastic, notwithstanding the day they were celebrating."[1]

The train arrived at Port Moody exactly one minute past noon. Premier Smithe extended to the Canadian Pacific Railway the felicitations of the provincial government, and Henry Abbott, general superintendent of the Western Division, announced the immediate inauguration of service to the East. The absence among the passengers of Sir John A. Macdonald, who had been detained in Ottawa, somewhat marred the celebration, but with a mood of exuberance and expectancy prevailing, it was easy to forget disappointment.

As western railway terminus, Port Moody had forged ahead of Granville during the past six years and it now looked forward to great expansion as a port commanding the coastal trade from Panama to Alaska. But the directors of the Canadian Pacific Railway had other plans. Their first intention was to make "The Queen's Highway" a great commercial route to the Orient; and for this project they needed a deep-sea port with better accommodation for ocean vessels. Van Horne had already conducted negotiations with the provincial government to permit the Company to extend the track a distance of twelve miles to Coal Harbour, adjacent to the Granville town-site; this fact was well known at Port Moody, but no one there believed as yet that "Vancouver", as Van Horne called his proposed new terminus, would supplant the original site.

The decision of the Railway Company to move the terminus was more than satisfactory to men like John Robson and Dr. Powell, who had long held land at Granville. The Oppenheimer brothers, David and Isaac, who had recently formed a syndicate to purchase some of the holdings of the Hastings Sawmill Company and who were now engaged in slashing timber between Carrall Street and Gore Avenue, were equally pleased. Hardly less so were the "Three Greenhorn Englishmen"—John Morton, Samuel Brighouse and William Hailstone—who still held the 550-acre pre-emption which they had taken up in 1862 between the two government reserves set aside by Colonel Moody. Not one of these property-owners found fault with the Smithe government for presenting to the Company a quite unnecessary subsidy of 6,000 acres of land at Coal Harbour; in fact, they all applauded the action of the legislature, and as a demonstration of their good will, each private owner donated to the Company one-third of his own lots.

The incorporation of the new city of Vancouver by special charter, dated April 6, 1886, signalled the coming decline of Port Moody. The wrath of speculators—and of Victoria merchants—flared into open defiance. In an attempt to force the Canadian Pacific Railway Company to make the statutory terminus the actual end of steel, Port Moody interests resorted to the courts; and with the intention of strangling business in an upstart community that had stolen the name of their Island, Victoria merchants threatened with a boycott all eastern traders who contemplated appointing agents in Vancouver. But neither the animosity of Port Moody nor the rivalry of Victoria could check the growth of the new city—within weeks of its incorporation, Vancouver had 800 business establishments and a population of 2,000.

Then, on a quiet Sunday afternoon in June, exactly 94 years after Captain George Vancouver's visit to Burrard Inlet, the city named in his honour was destroyed by fire. As a breeze freshened into a gale, flames spreading eastward from land-clearing operations near English Bay roared through tinder-dry slashings towards the little settlement. Forty minutes later, there remained of the new-born city of Vancouver only two sawmills, a hotel and a shack in the centre of town, and a few cottages on the shores of False Creek. That night, the survivors of the Great Fire—the men, women and children who had found refuge in wells and on rafts and ferry boats in the Inlet—slept in the deserted plant of Spratt's oil refinery, or in Hastings Mill, or at the Moodyville sawmill.

The disaster instilled an iron determination into every inhabitant. With the first rays of light on Monday morning, workmen began to reconstruct the city. By Wednesday evening, a three-storey hotel was open for business, and within a month, fourteen new hotels and hundreds of new stores were erected. "I never saw such enterprise amidst so much desolation," reported a visiting journalist.[2]

Even during these tense weeks, when the air was still thick with smoke and hot with flames, the fundamental cause for worry and concern in Vancouver was the continued delay in extending the track to Coal Harbour. With a persistence born of desperation, Port Moody investors had taken legal action to block the grant of the right-of-way, and although the Supreme Court of British Columbia had rejected their claim, they stubbornly clung to their rights, and carried an appeal to the Supreme Court of Canada.

At the head office of the Company in Montreal, the lifting of the legal injunction was awaited with impatience. The delivery in Montreal and New York of the first Canadian shipment of tea from Yokohoma had sustained the contention of George Stephen. He had held that his Company could shatter the transcontinental freight record and also establish such fast service between the Orient and Liverpool as to divert trade from the all-water route through Suez Canal to Europe. The Canadian Pacific had seven sailing ships ready to enter the China tea trade, and the only hindrance to the development of a successful new enterprise was the lack of a commodious deep-sea port on Burrard Inlet. Before the removal of the injunction, Van Horne began to lay track and to construct the Vancouver railway wharf; as soon as it was lifted, the work was speeded. Finally, he found it possible to arrange that the first passenger train arrive in the "City of Imperial Destiny" on May 23, 1887, eve of the celebration of Queen Victoria's Golden Jubilee.

The whole citizenry gathered on the railway wharf to greet the train. To emphasize the contribution being made by the Canadian Pacific Railway to the cause of national and Imperial unity, officials saw to it that Engine 374 was smothered with garlands and slogans. Not to be outdone, Vancouver had made its own preparations: the streets were resplendent with fir arches displaying appropriate mottoes and honouring great works brought to completion. With three cheers and a tiger,

the great crowd expressed to the Canadian Pacific Railway an appreciation that was all the more heartfelt for knowing that the *Abyssinia*, the first passenger ship from the Orient, was already on her way across the Pacific Ocean.

On May 24, there was rejoicing and thanksgiving throughout all parts of Queen Victoria's Empire; and in Vancouver a very special feeling of jubilation, a sense of the fulfillment of historic destiny. For the arrival of the first train had presaged the reopening of the North West Passage to Cathay.

A few weeks later, on June 14, the *Abyssinia* berthed at the Vancouver dock. She was a small ship—only 3,000 tons—but two other vessels, the *Parthia* and the *Batavia*, had also been chartered from the Cunard Line to ply the route. Her time from Yokohama was extraordinarily good—just 13 days, 14 hours. Every one of her 22 cabins was filled with first-class passengers, and in addition to tea (which reached Montreal 27 days after shipment from Japan) she carried the first trans-Pacific mail and the pioneer shipment of silk. Her sister ships were capable of equalling her sailing record, and all three ships were so well appointed that the first royal patron, the brother of the King of Siam, returning from the celebrations in London, booked his passage on the *Parthia*. Before the summer ended, the future of the trans-Pacific passenger and freight service was assured.

By the end of 1887, the population of the "Terminal City" had grown to 5,000. Every boat and every train arriving in Vancouver brought distinguished visitors—and what was more important, new settlers.

From every direction they came. From Yale and other deserted construction camps drifted engineers, carpenters and common labourers. From Manitoba arrived young English-men, many of them graduates of Oxford and Cambridge, who had been "busted" on prairie farms; from Winnipeg, lawyers, abandoning a collapsing boom for a new community replete with litigants; from Toronto, Hamilton and London, Ontario, journalists who were attracted by the wealth of fresh "stories"; from Brockville, shrewd real-estate men and brokers; from Montreal, officials of the Canadian Pacific Railway; from the Ottawa Valley and New Brunswick, lumbermen and loggers deserting timber limits that were becoming depleted; from the Maritimes and New England, fishermen and cannerymen; from Philadelphia, ambitious young business men, who guessed that rich profits were to be made from the China trade and the Hawaiian sugar trade; from San Francisco, capitalists who were willing to finance sawmilling and other ventures; and before very long, from St. Paul, lumber magnates. From Ireland came young men grown impatient with the Irish nationalist agitation; from England, upper-class families, contemplating a new life on western ranches; from Wales and Cornwall, unemployed miners; from Germany, bankers, investment dealers and brewers; from Italy, unskilled workmen; and from Hong Kong, boatload after boatload of Chinese coolies. All these newcomers—with the exception of the Chinese, as the riots of January, 1887, indicated—could be absorbed into the society of the newest and fastest growing city in Canada—a city which had sprung to life with all the trappings of the industrialist-capitalist system.

Editors of the great English newspaper chains, realizing that the interest of their readers in the Empire had been awakened by news of the first Colonial Conference, soon sent correspondents to report on the newly-completed Canadian transportation system, the burgeoning Pacific trade and the rise of the new seaboard metropolis. The tone of all their accounts was exhilarating.

Vancouver, they wrote, was "the seaport of the twentieth century! the Constantinople of the West!"[3] The noise of the blasting of tree trunks and the din of hammering continued without interruption night and day, and every week more of the forest and of the undergrowth of salal and branches disappeared. At the Lion's Gate there was emerging "a city of long streets, big blocks, handsome churches, and elegant villas."[4]

This was a city of contrasts: ocean liners made fast at one end of Granville Street, and at the other end a bridge led across False Creek to the forest. Many of the granite and brick buildings had "real architectural merit and individuality",[5] but "one lot would have a grand grey granite building in the primitive Romanesque style, costing 100,000 dollars; and the next a wretched little wooden shanty, or a bit of the original bush, with tall mountain ferns and mountain ashes and dogwoods...higher up, as you topped the hill to go over to False Creek there were stumps of trees in plenty—trees that had been a couple of hundred feet high in their day." The extraordinary thing was that "in the midst of all this wildness," the city was "so absolutely modern; no one would think of putting up a house without a telephone and electric light."[6]

Within two years of its founding, Vancouver had 36 miles of graded streets and miles of wooden paving; waterworks and sewerage; warehouses, foundries and factories; and the wharves, round-houses, office buildings and four-storey hotel built by the Canadian Pacific Railway. Its population was 8,000. There were two daily newspapers, a glee and madrigal society, and an amateur dramatic society. In 1889, a great natural park was encircled with driveways, a company was incorporated to provide tramway connection with New Westminster, and plans were drawn up for an opera house. The zest, self-assertiveness, enterprise and versatility of the citizens had already become noteworthy.

Most of the commercial life in these first years centred in the port. From Vancouver, the boats of the Canadian Pacific Navigation Company, founded by Fraser River steamboat interests, sailed daily for Victoria and at least weekly for the logging camps on Discovery Passage, Johnstone Strait and Bute Inlet. Wholesale grocers despatched supplies by boat to the sockeye-salmon canneries on the Fraser and Skeena Rivers; passengers and freight were carried north to Port Simpson and the Queen Charlotte Islands, and the keenest rivalry developed with American companies for the trade of the Puget Sound ports.

But more significant than the local trade was the expanding export market for lumber. Huge shipments of Douglas fir, red, yellow and white pine, cedar, hemlock, spruce and larch left almost daily for Peru, Chile, Australia, China and Great Britain. In the trans-Pacific trade, Vancouver had seized the initiative from Seattle, its senior by some twenty years, and even challenged the position of San Francisco.

The sight of the first of the "flying Empresses" rounding Brockton Point in 1891 gladdened every heart. For the next fourteen years, the *Empresses*—the *India*, the *China*, and the *Japan*—were never late in arriving or departing. Under the terms of the Canadian Pacific's agreement with the Postmaster General of Great Britain, they carried the Imperial mails from Hong Kong, and by arrangement with the Admiralty, they constituted an auxiliary naval reserve in the Pacific Ocean. With their white hulls, yellow funnels, long clipper stems and overhanging counters, they appeared to every school child as majestic yachts, and to greet their arrival, teachers were often persuaded to lead their classes down to the "Bluff" overlooking the dock.

No one objected to this diversion, for almost every father in town was also on hand to welcome passengers or check the cargo. In the waiting crowd, it was an easy matter to spot the real-estate men and other promoters. "The bare fact of a man's coming to Vancouver by train was almost sufficient introduction," declared an Australian reporter; "inside of an hour every real-estate man in the place would know him and his business in Vancouver, and probably whether he had any family or a hereditary disease. There was always grand excitement when a steamer came in from China or Japan.... The real-estate men dreamt of winging a first class globe-trotter, and the whole population expected something to turn up, though it usually was only silk and tea, which were shot into trucks as promptly as all the labour in the place could shoot them, sealed up, and sent tearing across to Montreal and New York as fast as engines could haul."[7]

1. *Victoria Daily Standard*, July 6, 1886.
2. Stuart Cumberland, *The Queen's Highway...*, London, 1887, p. 51.
3. Douglas Sladen, *On the Cars and Off...*, London, 1895, p. 360.
4. W. G. Blaikie, *Summer Suns in the Far West*, London, 1890, p. 119.
5. Henry T. Finck, *The Pacific Coast Scenic Tour...*, New York, 1891, p. 251.
6. Sladen, pp. 370–1.
7. Ibid., p. 373.

November Walk near False Creek Mouth

Earle Birney

I

The time is the last of warmth
and the fading of brightness
        before the final flash and the night

I walk as the earth turns
from its burning father
here on this lowest edge of mortal city
where windows flare on faded flats
and the barren end of the ancient English
        who tippled mead in Alfred's hall
        and took tiffin in lost Lahore
drink now their fouroclock chainstore tea
sighing like old pines as the wind turns

The beat is the small   slap   slapping
of the tide sloping   slipping
its long soft fingers into the tense
joints of the trapped seawall

More ones than twos on the beaches today
strolling   or stranded as nations
woolly mermaids   dazed on beachlogs
a kept dog   sniffing   leading his woman
Seldom the lovers   seldom as reason
They will twine indoors from now to May
or ever to never   except the lovers
of what is not city   the refugees
        from the slow volcano
        the cratered rumbling   sirening vents
        the ashen air   the barren spilling
        compulsive rearing of glassy cliff
        from city
they come to the last innocent warmth
and the fading
before the unimaginable brightness

II

The theme lies in the layers
made and unmade by the nudging   lurching
spiralling down from nothing

down through the common explosion of time
through the chaos of suns
to the high seas of the spinning air
where the shelves form   and re-form down
through cirrus to clouds on cracking peaks
to the terraced woods and the shapeless town
and its dying shapers

The act is the sliding out
to the shifting rotting
folds of the sands that lip
slipping to reefs and sinking cliffs
that ladder down to the ocean's abyss
and farther down through a thousand seas
of the mantling rock
to the dense unbeating black unapproachable
heart of this world

Lanknosed lady sits on a seawall
not alone   she sits with an older book
Who is it?   Shakespeare   Sophocles   Simenon?
They are tranced as sinners unafraid
in the common gaze to pursue
under hard covers their private quaint barren
affair   though today there is no unbusy body
but me to throw them a public look

        not this wrinkled triad of tourists
        strayed off the trail from the rank zoo
        peering away from irrelevant sea
        seeking a starred sign for the bus-stop
        They dangle plastic totems   a kewpie
        a Hong Kong puzzle for somebody's child
        who waits to be worshipped
        back on the prairie farm

        No nor the two manlings
        all muscles and snorkels and need to shout
        with Canadian voices   Nipponese bodies
        racing each other into the chilling waters
        last maybe of whatever summer's swimmers

        Nor for certain the gamey old gaffer
        asleep on the bench like a local Buddha
        above them   buttoned up mackinaw
        Sally Ann trousers   writing in stillness
        his own last book   under the squashed
        cock of his hat   with a bawdy plot
        she never will follow

A tremor only of all his dream
runs like fear from under the hat
through the burned face to twitch
one broken boot   at the other end
of the bench as I pass

dreaming my own unraveled plots
between eating water and eaten shore
        in this hour of the tired and homing
        retired   dissolving
        in the days of the separate wait
        for the mass dying

and I   having clambered down to the last
shelf of the gasping world of lungs

do not know why I too wait   and stare
before descending the final step
into the clouds of the sea

III

The beat beating   is the soft cheek
nudging of the sly   shoving   almost
immortal ocean at work
on the earth's liquidation

Outward the sun   explodes light
like a mild rehearsal of light to come
over the vitreous waters
At this edge of the blast
a young girl sits on a granite bench
so still as if already only
silhouette burned in the stone

Two women pass in a cloud of words
        . . . so I said   You're *not*!?
        and she said   I *am*!
        I'm one of the Lockeys!
        Not the Lockeys of *Out*garden surely
        I said   *Yes* she said   but I live
        in Winnipeg now   Why for heaven's *sake*
        I said   then you *must* know Carl *Thorson*?
        Carl? she said   he's my cousin by marriage
        He *is* I said   why he's *mine* too! So . . .

Born from the glare come the freakish forms
of tugs   all bows and swollen funnels
straining to harbour in False Creek
and blindly followed by mute scows
        with islets of gravel to thicken the city
        and square bowls of saffron sawdust
        the ground meal of the manstruck forest
or towing grids of the trees stricken

At the edge of knowledge the *Prince Apollo*
        (or is it the *Princess Helen?*)
floats in a paperblue fusion of air
gulf   Mykenean islands
and crawls with its freight of flesh
toward the glare and the night waiting
behind the   hidden Gate of the Lions

IV

The beat is the slap slip   nudging
as the ledges are made   unmade
by the lurching swaying of all the world
that lies under the spinning air

from the dead centre and the fiery circles
up through the ooze to black liquidities
up to the vast moats

where the doomed whales are swimming
by the weedy walls of sunless Carcassonnes
rising   rising   to the great eels waiting
in salt embrasures   and swirling up
to the twilit roofs that floor the Gulf
up to the crab-scratched sands
of the dappled Banks

into the sunblazed living mud
and the radiant mussels
that armour the rocks

        and I on the path at the high-tide edge
        wandering under the leafless maples
        between the lost salt home
        and the asphalt ledge where carhorns call
        call in the clotting air by a shore
        where shamans never again will sound
        with moon-snail conch the ritual plea
        to brother salmon or vanished seal
        and none ever heard
        the horn of Triton or merman

V

The beat is the bob   dip   dipping
in the small waves   of the ducks shoring
and the shored rocks that seem to move
from turning earth or breathing ocean
in the dazzling slant of the cooling sun

Through piled backyards of the sculptor sea
I climb   over discarded hemlock saurians
        Medusae cedar-stumps   muscled horsemen
        Tartars or Crees   sandsunk forever
and past the raw sawed butt
        telltale with brands
of a buccaneered boom-log
        whisked away to a   no-question mill

all the swashing topmost reach of the sea
        that is also the deepest
        reach of wrens   the vanishing squirrel
        and the spilling city
the stinking ledge disputed by barnacles
waiting for tiderise to kick in their food
contested by jittery sandfleas
and hovering gulls that are half-sounds only
traced overhead   lone as my half-thoughts
        wheeling too with persistence of hunger
        or floating on scraps of flotsam

VI

Slowly   scarcely sensed   the beat
has been quickening now as the air
from the whitened peaks is falling

faraway sliding   pouring down
through the higher canyons and over
knolls and roofs to a oneway urgent
procession of rhythms

blowing the haze from False Creek's girders
where now I walk as the waves stream
from my feet to the bay to the far shore
where they lap like dreams that never reach

The tree-barbed tip of Point Grey's lance
has failed again to impale the gone sun
Clouds and islands float together
out from the darkening bandsaw of suburbs
and burn like sodium over the sunset waters

Something   is it only the wind?
above the jungle of harbour masts
is playing paperchase with the persons
of starlings   They sift and fall
stall and soar   turning
        as I too turn   with the need to feel
        once more the yielding of moist sand
        and thread the rocks back to the seawall

shadowed and empty now
of booklost ladies or flickering wrens
and beyond to the Boats for Hire
where a thin old Swede clings to his chair
like hope to the last light

eyeing bluely the girls with rackets
padding back from belated tennis
while herring gulls make civic statues
of three posts on the pier
and all his child-bright boats
heave unwanted to winter sleep

        Further the shore dips   and the sea   sullen
        with sludge from floors of barges   spits
        arrogantly over the Harbour Board's wall
        and only the brutish prow of something
        a troller perhaps   lies longdrowned
        on an Ararat of broken clamshells
        and the flakings of dead crabs

        The shore snouts up again
        spilling beachlogs glossy and dry
        as sloughed snakeskins
        but with sodden immovable hearts
heigh ho the logs that no one wants
and the men that sit on the logs
that no one wants
while the sea repeats what it said
to the first unthinking frogs
and the green wounds of the granite stones

By cold depths and by cliffs
    whose shine will pass any moment now
        the shore puts an end to my ledge
and I climb past the dried shell
of the children's pool   waiting like faith
for summer   to where the last leaves
of the shore's alders   glistening with salt
have turned the ragged lawns
to a battlefield bright with their bodies

VII

For the time is after the scarring of maples
torn by the fall's first fury of air
on the nearest shelf above brine and sand
where the world of the dry troubling begins

        the first days of the vitreous fusing
        of deserts   the proud irradiations of air
        in the years when men rise
        and fall   from the moon's ledge

        while the moon sends   as before
        the waters swirling up and back
        from the bay's world
        to this darkening bitten shore

        I turn to the terraced road
        the cold steps to the bland new block
        the human-encrusted reefs
        that rise here higher than firs or singing
        up to aseptic penthouse hillforts
        to antennae above the crosses
        pylons marching over the peaks
        of mountains without Olympus

        Higher than clouds and strata of jetstreams
        the air-roads wait the two-way traffic
        And beyond?   The desert planets
        What else?   a galaxy-full perhaps
        of suns and penthouses waiting

        But still on the highest shelf of ever
        washed by the curve of timeless returnings
        lies the unreached, unreachable nothing
        whose winds wash down to the human shores
        and slip   shoving

into each thought nudging my footsteps now
as I turn to my brief night's ledge

in the last of warmth
and the fading of brightness
on the sliding edge of the beating sea.

Summer snowpack on Panorama Ridge, Garibaldi Provincial Park.

Broad-leaved willow herb and melting snowdrifts above Black Tusk Meadows in Garibaldi Provincial Park.

Mount Robson and Berg Lake from Mumm Peak, Mount Robson Provincial Park.

Elk in the Kicking Horse River Valley, Yoho National Park.

Cormorants and Pacific surf, Vancouver Island.

Willow in autumn, Columbia River Valley north of Golden.

Truck trail across open range on the Gang Ranch.

Fence and farmland, eastern outskirts of Vernon.

Brandywine Falls, south of Whistler.

Aerial view of sagebrush country near Savona, west of Kamloops.

Rolling sagebrush country above Canoe Creek in the Cariboo-Chilcotin region.

The Fraser River south of Lytton.

Aerial view of the Fraser River Valley west from Hope.

The Kicking Horse River at the Natural Bridge, Yoho National Park.

The Spectrum Range in Mount Edziza Provincial Park.

Cattle along Highway 97 south of Williams Lake.

Marmot with Takakkaw Falls in the distance, Yoho National Park.

Elizabeth Parker Hut and Cathedral Mountain, Yoho National Park.

Helmet Mountain in winter, Kootenay National Park.

Mount Yukness reflected in Lake O'Hara, Yoho National Park.

Aerial view of log booms in Howe Sound.

Howe Sound at sunset from near Lions Bay.

The Bear Glacier east of Stewart.

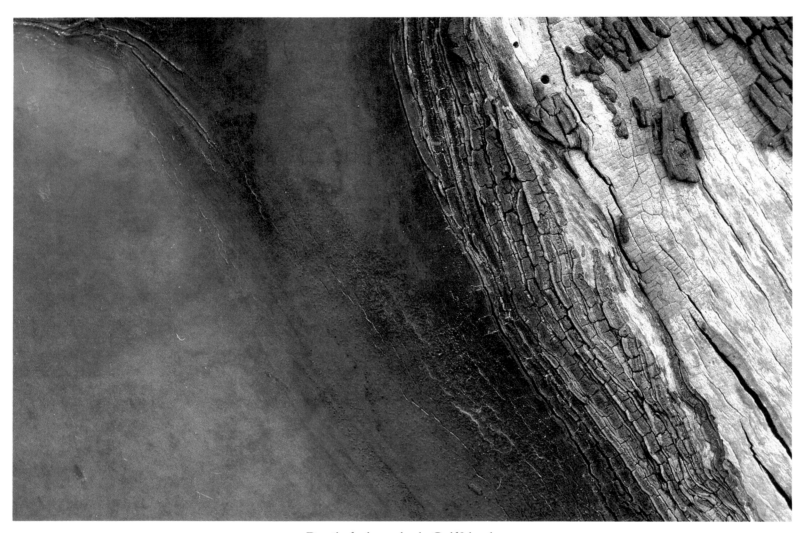

Detail of arbutus bark, Gulf Islands.

Driftwood detail, Lawyer Island, near Prince Rupert.

Stonecrop and sandstone along the shoreline of Galiano Island.

Arbutus trees, northern Galiano Island.

Farmland on the Saanich Peninsula north of Victoria.

Field with hay bales on the Gang Ranch.

PART TWO
Place & Persons

Swathed field along the terraces in the Fraser Canyon near Gang Ranch.

Touring B.C.

Dale Zieroth

1.

The rivers and the mountains
send out their summertime invitations and we
go to them, again and again we close the cabin door,
climb to the top of the world.
Sometimes we cast out across the water, sometimes
we even forget
how much we had to be there.

2.

The rain has washed across its face
but the mountain has not changed, it has
cracked and ripped open clouds of snow,
it has seen the trees approaching
but nothing has changed. The glacier
still stands on guard, aimed at the valley,
pointing down like a nerve.

3.

There is a wind in the desert
that whips and dances in the dunes. It
sticks in the roots of sage and it blasts off
the heads of trees. Sometimes it falls in the river
and leaves all the work for the sun.

Sometimes it passes through in the night,
sniffing at the sandtops, blowing them into the
lap of the moon.

4.

Inside each drop of rain,
the rain forest blooms. The sky pours down,
the ground swells with devil's club.
Somewhere, over there, day and night,
the trees struggle with their mosses.
Through the trees I get a
glimpse of animals, a moment that has
burst through from another world and I think
I am lucky, I am rich, I am hardly here at all.

5.

Here it is warm and ripe
but there is winter on a mountain not far away
and the trees know what happens next: the earth
takes back its leaves, makes a cover of
crisp gold, stitches the lake with ice.
Now we remember how we stood in the doorway one morning,
the wind blew the cabin with the
sticky smell of spruce and we
planned the last trip, talking,
not talking, then turned inside,
lit the first of the
white flames of winter.

Ebb Tide

Marjorie Pickthall

The sailor's grave at Clo-oose, Vancouver Island

Out of the winds' and the waves' riot,
Out of the loud foam,
He has put in to a great quiet
And a still home.

Here he may lie at ease and wonder
Why the old ship waits,
And hark for the surge and the strong thunder
Of the full Straits,

And look for the fishing fleet at morning,
Shadows like lost souls,
Slide through the fog where the seals' warning
Betrays the shoals,

And watch for the deep-sea liner climbing
Out of the bright West,
With a salmon-sky and her wake shining
Like a tern's breast,—

And never know he is done for ever
With the old sea's pride,
Borne from the fight and the full endeavour
On an ebb tide.

Salt Water and Tideflats

Roderick Haig-Brown

. . .The British Columbia coast is rocky and mountainous; miles upon miles of its length are deep inlets and sounds, always with mountains rising steeply from the water to four or five thousand feet, and a boat can pass safely almost anywhere within a cable's length of the shore. But at the heads of the inlets and bays, where the rivers come down, there are meadows and sloughs and tideflats. This is the country of ducks and geese and bears and salmon. It is beyond the reach of roads, and I love it.

There are well-known places at the head of one or two of the longer inlets, where hunters go every year in some numbers. Usually we stay away from these and hunt out new places, guessing at their virtue from maps and charts, from rumor, and more rarely, dependable hearsay. There are many places. A lifetime would not hunt them all, a dozen lifetimes could not learn a tenth of them thoroughly. Yet each is one's own place for the time one is there; rocks and sandbars and tide changes become familiar; the twisting river channels, the potholes and sloughs of the meadows are learned and understood in a day or two; even the flight lines and the feeding patterns of the birds begin to take on some measure of predictability and shape. And there is always something new for the next day; another fork of the river, a chain of lakes inland beyond the meadow, another bay within the bay where the geese lighted or the ducks rafted during the shooting.

I can think of one deep bay we go to, wide open to the northwesterlies, only a little better protected from the south-easters, where the widgeon feed by thousands. A little river comes in at the head of the bay and sandflats dotted with great rocks dry out from it for half a mile at low tide. Usually there are four of us hunting together and we go in very quietly, not shooting at all, two in the dinghy and two in the canoe. As we come near the head of the bay the widgeon begin to move, a few small flocks swing out past us, and the masses of birds feeding along the semicircular shoreline stir restlessly. Other flocks fly in and out, then one of the big concentrations, two or three thousand birds, takes wing in formidable sound. For a moment they are all together, white wing patches flashing, then they are a hundred smaller flocks swinging out, past us and over us. Other masses stir and go out until the beach is empty and something between five and ten thousand birds have left the stranded sea grasses at tide's edge.

Long before we can reach the head of the bay and set out decoys, flocks of seven and ten and twenty or more birds are coming in again, sometimes circling and going out again, sometimes pitching and going back to their feeding as though they had never been disturbed, sometimes rising almost as they pitch.

We set out our first decoys, rarely more than half a dozen to each of us, hide ourselves, and wait. At first we shoot seriously, picking the baldpate widgeon drakes, watching carefully for the occasional mallard or pintail or shoveler. But the flocks come in and in on their swift wing beats, riding up the left side of the bay, swinging across the front of us, flickering towards the decoys, flaring away, turning back to the next set, often pitching a little way out or in between the sets. It no longer seems important to shoot, only to see and see and see, to watch the lovely flight, the swift turns and changes and twists, the setting of wings, the sudden drop and hissing pitch to the decoys. It is important to see the white-crowned head of the drake in flight, to catch the shine of green along its side, to feel the richness of the warm red-brown of breast and flank. The whole bay is movement and color and light, in mood and values that are never twice the same because weather changes everything. We have shot the bay in the face of a heavy northwester that drove alternations of ice-cold rain and pale sunshine across it on a rising tide; that was a day when the widgeon flew and flew with a wild determination lovely to watch. We have shot the long foreshore at dawn on a dead low tide and in evenings when the rocks stood black against pale water and pale sand; there have been calm days when the flocks came in more cautiously and with longer circlings and hesitations, but they still came; and windy days when great tides crowded us back into the salal bush along the edge of the timber, and the ducks swung to decoys set in the lee of a fallen spruce whose trunk and broken limbs were shaggy with seaweed from the swells sweeping over them.

When the first freshness of the thing is over, I usually take the canoe up the river channel, across the flats, through the narrow gap in the timber that is the river's real mouth, and into the first big circular pool. Teal and bufflehead and occasional mergansers start from the water ahead of the canoe, circle once, and pelt back past me. In the pool there are always mallards and more teal. They rise boldly, thirty or forty birds making a great stir in the enclosed place. The teal drive out, low and fast through the gap; most of the mallards climb swiftly and head up along the line of the river towards the lakes, but a few always turn back towards the guns outside.

Later, when the tide has built the pool back into the grasses at its edge, scattered groups of mallard come down from the lakes, high and fast along the river, cutting down suddenly towards the pool, flaring and twisting away with the built-up speed still on them if we move to shoot. They are very difficult. But the last flight of the day is most difficult of all, so spectacularly difficult that we always hold off and wait for it and we rarely take more than two or three birds from it. It comes just at dark, as we stand with our backs towards the tall trees that close the pool off from salt-water, our eyes straining into the blue-grey of the sky upriver. Three hundred, five hundred, perhaps a thousand or more mallard, for many are beyond sight in the darkness, stream down from the lakes in twenties and thirties and fifties, flock after flock, very high, very fast. The whole problem is to see them soon enough, flickers of deeper darkness against darkness. In the moment of sight the gun must find shoulder and mark, then swing ahead faster than the mind can believe it should to loose the charge just short of the trees. Nearly always one is too late, often too late to fire at all. But once in half a dozen times sight may be quick enough, anticipation perfect, and a single bird will crumple and crash into the trees on the seaward side of the belt.

I have been told that geese use the bay sometimes, but have never seen them there or found sign of them. Yet geese are our true concern in these yearly hunts and any visit to the teeming bay is only incidental to this main search. The great western Canadas winter over in the lakes and salt-water meadows of nearly every coast valley in British Columbia, and the excitement of hunting them under these special conditions of wild and empty country, brown meadows, abrupt mountains, hidden lakes, and strong rivers, is as keen as anything I know. It is not easy hunting, nor especially productive; there is too much water and too much country for any casual party of three or four hunters to be sure of results. But the geese are always there and one plays for the breaks and chances—a skillful stalk, a lucky choice of position, or a moment of carelessness on the part of birds normally very cautious.

There is one estuary, a full mile width of flat clear meadows cut by a hundred deep sloughs, where the geese nearly always fly a line along the edge of the timber on a certain wind; that is as close as they come to predictability. There is another estuary of about the same width where a dozen shooters spread across the flats cannot be sure of anticipating their flight on any day that I have seen. There is a lagoon where they should come back through a narrow high-walled gut to open water—but often do not. There is a lake where they sometimes pitch in like mallards to a cluster of islands at the swampy end. There is a little narrow sound with high mountains at the head and along either side, and a sandspit stretching two-thirds of the way across it; it is an easy approach and should be a certain shot when geese are trapped in there. Yet I once saw a flock of fifty or sixty geese make a tight circle between the mountains and pass out over the sandbar so high that a rifle would hardly have reached them; I like to think they found some freak updrift that lifted them, because that place also should be predictable.

Lately we have hunted a short inlet where two creeks enter side by side at the head. The right-hand creek swings sharply southward to a high pass that leads through to the head of another small inlet. It is a swift stream, full of salmon and with bears everywhere alongs its banks; we found no place in its valley where geese would light. The other creek runs back a little way and turns through a right angle straight northward; its valley floor, between mountains as high as those of the other creek, is flat and wide. There is a big tidal meadow just beyond the right-angle turn and three lakes in less than three miles carry the valley almost through to a bay near the head of another long inlet. It is the perfect passageway for geese, and geese are always there, passing, resting, or feeding. We find them feeding in the meadows at dawn, find them again in the lakes, often see them passing high above the meadow through the day. Sometimes we get a shot at them; more often we do not.

It is hard to explain the fascination of Canada geese. I do not hunt primarily to kill them, but to be concerned with them. I am relieved rather than disappointed when the flock rises just beyond range, swings wide, or passes high; I love their name, their long black necks, the clean white cheek patches, the strong and heavy bodies. They mean courage to me, devotion, wisdom, endurance, and beauty, and I care not at all that the first three of these attributes should not normally be applied to creatures less than man. I go out to see them standing among tall grasses when they have not seen me, to find them floating serenely well out on still water and see them rise easily and powerfully from it. The measured slowness of the wing beat, the varying processional of ordered flight, the stretched necks, heads turning and watching, the voices talking, so plainly talking among themselves, all these things are strange and beautiful, with dignity and worth of their own. In cold reason, it seems fantastic to consider their destruction by gunshot; yet every emotion I feel from them is strengthened and deepened, at the moment and in recollection, by carrying a gun.

Later in the year we hunt another and smaller goose, the black sea brant. Brant are black and white birds and one hunts them in a black and white world. There are white snow and wet black rocks, white water, white snow flurries, black timber, white snow again on the open slopes of the mountains; grey sky, grey sand, grey beaches. The decoys, bobbing in strings and clusters in front of the blind, are black and white and the black heads of seals show often among them, stretching high out of the water to stare inquiringly at the blind, drawing calmly down without a sign of disturbed water, to show again still closer. White spouts and tall black fins of killer whales are often there and always black scoters, black cormorants, and black and white grebes. Sharpest black and white of all, seen against the pale water, are the little harlequin drakes that come in to ride with the decoys; white lines and dots of head and neck and breast and wing stand out plainly.

Yet the harlequin is not black but mainly blue-grey, with a handsome patch of glowing ruby on either flank; this shows brilliantly through glasses and is visible sometimes even in the black and whiteness if one looks for it.

I like to shoot brant early, in December and January, before the migrating birds start to come through from the south. It is often a slow sport then, but the wintering brant are fat, fine birds and it seems a better triumph to understand and solve the problems they offer than to take advantage of the greenness of migrants. The brant is a true sea goose, markedly unwilling to cross anything drier than a tideflat or perhaps occasionally a sandspit. They ride out open-water storms in rafted comfort and come near shore only to feed on eelgrass or to find sand or gravel.

Brant shooting is mostly waiting and watching, broken by more active spells of moving the decoys and the blind as the tide rises and falls. It is usually cold, and often wet, but in spite of this one watches well and sees everything, for brant may come at any time and they come in swiftly from a great distance. And the true reward is in watching. One sees first a wisp of black moving low over the water in the far distance — perhaps cormorants, perhaps scoters, perhaps brant. Then it is a line of dark birds in swift, even flight, not scoters because it rises or falls in flight, swings out and comes back to line; not cormorants because the rise and fall of flight is even, from level to level, where cormorants jerk upwards singly, bird by bird. They come on and on, twenty or thirty feet above the water, very swiftly, very gracefully; and suddenly are passing the decoys or swinging in to them.

When birds have passed or come in and been fired on, one waits again. Gulls hunt clams, fly up and drop them on rocks to break them open; crows shadow the gulls and wait their chance of theft or leavings. Eagles search over the water, ravens pass smoothly about their business, a hawk or a flicker shows on the landward side. In the water between one's feet are mussels, little crabs, barnacles, and sea anemones of many colors, purple or brown, translucent green or grey. A red-breasted merganser drops to the decoys and swims in puzzled friendliness up and down the bobbing line. A flight of black birds far out seems for a moment like brant, but the glasses show cormorants. A flock of Aleutian sandpipers pitches briefly on the beach in front of the blind, then rises and flickers away to pitch again two or three hundred feet farther along.

Last season we found a new sand beach and hunted it for brant. The weather was bad and they came sparsely, in twos and threes for the most part, often passing wide of us and carrying on to some more favored place. I began to think the beach was not as good as it seemed. The last evening we worked it was the day after a savage snowstorm with a fifty-mile easterly gale. It was a cold evening with a northeast breeze

and heavy snow clouds piled in enormous density over the Vancouver Island mountains. The sun went redly down behind them, somehow forcing its color through the mass. I watched a long reach of wave-rippled sand and tried to keep close enough to the edge of the tide as it drew swiftly away over the level beach. Then the brant came, a great flock of two hundred or more, black, slow-winged, and confident against the piled red clouds over the Golden Hind. They swung for the decoys, swung away, some of them calling, circled once, then pitched on the rippled water fifty yards outside my decoys. They packed immediately, as brant so often do, until there seemed no space between any two of them. But they were suspicious. Long necks raised uneasily. The flock let itself drift on the wind, a little towards shore but away from me at the same time, down towards the center of the sandy bay. I left the blind and began to stalk them over open sand, but they knew and drifted faster. There seemed no hope unless I could somehow herd them down towards Buckie and George on the point at the other side of the bay.

So I stood up and began to wade straight out until the wavelets splashed over my boot tops, then I turned towards the brant again. There was hope now. I was almost outside them, and upwind of them, with the dark of eastern sky and water behind me. Slowly I waded, herding them steadily downwind, towards the point half a mile away. They kept their distance, eighty or a hundred yards from me, watching me curiously, talking among themselves, riding the little swells with the lovely buoyancy that brant seem to have above all water birds. I saw Buckie move on the point and go back to cover. A hundred yards more, I thought, and someone must have a chance. The hundred yards became fifty. They had to rise into the wind, which would bring them past me unless they swung at once. And if they did that they would be within reach of the point. Twenty-five yards more. There was no change in the flock. They were still drifting at the same speed, still a little anxious, still talking among themselves. Then suddenly, all together, they rose, dead into the wind, wide of me, wide of the point. Jet black birds against the pale sky and water, a few voices kronking protest, slow wings; then they turned a little into the cold red sky and were gone.

It was a brant hunter's unorthodoxy, fifteen or twenty minutes of utter fascination, more memorable than any triumph that yielded dead birds.

On the Cape Scott Trail

Tom Wayman

July 1972, pushing through the trail in the rain forest
humped under the heavy packs, with mud and water
shin deep in the trail's centre, so skirting
the worst parts: walking around on thin plants at the edge
for more support, but slipping
so the weight of the pack shifts, throwing a leg
suddenly down over the knee in cold sucking mud
wrenching a hip pulling out again.
And the drizzle-soaked curtains of salmonberry
bushes to part, higher than our heads, clutching
at the bedrolls lashed on top of the packs;
salal, swordferns and wet moss, on through the dripping woods.

Twelve miles in the rain from the logging road past Holberg
nine hours in to Hansen's Lagoon. Hundreds of yards of the trail
under water, the small tributaries of
St. Mary's Creek and Fisherman River
flowing down the depression of the trail.

And the trail turning endlessly, like a track
unfolding in a dream: over a huge log
fallen across, along an earthen shelf
at the top of a gully, and toward the end
past Erie Lake, muskeg bog, then a climb
through a small forested rise, then working down
into a spongy muskeg clearing
again, missing the worst water, then up into the forest once more.

The trail is a ruin. Underfoot from the start
are wooden slats, shaped out of cedar logs, sunk in the mud.
Each stream crossing the trail was bridged;
the wrecks lie a little way upstream or down; logs
rotted through, or with their crossboards splintered
and gone. Sometimes the bridges still stand:
the earth vibrates under our sodden boots
moving over a small gorge, the wood
now so overgrown with moss and tiny white star-shaped flowers
that only holes in the ground
show where the boards below have crumbled away.

A mile or two from the sea, a farm.
Alone in the rain forest, old fenceposts first in the timber
then the flattened cabin: grey shakes and fallen beams
and the tangle of iron: rusted stoves and bedframes,
coffeepots, pans, bits of machinery. In a clearing behind
the single wall of a barn. Alder
has grown in the fields. But from here to the Lagoon
the old topographical map shows what is now trail
as *dry weather road*; the old town of Cape Scott:
five or six piles of collapsed lumber
with a roof half-on one of them, seen
through the thick screen of returned brush and trees, in the rain.

The road was theirs. Finns or Danes, people say
who broke into the wilderness for a while
as a hiker now might stay in a cabin
and lives and is gone. Or Indians settling here
at this end of the Island, and the air force
years ago maintaining the trail some.

At the Lagoon, a vast tidal marsh
carefully ditched and fenced, hay still growing across it
covered at high water. A wagon road
runs straight from the edge of the forest to
the furthest dike; where the trees end
is another demolished barn and an old buckboard parked
by some bushes, with the reins and traces
tossed into the back of it, when the last horses
were led off.
　　　　　　　In New Hampshire
in the woods near Gorham I was shown once
the trees were in lines: the end of somebody's orchard.
Near Kitwanga on the Skeena, one hot afternoon as a child
we found part of a cowhide left in an empty barn.
Slugging along in the rain here with shoulders and back weighted
under the pack's straps and buckles and pouches
I move again in the wilderness by all the work
of another man's settlement: hard for me to imagine
hacking a road and farm out of this useless land
the new fields stumped, ploughed, seeded
and losing it, hiking on
pulling through mud, in the steady rain
walking on the wet dead leaves of last summer's salal.

Mike
M. Wylie Blanchet

The first time we met Mike must have been the very first time we anchored in Melanie Cove. It was blowing a heavy south-easter outside, so we had turned into Desolation Sound and run right up to the eastern end. There the chart showed some small coves called Prideaux Haven. The inner one, Melanie Cove, turned out to be wonderful shelter in any wind.

We anchored over against a long island with a shelving rock shore. The children tumbled into the dinghy and rowed ashore to collect wood for the evening bonfire, while I started the supper. Away in at the end of the cove we could see what appeared to be fruit trees of some kind, climbing up a side hill. It was in August, and our mouths started watering at the thought of green apple sauce and dumplings. There was no sign of a house of any kind, no smoke. It might even be a deserted orchard. After supper we would go in and reconnoitre.

We were just finishing our supper when a boat came out of the end of the cove with a man standing up rowing — facing the bow and pushing forward on the oars. He was dressed in the usual logger's outfit — heavy grey woollen undershirt above, heavy black trousers tucked into high leather boots. As I looked at him when he came closer, Don Quixote came to mind at once. High pointed forehead and mild blue eyes, a fine long nose that wandered down his face, and a regular Don Quixote moustache that drooped down at the ends. When he pulled alongside we could see the cruel scar that cut in a straight line from the bridge of his nose — down the nose inside the flare of the right nostril, and down to the lip.

"Well, well, well," said the old man — putting his open hand over his face just below the eyes, and drawing it down over his nose and mouth, closing it off the end of his chin — a gesture I got to know so well in summers to come.

"One, two, three, four, five," he counted, looking at the children.

He wouldn't come on board, but he asked us to come ashore after supper and pick some apples; there were lots of windfalls. We could move the boat farther into the cove, but not beyond the green copper stain on the cliff. Later, I tossed a couple of magazines in the dinghy and we rowed towards where we had seen him disappear. We identified the copper stain for future use, rounded a small sheltering island, and there, almost out of sight up the bank, stood a little cabin — covered with honeysuckle and surrounded by flowers and apple trees. We walked with him along the paths, underneath the overhanging apple-branches. He seemed to know just when each tree had been planted, and I gathered that it had been a slow process over the long years he had lived there.

Except for down at the far end, where the little trellis-covered bridge dripped with grapes, the land all sloped steeply from the sea and up the hillside to the forest. Near the cabin he had terraced it all — stone-walled, and flower-bordered. Old-fashioned flowers — mignonette and sweet-williams, bleeding-hearts and bachelor's buttons. These must have reached back to some past of long ago, of which at that time I knew nothing. But beauty, which had certainly been achieved, was not the first purpose of the terraces — the first purpose was apple trees.

He had made one terrace behind the house first — piled stones, carted seaweed and earth until he had enough soil for the first trees. From there, everything had just gradually grown. Down at the far end, where terraces were not necessary, the trees marched up the hillside in rows to where the eight-foot sapling fence surrounded the whole place. "The deer jump anything lower," said Mike, when I commented on the amount of time and work it must have taken. Then he added, "Time doesn't mean anything to me. I just work along with nature, and in time it is finished."

Mike sent the children off to gather windfalls — all they could find — while he showed me his cabin. There was a bookshelf full of books across one end of the main room, and an old leather chair. A muddle of stove, dishpan and pots at the other end, and a table. Then down three steps into his winter living-room, half below ground level. "Warmer in winter," he explained. He saw us down to the boat, and accepted the two magazines. Then he went back to the cabin to get a book for me, which he said I might like to read if I were going to be in the cove for a few days.

"Stoort sent it to me for Christmas," he said. I felt that I should have known who Stoort was. I couldn't see the title, but I thanked him. The children were laden with apples — and full of them, I was sure.

Back in the boat, I looked at the book by flashlight. It was *Why be a Mud Turtle*, by Stewart Edward White. I looked inside — on the fly-leaf was written, "To my old friend Andrew Shuttler, who most emphatically is not a mud turtle."

During the next couple of days I spent a lot of time talking to old Mike, or Andrew Shuttler — vouched for by Stewart Edward White as being, most emphatically, worth talking to. The children were happy swimming in the warm water, eating apples, and picking boxes of windfalls for Mike to take over to the logging camp at Deep Bay.

In between admiring everything he showed me around the place. I gradually heard the story of some of his past, and how he first came to Melanie Cove. He had been born back in Michigan in the States. After very little schooling he had left school to go to work. When he was big enough he had worked in the Michigan woods as a logger — a hard, rough life. I don't know when, or how, he happened to come to British Columbia.

But here again, he had worked up the coast as a logger.

"We were a wild, bad crowd," mused Mike — looking back at his old life, a far-away look in his blue eyes. Then he told of the fight he had had with another logger.

"He was out to get me...I didn't have much chance."

The fellow had left him for dead, lying in a pool of his own blood. Mike wasn't sure how long he had lain there — out cold. But the blood-soaked mattress had been all fly-blown when he came to.

"So it must have been quite some few days."

He had dragged himself over to a pail of water in the corner of the shack and drunk the whole pailful...then lapsed back into unconsciousness. Lying there by himself — slowly recovering.

"I decided then," said Mike, "that if that was all there was to life, it wasn't worth living; and I was going off somewhere by myself to think it out."

So he had bought or probably pre-empted wild little Melanie Cove — isolated by 7,000-foot mountains to the north and east, and only accessible by boat. Well, he hadn't wanted neighbours, and everything else he needed was there. Some good alder bottom-land and a stream, and a sheltered harbour. And best of all to a logger, the south-east side of the cove rose steeply, to perhaps eight hundred feet, and was covered with virgin timber. So there, off Desolation Sound, Mike had built himself a cabin, hand-logged and sold his timber — and thought about life...

He had been living there for over thirty years when we first blew into the cove. And we must have known him for seven or eight years before he died. He had started planting the apple trees years before — as soon as he had realized that neither the trees nor his strength would last for ever. He had built the terraces, carted the earth, fed and hand-reared them. That one beside the cabin-door — a man had come ashore from a boat with a pocket full of apples. Mike had liked the flavour and heeled in his core beside the steps.

"Took a bit of nursing for a few years," said Mike. "Now, look at it. Almost crowding me out."

He took us up the mountain one day to where he had cut some of the timber in the early days, and to show us the huge stumps. He explained how one man alone could saw the trees by rigging up what he called a "spring" to hold the other end of the saw against the cut. And how if done properly, the big tree would drop onto the smaller trees you had felled to serve as skids, and would slide down the slope at a speed that sent it shooting out into the cove. He could remember the length of some of them, and how they had been bought for the big drydock down in Vancouver.

I got to know what books he had in his cabin. Marcus Aurelius, Epictetus, Plato, Emerson, among many others. Somebody had talked to him, over the years, and sent him books to help him in his search. He didn't hold with religion, but he read and thought and argued with everything he read. One summer I had on board a book by an East Indian mystic — a book much read down in the States. I didn't like it — it was much too materialistic to my way of thinking, using spiritual ways for material ends. I gave it to Mike to read, not saying what I thought of it, and wondered what he would make of it. He sat in his easy chair out underneath an apple tree, reading for hour after hour...while I lay on the rocks watching the children swim, and reading one of his books.

He handed it back the next day — evidently a little embarrassed in case I might have liked it. He drew his hand down and over his face, hesitated.... Then:

"Just so much dope," he said apologetically. "All words — not how to think or how to live, but how to get things with no effort!"

I don't think anyone could have summed up that book better than the logger from Michigan.

Atlantic Monthly, Harper's — he loved them. I would leave him a pile of them. At the end of the summer, when we called in again, he would discuss all the articles with zest and intelligence.

Mike's own Credo, as he called it, was simple. He had printed it in pencil on a piece of cardboard, and had it hanging on his wall. He had probably copied it word for word from some book — because it expressed for him how he had learnt to think and live. I put it down exactly as he had it.

"Look well of to-day — for it is the Life of Life. In its brief course lie all the variations and realities of your life — the bliss of growth, the glory of action, the splendour of beauty. For Yesterday is but a dream, and To-morrow a vision. But To-day well lived makes every Yesterday a dream of happiness, and every To-morrow a vision of hope. For Time is but a scene of the eternal drama. So, look well of to-day, and let that be your resolution as you awake each morning and salute the New Dawn. Each day is born by the recurring miracle of Dawn, and each night reveals the celestial harmony of the stars. Seek not death in error of your life, and pull not upon yourself destruction by the work of your hands."

This was just exactly how Mike lived — day by day, working with nature. That was really how he had recovered from the fight years ago. And later how he had pitted the strength of one man against the huge trees — seven and eight feet in diameter and two hundred or more feet high. Just the right undercut; just the right angle of the saw; just the right spots to drive in the wedges — using nature as his partner. And if sometimes both he and nature failed, there was always the jack — a logger's jack of enormous size and strength that could edge a huge log the last critical inches to start the skid.

He lent his books to anyone who would read them, but the field was small. For a time there was a logging outfit in Deep

Bay, three miles away. They used to buy his vegetables and fruit. Some of them borrowed his books. He talked and tried to explain some of his ideas to the old Frenchman in Laura Cove — old Phil Lavine, who was supposed to have killed a man back in Quebec. After Mike was dead, old Phil commented to me, almost with satisfaction, "All dem words, and 'e 'ad to die like de rest of us!"

But the next year when we called in to see him, old Phil had built book-shelves on his wall — around and above his bunk, and on the shelves were all Mike's books. Phil was standing there proudly, thumbs hooked in his braces, while some people off a yacht looked at the titles and commented on his collection. . . . Phil the savant — Phil who could neither read nor write.

Among Mike's circle of friends — lumbermen, trappers, fishermen, people from passing boats that anchored in the cove — not many of them would have stayed long enough, or been able to appreciate the fine mind old Mike had developed for himself. And the philosophy he had acquired from all he had read in his search to find something that made life worth living.

I can't remember from whom I heard that Mike had died during the winter. When we anchored there the next year, the cove rang like an empty seashell. A great northern raven, which can carry on a conversation with all the intonations of the human voice, flew out from above the cabin, excitedly croaking, "Mike's dead! Mike's dead!" All the cliffs repeated it, and bandied it about.

The cabin had been stripped of everything — only a rusty stove and a litter of letters and cards on the floor. I picked up a card. On the back was written, "Apple time is here again, and thoughts of ripe apples just naturally make us think of philosophy and you." It was signed, "Betty Stewart Edward White."

Apple time was almost here again, and the trees were laden. But apples alone were not enough for us. We needed old Mike to pull his hand down over his face in the old gesture, and hear his — "Well, well, well! Summer's here, and here you are again!"

Petroglyphs
Ken Cathers

images in stone
made by a dead people.

shapes they remembered
themselves by

are caught in this camera/
animals etched in light.

movements, lines that
taught men living

glimmer on this film,
travel with me

in my own country:
memories I look back to

      but can not know.

Blue Heron
Ken Cathers

thin boned thing
from the grey world
I grew out of

poised
in some dark
part of me

the sight of it
wheeling in atop
shore cedar

perched on the
sky. etched
image   remembered

from the first
shrill call   echoing
across these waters.

The Old Men of Telegraph Creek

Edward Hoagland

June 10, Friday.

I am staying at the Diamond C Café, "Pioneer Outfitters, Est. 1874". It's the only lodging in town, and is run by Edwin Callbreath's parents. The Anglican bishop is here for his annual visit, a stooping listener of a man; also a Kennecott survey team, so we're jammed. In the morning I climbed up the hill a couple of levels to the two McPhee brothers. Alec has the best vegetable garden in town. Dan, who lives up the last flight of stairs, is something of a landlord, owning a shack and two houses left him by friends who have died, in lieu of money that he had loaned. Both McPhees arrived in the West about 1904 and worked on the railway that runs to Prince Rupert and on a network of government trails to the north, building a wagon bridge across the Bell-Irving River, which hasn't been bridged since. While they were doing this, they'd walk back and forth across a cable, daredevil-style, balancing themselves with their loggers' peevies. In 1912, when they were cutting a trail in the valley of the Nass, which is only now seeing its first roads, the local Tsimshians rode out to intimidate them, circling them on horseback and firing their rifles. That winter was Alec's last visit south to a city.

Dan was the first to move to Telegraph Creek, although not until 1930, when he was put in charge of the maintenance crew on the village roads. He arrived on the riverboat, looked around at the size of the town and said to the Hudson's Bay man, "If I'm here next Saturday night, I'll kiss your blessed ass." ("Been here thirty-six years," he laughs.) He's a lean, wry, humorous man, haggy and coltish by turns. He looks like a canny grandpa from Tobacco Road — long nose, floppy hat, black shirt and pants — and when he tells a joke, he seems to swallow it, like a shot of whiskey, and feel it go down and simmer nicely. Dan always kept the security of the government job, but for the winter he picked up a trapline on the Scud River and Yehinko Creek from a moonshiner whom the Mounties kicked out. He used to average thirty marten a year. Martens are so dumb, he says, that if you see a marten's tracks that marten is yours. On the wall is a picture of him behind his dog team, in a high-collared native sweater, holding the hand grips and looking abrupt and rough and ready to shout. He had a half-breed wife who died three years ago and left him lonesome and rather itchy and at loose ends. One of his several sons still lives with him, bringing the money in, while Dan cooks. As the family absorbed his attention, he traded his trapline to another Scotchman for twenty-six cleared acres on the Chutine, intending to farm. The Chutine was better for farming than the Scud was, just as the Scud, with its twisting sloughs, was better for trapping. Nothing came of the trade, however, since Dan remained the road foreman and his wife

ran a small hotel in town; nor for the Scotchman, either, who drowned the next year in his new territory while cranking his motor. This was the way it usually happened. The outboard would stall, and the man couldn't keep hold of the oars at the same time as he cranked. The boat swung into a riffle and the river swept him under a driftpile, where it didn't make any difference if he could swim or not.

It's hard to elicit descriptions of the other people on the Chutine. Some were wanderers, always out after gold or hunting somewhere, living from hand to mouth on what they could get at the moment. Others organized their lives as a farmer does, raising a regular schedule of vegetables, which they canned for the winter, filling the potato house with potatoes and onions and salting away a winter's supply of fish. . . .

Alec McPhee is a shorter, more ebullient man. He has blue eyes, yellow-silver hair, and a red toothless mouth, and he scrunches over his crossed knees like a boy, sniffs a breath in through his nose, and stares boldly out of the window to see who's going to be coming past next. When he speaks he shakes his head and his whole body shivers delightedly, because everything that he finds to say amazes and amuses him. He was the town's gravedigger; he was the carpenter and electrician; he was the powder man on the public-works crew whose job was clearing the river of snags. So he's the fortunate man, he says, never to have blown himself up, or to have caught a fever from a corpse. When he was stringing wiring to the school from the government generator near the Mountie's house, he slipped on the icy steep slope, tangled the top of his hand in the spool, and although he was wearing mittens, lost only a single finger. Explain that good luck if you can. Never having married, he has an uncared-for, jumpy air that brings him cookies and stews from the widow next door and the nurse down the hill. He's an irresistibly blithe man, an urchinlike man. Apparently he did approach marrying an Indian girl once, but in some way she banged her head on the gunwale of the boat when they were down by the Iskut, and fell overboard in a rapids and drowned.

In the winter of 1932, with a responsible job in the Prince Rupert area, Alec was out prospecting along the Nass together with a friend. It wasn't the right season for prospecting, but it was their only chance. They had a dog team and were having a lark, crossing into land new to them, Damdochak Lake, Muckaboo Creek. They kept postponing returning, and since Alec's brother already had gone to live in Telegraph Creek, all of a sudden, when they noticed that they were on the Telegraph Trail, they decided to forget the ties which they had and hike to the Stikine. This they did, potting game as they went and bumming tobacco from the relay men on the line. They had so much fun and poked up so many side creeks, dawdling along, that they were at it 105 days, all told. Not until 40 miles out of Telegraph Creek did they run out of snow. They simply packed the stuff that was left on the backs of the dogs. They couldn't stop, they were so attuned to moving. After seeing how Dan was, they went right on to the Jennings River country, which is 160 to 170 miles farther north, and back again. On Level Mountain (the historic hunting ground of the Tahltan) one spring night, sitting in front of their tent, they watched every imaginable sort of game cross before them: caribou, moose, deer, black and brown bear, mountain sheep, mountain goats, like a splendid parade, as if on display.

He was in his forties by then. This lilting, long, weightless trip was just the latest of many for him, and as handy and busy as he was about town, he kept going out. He prospected to the Big Muddy River and the Turnagain River, 150 miles to the east, a rugged country of big boulders and scrub spruce where he saw not a soul for weeks, not even a Siwash — may be a rusted old stone in a lean-to or a rotted deadfall. He wound back by way of Cold Fish Lake and the valley of the Klappan and the high source plateau of the Iskut. Another year, in the winter, he traveled northeast a couple of hundred miles to the Rancheria River in the Yukon where there was a strike — this the teeming caribou country, so that every night he was able to shoot one and camp right beside it, gorging himself and his dogs. When he was out in the fall, in some places he hadn't been able to find a drink of water for miles, but next April, on the return, he could hardly struggle through the very same streams which had been dry, and in every half-promising creek a man would be gophering with a shovel and sluice, throwing up sand. It amounted to working for wages, like other work, since each creek settled into providing a set rate of pay, which then diminished gradually over the years until it wasn't enough to live on, although the gold dust on the bottom continued to sparkle.

Alec's registered trapline was in another direction entirely, down by the Boundary on the Stikine, and included the Katete to its head as well as the first seven miles of the Iskut River. For years he averaged as many as one hundred beavers a season, each worth about $30, and perhaps fifty marten ($15), and thirty-five mink ($20), and two or three otter ($10), and one or two fisher ($75). He'd fish through the ice for rainbows and cutthroats and Dolly Varden, besides shooting a couple of moose. Down where he was, ten feet of snow lay on the ground by February and the moose endured by huddling in the spring-fed sloughs alongside the river, which didn't freeze over, or else under the thickest cover of spruce. Whenever they were forced to cross between sanctuaries they were helpless, wallowing like an overstrained snowplow, leaving a mournful, deep trench exactly the shape of their bodies, whereas he ran lightly on top on his snowshoes. The wolves traveled the open ice where the wind scoured it bare. He used to see twelve or fifteen at once playing on the sandbar across from him, big ones with little ones. Eight wolves, loping tightly in a pack like a gang of sleigh dogs, came up the river

from the direction of Wrangell one day. He thought a friend of his was arriving to visit. Dirty and shaggy, they wheeled into the yard and sniffed his two bear dogs, a unique and spindly little breed about the size of a terrier, developed by the Tahltans. The wolves didn't kill them, and when he clapped his hands, they turned and ran for the opposite bank of the river and got into the woods and howled. Another time, in the spring, a grizzly got caught in a beaver trap and so tangled up in the willows that it didn't have leverage enough to break free. The willows were weaving as though in a wind. John Creyke, who was staying overnight, went down and shot the bear with nothing more redoubtable than Alec's trapline .22.

Grizzlies are the gorillas of the continent, the man-of-the-mountains, of interest to everybody, but Alec speaks of all these animals and people with equal affection and gaiety, poofing his words out, laughing, nodding, shaking his head, recrossing his legs and swinging the top one, blinking, and looking boldly out of the window. He says he's seen an eagle dive on a salmon and get taken under when the salmon sounded. He says the Siwash kids will be in his yard after his radishes as soon as they're up and he just wonders whether he's planted enough for both them and him. When he was on the lower Stikine, he might not see man, woman or child for seven months in the year, unless maybe he snuck into Wrangell. It got a bit stiff towards the end, but it was the richest territory anybody had, and when you're alone you keep busier. It's surprising the company a bunch of sleigh dogs is. He had a jovial four-dog team that could pull a quarter of a ton. In difficult snow he'd break trail ahead of them, as when they went to his overnight cabin up the Katete. Once out of the coastal belt, though, running for home on the ice, he went seventy exuberant miles with them in a day — jogging behind the sled, jumping on, jogging again, and jumping on. When he trapped, he had his summers off except for being powder man, and when he was prospecting, if he made any money he took the winter off, except for wiring and carpentering the town. He sold his furs to the local man, but his friend Gus Adamson preferred to ship to Montreal in hopes of a better price. One particular year the bottom fell out of the market when Gus did this, so that the catch he was offered $1500 for in town had fallen in value to $900 by the time it got East.

Dan McPhee even prospected for sturgeon in some of the lakes. Since these can go over a thousand pounds, it wouldn't need many to set you up. The Bear Lake Indians caught one very occasionally and kept it alive as long as they could, tied in the shallows, cutting steaks off its sides. Both McPhees have a smile they reserve for such antics. Dan's is ironic and civilized and Alec's is curious and buoyant. Tired from my visit now, they both look like small hooligans, Dan rather trembly and drawn. His word for most people I ask about is "born locally", with a pursed smile, meaning illegitimately, but his smile means mostly that he wishes that he'd had a hand.

The Forest Jungle
Emily Carr

Working on jungle. How I want to get that thing! Have not succeeded so far but it fascinates me. What most attracts me in those wild, lawless, deep, solitary places? First, nobody goes there. Why? Few have anything to go *for*. The loneliness repels them, the density, the unsafe hidden footing, the dank smells, the great quiet, the mystery, the general mix-up (tangle, growth, what may be hidden there), the insect life. They are repelled by the awful solemnity of the age-old trees, with the wisdom of all their years of growth looking down upon you, making you feel perfectly infinitesimal — their overpowering weight, their groanings and creakings, mutterings and sighings — the rot and decay of the old ones — the toadstools and slugs among the upturned, rotting roots of those that have fallen, reminding one of the perishableness of even those slow-maturing, much-enduring growths. No, to the average woman and to the average man, (unless he goes there to kill, to hunt or to destroy the forest for utility) the forest jungle is a closed book. In the abstract people may say they love it but they do not prove it by entering it and breathing its life. They stay outside and talk about its beauty. This is bad for them but it is good for the few who do enter because the holiness and quiet is unbroken.

Sheep and other creatures have made a few trails. It will be best to stick to these. The salal is tough and stubborn, rose and blackberry thorny. There are the fallen logs and mossy stumps, the thousand varieties of growth and shapes and obstacles, the dips and hollows, hillocks and mounds, riverbeds, forests of young pines and spruce piercing up through the tangle to get to the quiet light diluted through the overhanging branches of great overtopping trees. Should you sit down, the great, dry, green sea would sweep over and engulf you. If you called out, a thousand echoes would mock back. If you wrestle with the growth it will strike back. If you listen it will talk, if you jabber it will shut up tight, stay inside itself. If you *let* yourself get "creepy", creepy you can be. If you face it calmly, claiming relationship, standing honestly before the trees, recognizing one Creator of you and them, one life pulsing through all, one mystery engulfing all, then you can say with the Psalmist who looked for a place to build a tabernacle to the Lord, I "found it in the hills and in the fields of the wood."

Target Practice at Findlay Creek
Dale Zieroth

The old cabins along the creek
stopped us, like the 1933 licence plate
and the homesteads on the alkali flats.
The men who panned this creek for gold
when the bright veins at Wild Horse ran out,
where did they finally die
and would they remember their work here
or imagine the way it is now? collapsing, almost
gone, the rot and the rust, the animals
and the trees coming back. And two strangers
crossing their land with guns
looking for targets and a little peace.

It had been five years but the feeling of the gun
was still familiar: the sound
and the surprise against your shoulder.
Neither of us imagined I would shoot
so well. I shot down deer, and grouse
at fifty yards. I shot down the differences
between us. I shot down time.
We were boys again, shooting crows for
ten cents a pair of legs, and squirrels for supper.
We were Findlay Creek men, living only as well
as we hunted, and living well,
each small round hole something wounded
or dead, this time at least
a sign of friendship between men.

When we left the high country,
we passed the sluice boxes and the ditches
one last time and did not reach the valley floor
until the shadows touched across the road.
We were almost home and thinking of
other homes, years back, full of strangers now
but we did not ask what it meant, we drove,
we could not afford to remember much more.
We drove, the rifle on the seat between us,
the smell of gunpowder on our hands, wondering how
long it would take to go all the way back.

Sailing to the Logging Camps

M. Allerdale Grainger

In Vancouver

As you walk down Cordova Street in the city of Vancouver you notice a gradual change in the appearance of the shop windows. The shoe stores, drug stores, clothing stores, phonograph stores cease to bother you with their blinding light. You see fewer goods fit for a bank clerk or man in business; you leave "high tone" behind you.

You come to shops that show faller's axes, swamper's axes—single-bitted, double-bitted; screw jacks and pump jacks, wedges, sledge-hammers, and great seven-foot saws with enormous shark teeth, and huge augers for boring boomsticks, looking like properties from a pantomime workshop.

Leckie calls attention to his logging boots, whose bristling spikes are guaranteed to stay in. Clarke exhibits his Wet Proof Peccary Hogskin gloves, that will save your hands when you work with wire ropes. Dungaree trousers are shown to be copper-riveted at the places where a man strains them in working. Then there are oilskins and blankets and rough suits of frieze for winter wear, and woollen mitts.

Outside the shop windows, on the pavement in the street, there is a change in the people too. You see few women. Men look into the windows; men drift up and down the street; men lounge in groups upon the curb. Your eye is struck at once by the unusual proportion of big men in the crowd, men that look powerful even in their town clothes.

Many of these fellows are faultlessly dressed: very new boots, new black clothes of quality, superfine black shirt, black felt hat. A few wear collars.

Others are in rumpled clothes that have been slept in; others, again, in old suits and sweaters; here and there one in dungarees and working boots. You are among loggers.

They are passing time, passing the hours of the days of their trip to town. They chew tobacco, and chew and chew and expectorate, and look across the street and watch any moving thing. At intervals they will exchange remarks impassively; or stand grouped, hands in pockets, two or three men together in gentle, long-drawn-out conversations. They seem to feel the day is passing slowly; they have the air of ocean passengers who watch the lagging clock from mealtime to mealtime with weary effort. For comfort it seems they have divided the long day into reasonable short periods; at the end of each 'tis "time to comeanavadrink." You overhear the invitations as you pass.

Now, as you walk down street, you see how shops are giving place to saloons and restaurants, and the price of beer decorates each building's front. And you pass the blackboards of employment offices and read chalked thereon:

50 axemen wanted at Alberni
5 rigging slingers $4
buckers $3½, swampers $3.

And you look into the public rooms of hotels that are flush with the street as they were shop windows; and men sit there watching the passing crowd, chairs tipped back, feet on window-frame, spittoons handy.

You hear a shout or two and noisy laughter, and walk awhile outside the curb, giving wide berth to a group of men scuffling with one another in alcohol-inspired play. They show activity.

Then your eye catches the name-board of a saloon, and you remember a paragraph in the morning's paper—

> In a row last night at the Terminus Saloon several men . . .

and it occurs to you that the chucker-out of a loggers' saloon must be a man "highly qualified."

The *Cassiar* sails from the wharf across the railway yard Mondays and Thursdays 8 p.m. It's only a short step from the Gold House and the Terminus and the other hotels, and a big bunch of the boys generally comes down to see the boat off.

You attend a sort of social function. You make a pleasing break in the monotony of drifting up the street to the Terminus and down the street to the Eureka, and having a drink with the crowd in the Columbia bar, and standing drinks to the girls at number so-and-so Dupont Street—the monotony that makes up your holiday in Vancouver. Besides, if you are a *woodsman* you will see fellow aristocrats who are going north to jobs: you maintain your elaborate knowledge of what is going on in the woods and where every one is; and, further, you know that in many a hotel and logging-camp up the coast new arrivals from town will shortly be mentioning, casual-like: "Jimmy Jones was down to the wharf night before last. Been blowing-her-in in great shape has Jimmy, round them saloons. Guess he'll be broke and hunting a job in about another week, the pace he's goin' now." . . .

So you all hang around on the wharf and see who goes on board, and where they're going to, and what wages they hired on at. And perhaps you'll help a perfect stranger to get himself and two bottle of whisky (by way of baggage) up the gang plank; and help throw Mike M'Curdy into the cargo-room, and his blankets after him.

Then the *Cassiar* pulls out amid cheers and shouted messages, and you return up town to make a round of the bars, and you laugh once in a while to find some paralysed passenger whom friends had forgotten to put aboard. . . . And so to bed.

The first thing a fellow needs when he hits Vancouver is a clean-up: haircut, shave, and perhaps a bath. Then he'll want a new hat for sure. The suit of town clothes that, stuffed into the bottom of a canvas bag, has travelled around with him for weeks or months—sometimes wetted in rowboats, sometimes crumpled into a seat or pillow—the suit may be too shabby. So a fellow will feel the wad of bills in his pocket and decide whether it's worth getting a new suit or not.

The next thing is to fix on a stopping-place. Some men take a fifty-cent room in a rooming-house and feed in the restaurants. The great objection to that is the uncertainty of getting home at night. In boom times I have known men of a romantic disposition who took lodgings in those houses where champagne is kept on the premises and where there is a certain society. But that means frenzied finance, and this time you and I are not going to play the fool and blow in our little stake same as we did last visit to Vancouver.

So a fellow can't do better than go to a good, respectable hotel where he knows the proprietor and the bartenders, and where there are some decent men stopping. Then he knows he will be looked after when he is drunk; and getting drunk, he will not be distressed by spasms of anxiety lest someone should go through his pockets and leave him broke. There are some shady characters in a town like Vancouver, and persons of the underworld.

Of course, the first two days in town a man will get good-and-drunk. That is all right, as any doctor will tell you; that is good for a fellow after hard days and weeks of work in the woods.

But you and I are no drinking men, and we stop there and sober up. We sit round the stove in the hotel and read the newspapers, and discuss Roosevelt, and the Trusts, and Socialism, and Japanese immigration; and we tell yarns and talk logs. We sit at the window and watch the street. The hotel bar is in the next room, and we rise once in a while and take a party in to "haveadrink." The bartender is a good fellow, one of the boys: he puts up the drinks himself, and we feel the hospitality of it. We make a genial group. Conversation will be about loggers and logs, of course, but in light anecdotal vein, with loud bursts of laughter....

About this time it is as well to hand over your roll of bills to Jimmy Ross, the proprietor. Then you don't have to bother with money any more: you just wave your hand each time to the bartender. *He* will keep track of what you spend...

Now you are fairly on the bust: friends all round you, good boys all. Some are hard up, and you tell Jimmy to give them five or ten dollars; and "Gimme ten or twenty," you'll say, "I want to take a look round the saloons"—which you do with a retinue.

The great point now is never to let yourself get sober. You'll feel awful sick if you do. By keeping good-and-drunk you keep joyous. "Look bad but feel good" is sound sentiment. Even suppose you were so drunk last night that Bob Doherty knocked the stuffing out of you in the Eureka bar, and you

have a rankling feeling that your reputation as a fighting man has suffered somewhat—still, never mind, line up, boys; whisky for nine: let her whoop, and to hell with care! Yah-hurrup and smash the glass!!

If you are "acquainted" with Jimmy Ross—that is to say, if you have blown in one or two cheques before at his place, and if he knows you as a competent woodsman—Jimmy will just reach down in his pocket and lend you fives and tens after your own money is all gone. In this way you can keep on the bust a little longer, and ease off gradually—keeping pace with Jimmy's growing disinclination to lend. But sooner or later you've got to face the fact that the time has come to hunt another job.

There will be some boss loggers in town; you may have been drinking with them. Some of them perhaps will be sobering up and beginning to remember the business that brought them to Vancouver, and to think of their neglected camps up-coast.

Boss loggers generally want men; here are chances for you. Again, Jimmy Ross may be acting as a sort of agent for some of the northern logging-camps: if you're any good Jimmy may send you up to a camp. Employment offices, of course, are below contempt—they are for men strange to the country, incompetents, labourers, farm hands, and the like.

You make inquiries round the saloons. In the Eureka someone introduces you to Wallace Campbell. He wants a riggin' slinger: you are a riggin' slinger. Wallace eyes the bleary wreck you look. Long practice tells him what sort of a man you probably are when you're in health. He stands the drinks, hires you at four and a half, and that night you find yourself, singing drunk, in the *Cassiar*'s saloon—on your way north to work.

Going North

I was not singing drunk myself, nor was I on my way to securely promised work, as I stood upon the deck of the steamer *Cassiar* one evening and watched the lights of Vancouver disappear. In fact, I was depressingly sober, as it is my habit to be; and I began to think with some anxiety of my immediate affairs and to make a series of hurried calculations.

My steamer fare had cost five dollars and a half. But there was a pound of cheese and two packets of grape-nuts in my bag, and so I knew I could avoid the fifty-cent meals aboard the boat. Thus Friday night would see me landed at Hanson Island Hotel with sixteen dollars and a half in pocket.

Now on what system did they run that hotel? What would they charge? Meals would be fifty cents; that I knew. But would they throw in sleeping accommodation—bed or floor—free gratis as at Port Browning? If so, I could allow myself to eat two meals a day, and so last out for eleven days, and still have five and a half dollars for the return trip to Vancouver should that be necessary.

"Why all these considerations?" you will ask. "Why think of the return journey?"

Well, you see, my prospects were uncertain. Two months had gone since Carter had asked me to work for him. Carter might have changed his mind. Carter might be ill. Carter might have decided to shut down camp this winter. And so at Hanson Island I might find myself among strangers, with no one to give me work. Indeed, all sorts of unpleasant things might happen. I had left my last job and been laid up for several weeks on account of a damaged foot; and the foot was still troublesome. And so I could not venture to undertake any work that should require real activity. There were thus few jobs possible for me in that logging country....

The wind began to feel cold and we went inside the saloon. The boat was really very quiet now. In the smoking-room there sat a coterie engaged at whisky, but at the stern their bursts of laughter and loud talk were made remote by the steady throbbing from the engineroom and by the snores of sleeping men. There was no temptation to waste money on a berth, for all the little cabins were taken and several men were sleeping on the passage floors. By good luck I found a bench unoccupied, and lying down, drew some oilskins over me and set myself to sleep. Some time in the night I remember a gentleman lifting off my covering and looking at my face. He was speechlessly drunk, I think, and he patted my head. I think I fell asleep while he was doing it.... Next morning I awoke to eat my cheese and grape-nuts and to look upon a glorious dawn. The sea, in the narrow channels that we threaded, was glassy calm, except where our churning wake lay white behind us, and where the steamer's bows sent a small swell to swash against the near-by rocks. There is deep water close to shore almost everywhere along the coast....

There was green forest—and it looked like a moss upon the higher slopes; and the bristling dead poles of burnt forest showing against the bare mottled rock: standing timber, fallen timber, floating logs, and tree tops; and drift logs piled white upon the beach. There were long stretches of coast along which, every few yards, little lanes seemed to have been cut in the water-side forest. And now we were well into the northern logging country; for these little lanes marked the work of hand-loggers, and were the paths down which big logs had crashed their way into the sea....

Every now and again we would see the distant roof of a logging camp shining yellow through the trees, and hear the whistle of a donkey-engine from where white puffs of steam would show against the forest green. Then the *Cassiar* would toot and slow down, and the camp rowboat would put out to intercept us. A whole fleet of hand-loggers' boats would come out too, and tie up to the steamer's side for a few hurried minutes while meat and supplies and mail were being thrown into them. We passengers would all lean over the deck rail above and laugh at little breakages that would occur to freight,

and recognize acquaintances in the boats alongside and shout the latest news from Vancouver to them....

Down on the *Cassiar*'s lower decks were rows and rows of huge quarters of beef for the camps, and piles of heavy boom chains and coils of wire cable and groceries galore, in boxes and in sacks. There were new rowboats fresh from the builders in Vancouver, and old rowboats belonging to passengers who were going timber-cruising.... The lower deck, in fact, was just a cargo-room, with a space partitioned off to hold the liquor and the bartender. Aft of the cargo-room were the oily-smelling engines, and the little rooms where Chinamen and Japanese cooked and washed dishes and peeled potatoes. There too was the skookum box—that is, the *strong room* or lock-up. To it the first mate of the *Cassiar* is wont to shoot too noisy drunks, pushing them before him at arm's length, with that fine collar-and-trouserseat grip of his that is so much admired....

Just beyond Church House we lay at anchor for an hour or two, waiting for slack water in the Euclataws. The northern and the southern tides meet here, and in the narrow channel whirlpools form. There's something in the sinister, all-powerful thrust and sweep of such water that puts the fear of God into a man in a rowboat—if he is a little bit late for slack water. But of course the *Cassiar* doesn't mind going through, as long as the tide hasn't turned very long....

The White Frenchman came out in his boat for supplies. In the last month, I notice, he has collected quite a few logs—all lonely himself in that dismal place. For his shack is on the mountain slope just below the rapids: the situation chosen for beachcombing purposes. When a tug towing a raft gets into trouble at the Euclataws and loses logs Auguste is sure to pick up some....

At Hanson Island Hotel

At eleven o'clock, in the pitch darkness of that Friday night, the *Cassiar* drew near to Hanson Island and made the hilly shores of the narrow channel re-echo with her siren. We passed a dark headland and saw the lights of the hotel.

Several lanterns were flickering about along the beach, and we could judge that men were launching rowboats and hurrying to meet us at the raft. For at Hanson Island there is no wharf. A large raft anchored in the sea serves for the landing stage; a shed built thereon serves as warehouse....

The *Cassiar*'s searchlight glared upon the raft where men stood waiting to catch the mooring ropes. The steamer edged her way gingerly alongside and was made fast; the doors of the cargo-room were opened, freight was poured out upon the raft, hurriedly; and we passengers let ourselves down upon the boxes and bales that lay piled in rank confusion. All was black shadow, and dim forms and feeble lantern gleams.

I was surprised, for a moment, to find that a man had seized my blanket roll and pitched it into the far darkness; but then I found a boat was waiting there. Someone flashed a lantern; I jumped into the boat. I saw a solemn, fat old Dutchman tumble in behind me; other men came pushing in. Soon in that boat we were a solid mass of men and bundles. Then we began to move, and I heard a weak, drunken voice appealing for more room to work his oars. Heavens! I recognized those wheedling tones at once. The oarsman was my old acquaintance Jim; Jim the "engineer"; Jim, ex-coal-trimmer from the White Star Line.

My old acquaintance Jim was dreadful drunk, but not too drunk to know his duty. He held to a design to row the boat ashore, aiming for where the hotel lights shone bright above the beach. We moved through utter darkness, Jim's oars waggling feebly in the water. . . .

Then we went bump and bump again, and reaching out our hands, we felt a floating log that barred our path. We seemed to get entangled with logs; logs everywhere. Jim, with sudden fury, tried to row over them. Then he gave up the attempt and told us to walk ashore upon the logs. But a tearful-drunk old voice wailed against the idea in foreign-sounding cockney accents, and other voices made an angry chorus, saying that their boots were not spiked and that they would walk no slippery logs in darkness, and they swore. So the engineer became absorbed again in trying to row over logs, bump, bump, bump. . . until he felt it futile and reached the querulous verge of tears. . . . I jumped, thigh-deep, into the water then and took my stuff ashore, leaving the fools in drunken argument. . . .

I opened the front door of the hotel and walked, half-blinded by the dazzle of acetylene, into the public room. Noise was my first impression—noise of shuffling feet, stamp of dancing men, loud talk and shouted cuss words. Then I saw that the room was crowded.

A red-hot stove stood in one corner, and round it men sat in chairs or stood warming themselves or drying their wet clothes. A card game was going on at a small table, and men stood around, three deep, to watch the play. Large sums were in the pool. There was an incessant coming and going of men between the barroom and the public room, and men loafed about the rooms and passages and talked, or argued, or scuffled playfully. Some danced to the tunes of a fiddle played by an old man who swayed with shut eyes, rapt in his discordant scraping.

In fact, the hotel was doing good business that night. The whirlpool, as a temperance tract might say, was a-booming and a-boiling, sucking down men's wages and perhaps their health; the boys were "on the tear," and the hotel resounded with their revelry. Those who had fallen lay splayed out upon the floor in drunken sleep; those who were sick lay outside in the night. The scene reminded me a little of boating suppers and undergraduates; but the action, of course, was much more vigorous, as befitted grown-up men.

Swan Song
Gary Geddes

Ten years ago, standing
on a rock on Texada,
watching two drunks set out
in a gill-netter for Westview,
beer in one hand, helm in the other,
snatches of Annie Laurie caught
in the wind.
    A mile out,
the mast a crazy metronome
      cutting the air,
they turned over and were gone,
the barnacled hull glistening
      for a moment
like a blackfish in the sunlight.
I must have stood there an hour,
feeling myself too small an audience
      for their last great binge.

The Last Spar-Tree on Elphinstone Mountain

Peter Trower

The last spar-tree on Elphinstone Mountain
through drunken Sunday binoculars
pricks the blue bubble of sky
on the final ridge where the scar tissue peters out.

Been four years quiet now on the battered mountain's back
except for shakecutters, hunters, and stray philosophers.
The trucks are elsewhere—some of the rivers dead
and the donkeys gone to barber another hill.

I'm always shouting my mouth off about mountains
sometimes climbing them
sometimes just distantly studying them like this.
My eyes need no caulk boots
I can vault to that ridge in my mind,
stand at the foot of that tree forlorn as a badly-used woman
demoted to landmark and ravenperch.
I can touch its bark warm as flesh
feel the engines still shaking it functional
with vibrations that never quite die.

It's either a cornfield or a catastrophe.
Either a crop or a tithe or a privacy
has been taken from this place.
What matter? It's done. Beyond this ridge is a valley
I helped hack and alter. There's a gully there
two hundred feet deep in places
where we tailholted on its rim.
Dizzy abyss that scared the wits out of me—
you furrow down that mountain like God's own drainage-ditch
and stopped a forest fire in 1965.

At your feet is the dirtiest show of them all
where we logged in the box canyon with debris crashing down
and the rotten hemlock snags trembled over us,
the haulback stumps pulled out like bad teeth.
The hooktender said: "She's a natural born bitch!"
The lines broke—the omens spoke
and I quit from fear to become a brief boomman.

I'm getting melodramatic again but it's hard not to be.
Logging's larger than life. Keep your sailors and cowboys!
I'm always stressing the sombre side
but there's much companionship and laughter—
great yarns beside noon donkeys, high humour between turns,

excellent shits behind stumps with the wind fanning the stink away,
sweat smelling good and cigarette smoke celestial.

Dream on in peace old tree—
perhaps you're a truer monument to man
than any rocktop crucifix in Rio de Janeiro.

A Summer Journey
Emily Carr

June 7th [1933]—Pemberton, B.C.

I left home on May 15th and went to Brackendale first, . . . along with vast quantities of prospectors going to the mines with their packs on their backs. I rejoiced that their packs were even worse to behold than mine. . . .

I stayed five days at Lillooet and then came on down to Seton. Seton and Anderson lakes used to be one till a mountain sat down in its midst and divided it squarely amidships, leaving each lake eighteen miles long. The Durban's stopping place was full of prospectors coming and going in a steady stream, men seeking for gold, strong men, glad to get away from city fuss into the great open, to shoulder their packs, make themselves into beasts of burden, struggle up the stony, steep mountainsides, enduring hardship, cold, hunger, tiredness, always with that gold god ahead, planning their lives when they would find the gold, and building airy castles for themselves, and wives, children, aged parents, and who-not, generous in their imagined affluence. Then, when they do not strike it lucky, collapsing like burst bubbles. Some, not having the courage to face those at home who they bragged to, end it with a bullet. Others will come again next year and the next. Others will stake unworthy claims and bamboozle some poor fool to buy them.

The Durban House at Seton looked like an erupted volcano. Specimens of rock everywhere, on tables, shelves, seats, verandahs. Men pounded them in mortars, making horrid noises, and washed them in pans, making sloppy the porch. They did up bundles and parted them. They carried little canvas sacks full. Indians brought ponies with pack saddles to the front and outfits with frypans, blankets, grub, and always the axe, pick and shovel; loaded the beasts till only their ears and tails were visible. The Indian superintended, then the laden beasts, tied in a string one behind the other, started up the trails. You met them a few days later wearily returning, empty of their packs, the Indian cheerful—he had his money safe in his pouch, no digging for gold for him!

One boy had brought an old friend down in a coffin, returning him to his wife in Vancouver. Disheartened, so a bullet in his brain. The boy had had it all to see to, broke the shack door open just as the gun went off. He had had to make the poor body decent, to help make a coffin, to get others to help carry him one and a half miles down the rough trail, to make arrangements. For he had known this middle-aged man since he himself was a boy of sixteen—he had been to him like a father—and the poor suicide had left a message that he was to take his body down to Vancouver to his wife. There were circles round the boy's eyes. He talked incessantly at dinner

(there were only two of us that night) and he played the piano and was restless.

The boy told me of the inside of the big Pioneer mine and I wondered how they had the grit to go down into the blackness, to sink down, down that awful shaft on a lift—only a platform, no cage, no sides. If anything went wrong with the lift there were ladders perpendicular up the sides of the shaft—their only way of coming up—a ladder of a certain length, then a plank to rest on, another ladder and a plank, and so on and so on, and that awful, awful black hole if one slipped or got dizzy. The telling sickened me. If a man's light went out he must stand perfectly still and shout. He said the blackness was different from any other, a smothering density you could feel. This boy's job was to set and fire the blasts. It must be done with exact precision and the mad rush to get away, far, far as possible. The succession of concussions that split your ears and knocked you down. Oh, is there any gold in the world worth all that?

Everyone got up early at the Durban. The walls were so thin you heard the sighs and yawns from 5 A.M. The men washed in the open hall, I in my room, so it was befitting I should be the last to go down the hall to breakfast. I usually did that at 7 or 7.30. There were seldom the same men for two days. I, being the one woman, wielded the maternal teapot. Everyone loved Tantrum and had a smile for or at him.

Today I moved on to Pemberton and it is pouring rain.

June 10th—Pemberton.

Here we are. Three days at Pemberton have passed already. It is beautiful and exhausting. First day they told me of a walk. Said it was four miles. It proved to be six and I got home exhausted and mad, also late. Today I went up Harvey Mountain, supposed to have one of the grand views. They said it covered all the peaks. I expected a glorious panorama and to walk five miles. I crossed three railway bridges, beastly things, scuttling over them lugging Tantrum and all my gear, counting my steps and reckoning each one aloud to Tantrum. I met two patrollers and stood on edges of track to let them pass. The mountains glorious, tossing splendour and glory from peak to peak. Yesterday there was fresh snow. They were half white and half navy blue and the beastly, treacherous Lillooet river snaked through the willows and meadows. I don't like these rivers. They are oily smooth and swift but swirling, with mean currents and whirlpools. You feel as if they asked you sneakily and stealthily to fall in and be swallowed, swept away swiftly to nothingness. There is meanness in their muddy green-grey water and shelvy sand banks. I never go to the rivers about here or want to look at them or hear them.

Well, after miles and miles along the tracks, I climbed the waggon road to Harvey Mountain. At the summit I sat to rest and made a sketch. The view was certainly fine in a middling way but not all the wonder they raved over, so I supposed this was only the beginning and the trail went up from there. A boy came along on a mule with a bear skin, still newly wet, in a sack. He told me he had just shot the bear. It had been fighting and was in a mean temper. It turned on him so he had shot even though it was off season. I asked about the trail and he showed me where it started up a few rods away, and off I started, on and on and on. It got worse and worse, perpendicular, stony, ghastly. Still I struggled on. From the amount of bear spoor there must have been millions about. It was fresh. Would I meet one? Would it be ugly and attack? Surely, I thought, this is a queer trail to set a woman of sixty off on alone.

There seemed to be no top. I plunged into valley after valley, spooky, silent, grey places. Tantrum heeled splendidly, but he looked into the forest and growled. The mosquitoes were the only life except one startled hawk. I felt as if bear eyes were peeping in all directions and as if my back hair might be clawed and the hot snorting breath of a beast might suddenly touch my ear. But I hated to be a slacker and turn back so I toiled on. Evidently no one had been there recently for trees were across the way. It was very stony, mostly a sort of stony ditch and steep gully. I reached a place where the trail stopped, was lost in undergrowth, and dipped into another valley. I tied

my handkerchief to a tree and scouted round for a trail. There was no light showing, as if I was near the top. I'd had enough. Slowly I retraced my steps, counting myself a slacker, but to be lost on that mountain in a regular bear 'rancherie' did not seem good enough to risk.

Some way back I had noted a bare bluff, so I tore paper and marked bushes and, leaving a trail, I climbed up. The view was good but the place creepy in the extreme. I ate and took out my sketch things. I was too tired and too creepy to work or to rest. The dog stared into the forest and growled and barked. "I'm getting out," I said, and, consigning my informants in the hotel to hot places, I started the descent and kept going without pause. Somehow I missed the trail. When I got to the road again it was in totally different country; however the track was there, so I knew I could make Pemberton by walking along it far enough. I could have kissed the beastly bridge, it was so good to be sure where I was.

When I limped back into the hotel kitchen they were appalled. "My goodness," said the daughter, "you'd got to the top that we meant, when you 'started' on the trail. You must have got on the old McCulloch trail up to an old mine. Why, I wouldn't dream of going up there without a man." Counting that awful climb, I must have gone nine or ten miles. I ache dreadfully.

Encounter with an Archangel
George Woodcock

When my wife and I returned to Canada in the spring of 1949, I found that on Vancouver Island, where we settled, there was a small group of Doukhobors who had migrated from the interior of British Columbia and had founded a colony at Hilliers, sixty miles north of the village where we were clearing land and carpentering a house in search of that Tolstoyan *ignis fatuus*, the marriage of manual and mental work.

The people of our village talked reluctantly about the Hilliers community, yet even their rare hostile comments told us something. The leader of the group—a heretical offshoot—was a prophet who called himself Michael the Archangel. He openly preached the destruction of marriage, and this our neighbours vaguely envisaged as a complex and orgiastic pattern of shacking-up which provoked and offended their Presbyterian imagination at one and the same time.

Since Hilliers was near, we could easily go there to see for ourselves, but we knew already that chronic bad relations with the Canadian authorities had made the Doukhobors distrustful of strangers. However, I wrote to the community, and by return I received a letter from the secretary, whose

name was Joe. He not only welcomed my interest, but invited us to stay at Hilliers as long as we wished. I was a little surprised at the enthusiastic tone of his letter, but the reason became evident once we reached Hilliers.

One day in August we set off northward. For lack of money, we hitchhiked, and it was late afternoon when the last driver turned off the sea-coast road into the broad valley, hot and still of air, where Hilliers lies in the lee of the hard mountain spine that runs down the length of Vancouver Island. The older, non-Doukhobor Hilliers was a whistle-stop on the island railway, and the entrance to the community stood opposite a siding filled with boxcars. A high cedar fence faced the road. A large board had been nailed to it. UNION OF SPIRITUAL COMMUNITIES OF CHRIST, it said, in Russian and English. The wide gates stood open; looking between them, the eye encompassed and then recognized with some surprise the unconscious faithfulness with which a Russian village of the Chekhov era had been reproduced. Low cabins of logs and unpainted shakes were scattered along a faintly marked trail that ran between grass verges to end, a furlong on, at two larger two-storeyed houses standing against the brown background of the mountains, with the grey bubble of a communal baking oven between them. Each cabin was surrounded by a picketed garden, where green rows of vegetables and raspberry canes ran over the black earth in neatly weeded symmetry, and ranks of sunflowers lolled their brown and yellow masks towards the light.

An old woman with a white kerchief shading her face was hoeing very slowly in the nearest garden. She was the only person in sight, and I went up to her fence. Could she tell me where to find Joe? Her English was so broken that I could not follow what she was trying to tell me. By this time our arrival had been noticed in the cabins, and a little wave of younger women in bright full petticoats, and of blond, crop-headed small boys, came towards us hesitantly. There was nothing of the welcome we had expected. Inge spoke to one of the women. "Joe ain't here," she answered. "He's at the other place." She waved vaguely northward. A pick-up truck drove in through the gates, and two young men got out. The women called to them, and they talked together in rapid, anxious Russian. Then one man got back into the truck and drove off, while the other came up to us. He was dark and nervous, dressed in an old blue serge suit with chaff whitening the wrinkles. "I'm Pete," he said. "Joe's brother. Joe's coming." He paused. "Afterwards...you'll see Michael...Michael Archangel," he added hesitantly, and then fell silent. The small boys gave up interest and went to play on the boxcars.

Joe was so different from Pete that it was hard to believe them brothers—blue-eyed, wiry, jumping out of the truck to run and pump our hands. "Michael Archangel knew you were coming. A long time ago," he shouted. I had written only a week before. "A long time ago?" I asked. Joe looked at me and then laughed. "Yes, before you wrote!" Then he grabbed our rucksacks, helped us into the truck, and drove wildly for a couple of miles along a rough track beside the railway to a large old farm house in a quadrangle of shacks and barns surrounded by propped-up apple trees that were ochre-yellow with lichen. "This is the other place," Joe explained. "Most of the young people stay here. The old 'uns live up there with Michael Archangel."

We went into the kitchen. Two young women, fair and steatopygous as Doukhobor beauties are expected to be, were preparing the evening meal. A small girl showed us to our room, and stood, avid with curiosity, while we unpacked our rucksacks and washed our faces. Then Joe took us around the yard, showed us the new bakehouse on which a hawk-faced old man like a Circassian bandit was laying bricks, and tried to entice us into the bathhouse. I looked through the doorway and saw naked people moving like the damned in the clouds of steam that puffed up whenever a bucket of water was thrown on the hot stones. In a couple of seconds I withdrew, gasping for breath. The bricklayer laughed. "You never make a Doukhobor," he said. "Add ten years to your life," said Joe coaxingly.

When everyone stood in a circle around the great oval table for the communal meal we began to see the kind of people the Doukhobors were. There were twenty of them, singing in the half-Caucasian rhythm that penetrates Doukhobor music, the women high and nasal, the men resonant as bells. Most had Slavonic features, their breadth emphasized among the women by the straight fringes in which their hair was cut across the forehead. But a few, like the bricklayer, were so unRussian as to suggest that Doukhobors had interbred with Caucasian Moslems during their long exile in the mountains before they came to Canada. They sang of Siberian and Canadian prisons, of martyrs and heroes in the faith. "Rest at last, ye eagles of courage, rest at last in the arms of God," they boomed and shrilled.

The singing was solemn, but afterwards the mood changed at once and the meal went on with laughter and loud Russian talk; now and then our neighbours would break off repentantly to translate for our benefit. The food was vegetarian, but the best of its kind I have ever tasted; bowls of purple borscht, dashed with white streaks of cream, and then casha, made with millet and butter, and vegetables cooked in oil, and pirogi stuffed with cheese and beans and blackberries, and eaten with great scoops of sour cream. Slices of black bread passed around the table, cut from a massive square loaf that stood in the middle, beside the salt of hospitality, and the meal ended with huckleberries and cherries.

Afterwards Joe and Pete took us to drink tea in a room they used as an office. It was furnished with a table and benches of thick hand-adzed cedar, but a big blue enamel tea-pot served instead of a samovar. This was the first of a series of long conversations in which the ideas of the community were imparted to us, principally by Joe, who spoke English more fluently than anyone else at Hilliers. Except for a few phrases, the details of the dialogues have become blurred in my memory during the thirteen years that have passed since then, but this, in substance, is what we were told on the first evening.

The community began with the experiences of Michael Verigin, a backsliding Doukhobor. Michael had left his home in the mountains, opened a boarding-house for Russians in Vancouver, and prospered there. After a few years Michael began to feel the malaise which many Doukhobors experience when they go from their villages into the acquisitive outside world, and he returned to the mountain valley of Krestova. Krestova is the Mecca of the Sons of Freedom, the fire-raising and nude-parading radical wing of the Doukhobor sect. Michael rejoined the Sons of Freedom and was regarded with deference because he bore the holy name of Verigin and was a distant cousin of Peter the Lordly, the Living Christ who presided over the Doukhobors' first years in Canada, and died mysteriously in a train explosion during the 1920s.

"Then Michael had a vision."

"A dream?"

"No, a vision. He was awake, and he said there was a voice and a presence."

"He saw nothing?"

"That time he didn't. The vision told him he was no longer Mike Verigin. Michael the Archangel had gone into him. He was the same man, but the Archangel as well."

"How did he know it was a real vision?"

"He just knew." Joe looked at me with the imperturbable blue-eyed confidence of a man used to assessing the authenticity of supernatural messages. "The vision said Michael must prepare the world for the Second Coming."

The Second Coming did not mean the return of Christ. According to Doukhobor beliefs, Christ is returning all the time in various forms. The Second Coming meant the establishment of God's earthly kingdom and the end of time and mortality.

As the chosen pioneers in this great mission, the Doukhobors must purify themselves. The Archangel began by proclaiming that they must renounce not only meat and alcohol, but also tobacco and musical instruments. A radio was playing loudly in the kitchen as Joe explained this. "That's о.к.," he reassured us. "A radio ain't a musical instrument."

Above all, the lust for possession must be rooted out. This meant not only a return to the traditional communistic economy from which the Doukhobors had lapsed under evil Canadian influences, but also the destruction of that inner citadel of possession, marriage. No person must have rights over another, either parental or marital. Women must be liberated, sexual relations must be free, families must wither away.

Two or three hundred of the Sons of Freedom, mostly seasoned old veterans of the nude marches and the pre-war internment on Piers Island, accepted the Archangel's teaching. Their neighbours showed disagreement by burning down the houses of those who followed Verigin. At this point the Archangel very conveniently had another vision.

Two of his followers must visit Vancouver Island. There they would find a town where a clock had stopped at half-past two, and then they must proceed eastward until they saw a white horse by the gate of a farm. Joe and another man went on the expedition. They found the clock at Port Alberni, and the horse by the gate of a three-hundred-acre farm that was up for sale at a knockdown price. And, for what the fact is worth, I should record that after I had heard Joe's story I happened to visit Port Alberni, and there, on the tower of a fire-hall, I saw a dummy clock whose painted hands stood unmoving at half-past two.

The farm was bought with the pooled resources of the faithful, and Michael the Archangel led two hundred of his disciples on the exodus to Vancouver Island. Immediately after leaving the mainland he added to all the other prohibitions a ban on sexual intercourse—to conserve energies for the great task of spiritual regeneration. Complete freedom was only to be won by complete self-control. So much for the stories of Free Love rampant!

I wanted to find out the actual nature of the power that enabled Michael the Archangel to impose such restrictions. Tolstoy once thought that, because they opposed the state, the Doukhobors lived without rulers. Other writers had suggested that Living Christs, like Peter the Lordly Verigin and his son Peter the Purger, had been rulers as powerful as any earthly governor.

"He is just our spiritual leader," Joe explained blandly.

"But he still seems to have a big say in your practical affairs."

"It depends on what you mean by say. He gives no orders. We are free men. We don't obey anybody. But he gives us advice."

"Do you always accept it?"

"If we know what's good for us, we do."

"Why?"

"Because we know Michael the Archangel is always right."

"How do you know?"

"We just know."

The next day we met the Archangel. He had sent a message early that morning summoning us to his presence, and Joe drove us to the hamlet where we had arrived originally. The Archangel's house was one of the larger buildings, but we were not allowed to go in. We waited outside. The Archangel would meet us in the garden.

A tall man in his late fifties came stepping heavily between the zinnia borders. A heavy paunch filled his knitted sweater, and his shining bald head loosened into a coarse, flushed face with a potato nose, a sandy moustache, and small eyes that glinted out of puffy sockets. It was a disappointing encounter. The Archangel bowed in the customary Doukhobor manner, but without the warmth most Doukhobors put into their greeting. He shook hands limply. He spoke a few sentences in Russian, welcoming us and wishing us good health, and he affected not to understand English, though we learned later that he was effectively bilingual. He picked two small pink roses from a briar that ran along the fence and gave one to each of us. In five minutes he was gone, retiring with dignified adroitness and leaving all our intended questions about archangelic power unanswered. Joe led us away, loudly declaring that the Archangel had been delighted with us, and that he had given many messages which he, Joe, would transmit in due course. Our whole relationship with the Archangel took on this elusive, indirect form, with Joe acting like a voluble priest interpreting and embellishing the laconic banalities of the oracle.

For the rest of the second day we wandered around the community, talking to the people we encountered. I pumped the handle of a primitive hand washing-machine, and learned from the girl I helped a curious instance of Doukhobor double-think. A spaniel bitch trotted over the yard, followed by a single pup. "She had four," the girl volunteered. "Did you give the rest away?" "No, they were drowned." "I thought you didn't believe in killing." "We didn't kill 'em. That Mountie sergeant drowned 'em for us." She chuckled, and quite obviously felt no guilt for merely condoning a killing someone else had carried out.

Under the prophetic discipline there were certainly signs of strain. I found empty beer bottles under the bushes in a corner of one Doukhobor field, and in the shelter of the ten-feet plumes of corn which were the community's pride a young man begged a cigarette and smoked in hasty gulps to finish it before anyone came into sight. Yet there was also an atmosphere of dogged devotion. Much of the land had been irrigated, and it was growing heavier crops of corn and tomatoes and vegetables than any of the neighbouring farms, while the houses were surrounded by rows of hotbeds and cold frames where melons and gherkins ripened. The younger people talked constantly of schemes for new kinds of cultivation and for starting up light industries, but the younger people were so few. There were too many children, too many old visionaries.

Sunday was the climax of our visit. Our arrival had coincided with the community's first great festival. In the afternoon the only child so far born there was to be handed over to the care of the community as a symbolic demonstration against conventional ideas of motherhood and the family. Since the Archangel had forbidden fornication, we were rather surprised that a child whose very presence seemed to defy his will should be so honoured. From my attempts to discuss the situation I gained an impression that the Doukhobors applied a rather Dostoevskian equation—considering that, if the ban itself was sacred, so must be the sin against it. "Free men ain't bound by reason," as one young man rather unanswerably concluded a discussion on this point.

The day began with morning service in the bare meeting house. Flowers and plates of red apples had been brought in, and the sunlight played over the white head-shawls and bright cotton dresses of the women. Bread and salt stood symbolically on the small central table, and also a great ewer of water from which anybody who happened to feel thirsty would stop and drink as the service went on. The women ranged to the right of the table and the men to the left. On entering the hall each person bowed low from the waist, and the bow was returned by the whole assembly; the salutation was not to the man, but to the God within him. The Archangel stood at the head of the men, benign and copiously sweating; despite his celestial nature, he did not attempt to offend Doukhobor precedent by acting like a priest. Today, in fact, as a child was to be the centre of the festival, the children led off the service, choosing and starting in their sharp, clear voices the Doukhobor psalms and hymns for the day. Almost every part of the service was sung, and the wild and wholly

incomprehensible chanting of the two hundred people in the small meeting house produced in us an extraordinary sense of exaltation such as I have only experienced once since then, in a church full of Zapotec peasants at a festival south of Oaxaca. At the end of the service, we all linked arms at the elbows and kissed each other's cheeks, first right then left, in traditional token of forgiveness.

Later in the day we re-assembled in the open air, forming a great V with the bread and salt at the apex. The singing rose like a fountain of sound among the drooping cedar trees, and between lines of women waving flowers and men waving green boughs the mother carried her child to the table. She was one of the young women we had met at the farmhouse on our arrival. As she stood there, her fair face grave and melancholy within the white frame of her head-shawl, she looked like the dolorous mother of some naive ikon. The singing ended, the old hawk-faced bricklayer prayed before the table, and the mother, showing no emotion, handed the child to another of the women. The Archangel began to speak, in high, emotional tones; Pete, standing beside me, translated. The child would be named Angel Gabriel. The fruit of sin, he contained the seed of celestial nature. It was he who would fulfil the great destiny of the Doukhobors and lead mankind back on the great journey to lost Eden.

The women brought out pitchers of kvass and walked among the people as the orators began to speak. Emblematic banners were unfurled before the assembly. One, representing women dragging the ploughs that broke the prairies during the hard early days of the sect in Canada, was meant to celebrate the coming liberation of the sect from all forms of bondage. Another, covered with images of clocks and other symbols of time, was carefully expounded by the Archangel, who found in it the fatal dates that charted the destiny of the world. Then everyone spoke who wished—elders and young women; a Communist lawyer who had come in from the blue; even I, under moral coercion, as the enquiring Tolstoyan I then was. It was hot and tedious work as the sun beat down into the bowl among the mountains and Sunday trippers from Qualicum Beach gazed in astonishment through the palisades.

We walked back to the farmhouse with a Canadian woman who had married into the Doukhobors. "You've seen what Mike wants you to see," she said, bitterly. "You don't know all there is to know about that girl. Today they've taken her child. Now she'll go to stay up in Mike's house. They won't let her talk to anyone, and they'll pay her out in every way they can for having a child by her own husband. Purification! That's what they talk about. I call it prison!" The mother of the Angel Gabriel was not at the evening meal, and we never saw her again. We asked Joe what had happened to her. She had gone willingly into seclusion, he answered, for her own good, of course.

Indeed, Joe had much more important things to talk about

in that last conversation. "You have a great part to play in the future of mankind." He fixed me with a sharp, pale eye. "Michael's vision has told him that the end of the world is very near. Now we have to gather into Jerusalem the hundred and forty-four thousand true servants of God mentioned in the Book of Revelation. This time Jerusalem will be right here."

"Here? On Vancouver Island?"

"On this very spot."

"But how do you *know?*"

"We ain't worrying. We just know. And the Archangel had a vision about you. He knew you were coming a long time ago. He knew you were a writer. He knew you were being sent here so you could tell the world what we're doing."

I must have looked at him very dubiously for he flapped his hands reassuringly. "I ain't asking you to do it. Nor is Archangel. We just know you will. You'll write about us, and people will come to us, and then you will come back and be marked with the sign and live for ever among the servants of God."

We left the next day. The Archangel saw us once more in his garden, gave us a white rose each, and said we would meet again before long. "It's a prophecy," Joe whispered.

And indeed it was. One day, months later, I was broadcasting in Vancouver when Ross McLean, who was then a radio producer, said he had heard Joe was locked up in the court house. I went over, but I could not see him. The Mounties were holding him incommunicado. But as I was leaving the station Michael the Archangel was brought in, and for a couple of minutes, in that grim barred room, I was allowed to talk to him. He was pleased to be recognized, and even willing to talk a little English. "I am free soon," he said, as he was led away to the cells. Not long afterwards he and Joe were sentenced on some rather nebulous charges of disturbing public order. And a few months later Michael the Archangel Verigin died in jail.

Ten years afterwards we drove through Hilliers, turning off our road on a nostalgic impulse. The palisade was still there, opposite the railway siding, and for a moment everything looked unchanged. But inside, where Jerusalem should have been rising, there was only the ghost of what we had seen on the day the Angel Gabriel was named. Most of the buildings had gone, but falling fences and squares of thistles still marked out the theocracy where the Archangel had ruled.

Prospector
Patrick Lane

Old man you prospected summer
country of caves and gold.
With the rattlesnake and spider
you were a black widow without a mate
gone deep chrome yellow.
You shared with the sun
a babble of flowers and full
brown flawless centres where
you walked in a wilderness
of golden sleep.

Once I was a child
and saw you touch a mountain
wasp with your finger
tip to wing he didn't move
but shivered gently his petal shells
of yellow and black in the wide corner
of August. You watched solitary
wasps float down sunflower fields.

Old man I dreamed you
wandered the mountains
in spring and planted
the hills with golden flowers.
When they found you
they said you were dead
but I knew that the wasps
had planted their eggs in you
and flowers were growing
out of your sleeping eyes.

The Mountains;
The Valley
Peter Trower

Constant as clockwork
the loaded logging trucks
rumble down the gut
of the hot valley,
shout their radio warnings
along the river.

We dodge one after another.
Janosch our guide, expatriate alpinist
who knows the Matterhorn, the Eiger,
lauds the mountains we move among,
has scaled their walls,
skied their ridges.

They own the valley, those peaks;
waterfalls whiten their cliffs
as the snows weep under summer.
The road narrows, forks;
above low trees
the strange pinnacle rises.

It's a rotting tooth of decaying rock—
Janosch admits he doesn't care
or dare to tackle that one—
it's a crumbling witchtower
eroding into rubble
among the healthier hills.

The road snakes right again
through logged-off vistas
green with fireweed and reseeded fir
not battleground-ugly in distance
but like miles of alpine meadow
tipping up to scrub and more white summits.

Around us now
the househuge boulders
of an ancient rockslide
that built its town of ruin before men came—
beyond, a glory hole of stumps
pitching to the glacial river.

Far ahead, a black monolith
moults snow in remote ranges.
It's a volcanic plug, Janosch tells me,
jammed like a gigantic cork
in the mouth of a dead crater—
he has trodden its lava-top too.

High to our right, a shale-sided Sphinx
broods against blue
below it, a pencil-small steel spar
fishes far slopes
whistles float down, lines twitch silver,
kicking across the hill the catch comes in.

Homebound down the valley,
Janosch, whose task is to heal and restore,
who is the mountain-walker and valley-mender,
tells me of the beekeeper
who plants his hives in the fireweed forests
stealing simple honey from these hills.

Wild Horses
Patrick Lane

Just to come once alone
to these wild horses
driving out of high Cascades,
raw legs heaving the hip-high snow.
Just once alone. Never to see
the men and their trucks.

Just once alone. Nothing moves
as the stallion with five free mares
rushes into the guns. All dead.
Their eyes glaze with frost.
Ice bleeds in their nostrils
as the cable hauls them in.

Later, after the swearing
and the stamping of feet,
we ride down into Golden:

'Quit bitchin.
It's a hard bloody life
and a long week
for three hundred bucks of meat.'

That and the dull dead eyes
and the empty meadows.

Canadian Pacific Camp
Daphne Marlatt

Sun shining upstream on the Fraser River, October, on the south shore of Lulu Island, river running by. A drying shed. A wharf, some poles with nets slung over, somebody's boat on blocks. *Crystal S.* and further, hidden by nets and the shed to some extent, *Lady Tara.* Out of their element. Curve of hull, belly solid and somewhat naked up there in the air, wind blowing sharp across our ears in the nevertheless warm sunlight.

We're here to talk to fishermen about the old days, standing, near the close of fishing season, on the worn wood of their dock. Twenty-four-hour fishing schedules have been posted down at Star Camp and duck-hunting season opens Saturday. For those who are here it's a good day for mending nets.

Henry Kokubo grins up at us from under his Ohmi netting cap, "Yes? You want to see the net shed?" He moves briskly, cheerfully, sleeves rolled up to above the elbow. Nisei, weathered to a thin resiliency, standing under the rafters in a cascade of green nylon surprisingly soft after salt-water use. He explains there are different sizes of mesh for different fish, different shades of green, too, for varying depths of water. When he was young, he tells us, the nets were made by hand through the winters, made with linen and a long needle; you would start to work at 8 in the morning and, stopping only for lunch and coffee, knot until 8 or so at night, your hands always moving, only your hands, for weeks, making the net. Now everything is made by machine and imported from Japan.

Outside on the wharf, nets are stretched on long poles. Several men bend over them, snipping frayed strands with tong-like Japanese scissors, and knotting new nylon onto the old. Each works in a kind of attentive solitude, with only the sound of gulls and an occasional plane above to mark the passing of time. But there is conversation, too, and bantering as other men arrive. Out here there are also a couple of punts like the one inside the shed, shallow things, their gunnels stuck with sheaves of dry reeds so that, in the river, one can imagine a gliding island and the man inside hidden, silent, waiting for the first V to cross the horizon.

Harry Sameshima seems busy with his net but will answer some questions, and Bill Maeda, who is quietly listening while he knots, is also drawn into the conversation. Both of them in peaked caps, measured and deliberate in their talk, as their hands move easily with the skill of long-doing.

"There were over 2,000 Japanese in here before the war."

"Were you born here?"

"I was born right here, by that boathouse. It was a company house."

"Did you pay rent for the house?"

"By the number of fish you caught. They deducted 5 cents from the price of each fish for the rent, so if you caught a thousand fish that meant $50 for the rent. And you had to pay water separate, $24."

"Did you want to be a fisherman?"

"We had no choice in our days, you know. I mean those prewar days...there was a lot of prejudice and you couldn't get jobs the way the third generation can get now. Third generation now, well, they're on an equal footing with everyone else and they can get it; long as you got the education and the qualifications you can get a job. Our days you couldn't do that. I mean to be a fisherman you don't have to have brains, so for us I guess it was the easiest thing to get into."

The gulls wheel and cry, a plane on the other side of the river flies so low that it's difficult to hear the men.

"So things are better now?"

"You make more money, but everything else is up accordingly. I still say you're farther ahead now, though. 'Cause, for example, chum salmon that we're catching now—before the war you could get maybe 15 cents a piece for them and right now we're getting 30 cents a pound. And pink salmon—I remember days when they were down to one-half cent a piece, and we get about 16 cents a pound now. So those days you had to get a boatload to make any money."

There is a literalness to their speech that stays close to what is known and obvious, public knowledge. They don't wish to speak of the *experience* of fishing, introspective as that must seem to them. What counts is what you can do, however skilfully, in the face of necessity. "You don't cook, you don't eat."

"You eat fish most of the time when you're fishing?"

"No, we don't. I very seldom eat fish out there. No, mostly out of cans. Saves cooking." One gets on with the business at hand.

Harry Sameshima spends three months of the year fishing off the west coast of Vancouver Island, but it's "not good for family life, you come home once a month maybe." Does Bill Maeda want his son to be a fisherman? "No. And I don't recommend him being a fisherman either. Well, fishing's all right if you like it, but it's a rough way of making a living." Henry Kokubo interjects, "You're your own boss." Sure you are, and when it comes right down to it, they like fishing. "Sure, you grow attached to your boat like you grow attached to a car."

Boats. How small the boats were in the old days. Columbia River type, they were simply skiffs with sail, each operated by a "boss" who fished while his partner ("puller") rowed. And the canneries, small and numerous, lined the riverbanks on pilings, 20, 30 of them in the town's heyday. Henry lists them off in order down the riverbank, those that existed before the war: Winch Cannery, then Beaver, Colonial, Alexandria, Ben, Phoenix, Imperial, Star, Gulf of Georgia, Atlas, Scott, Burrard. Each cannery had a cluster of company bunkhouses or cabins like the abandoned ones still at Star Camp. "They rented for $24 or 30 a month, and then you pay your water and light separately, but in the old days they used lamps, lanterns, and cooked on wood stoves using driftwood."

In prewar days the town served some 2,000 Japanese with grocery stores, poolrooms, barber shops, hotels, general stores, and the Japanese Hospital for births and illness, and the Japanese School which changed to English school when Henry was in the fifth grade. You took the tram-line to Eburne and Marpole if you wanted to go to Vancouver. But you could get everything you needed in Steveston because, besides the three fish markets, there were machine shops, drugstores, hardware, and one bank. And there were door-to-door suitcase salesmen who brought samples of ready-made clothes and underwear, though most of the women made their own (there was even a dressmakers' school in Steveston). In winter the women sewed while the men cut firewood or made their nets. In summer they worked in the canneries while the men went fishing.

Life was hard. You got 15 cents a piece for dog-salmon. And though it cost you less to live (you could get your fishing license for $1 a year while now it costs $200), still, says Bill Maeda, we're ahead now.

Where did the people go from Star Camp? "Oh, they own their own houses now." All those modern suburban houses, those split-levels along Steveston Highway? Yes, many of them are owned by fishermen.

But Harry Sameshima's words echo—fishing's going bust. Are there less fish now? Some people say so. Some say it depends on the year, as always. Why is the Government cutting back on the boats? Maybe too many boats. Maybe less fish. It's hard to imagine when your livelihood depends on the fish running and your history is almost that of the industry itself—how it developed and you survived, as "cannery slave", as wartime "Jap", and now, finally, union fisherman, citizen, property-owner.

What Do I Remember of the Evacuation?
Joy Kogawa

What do I remember of the evacuation?
I remember my father telling Tim and me
About the mountains and the train
And the excitement of going on a trip.
What do I remember of the evacuation?
I remember my mother wrapping
A blanket about me and my
Pretending to fall asleep so she would be happy
Though I was so excited I couldn't sleep
(I hear there were people herded
Into the Hastings Park like cattle.
Families were made to move in two hours
Abandoning everything, leaving pets
And possessions at gun point.
I hear families were broken up.
Men were forced to work. I heard
It whispered late at night
That there was suffering) and
I missed my dolls.
What do I remember of the evacuation?
I remember Miss Foster and Miss Tucker
Who still live in Vancouver
And who did what they could
And loved the children and who gave me
A puzzle to play with on the train.
And I remember the mountains and I was
Six years old and I swear I saw a giant
Gulliver of Gulliver's Travels scanning the horizon
And when I told my mother she believed it too
And I remember how careful my parents were
Not to bruise us with bitterness
And I remember the puzzle of Lorraine Life
Who said "Don't insult me" when I
Proudly wrote my name in Japanese
And Tim flew the Union Jack
When the war was over but Lorraine
And her friends spat on us anyway
And I prayed to the God who loves
All the children in his sight
That I might be white.

Fog
Ethel Wilson

For seven days fog settled down upon Vancouver. It crept in from the ocean, advancing in its mysterious way in billowing banks which swallowed up the land. In the Bay and the Inlet and False Creek, agitated voices spoke to one another. Small tugs that were waylaid in the blankets of fog cried shrilly and sharply "Keep away! Keep away! I am here!" Fishing-boats lay inshore. Large freighters mooed continuously like monstrous cows. The foghorns at Point Atkinson and the Lions' Gate Bridge kept up their bellowings. Sometimes the fog quenched the sounds, sometimes the sounds were loud and near. If there had not been this continuous dense fog, all the piping and boo-hooing would have held a kind of beauty; but it signified danger and warning. People knew that when the fog lifted they would see great freighters looking disproportionately large riding at anchor in the Bay because passage through the Narrows into the harbour was not safe. Within the harbour, laden ships could not depart but remained lying fog-bound at great expense in the stream...booo...booo...they warned. "I am here! Keep away!" All the ships listened. The CPR boat from Victoria crashed into the dock. Gulls collided in the pathless air. Water traffic ceased and there was no movement anywhere offshore.

In the streets, cars crawled slowly. Drivers peered. Pedestrians emerged and vanished like smoke. Up the draw of False Creek, fog packed thick on the bridges. Planes were grounded. People cancelled parties. Everyone arrived late for everything.

Mrs Bylow was an old woman who lived in a small old house which was more cabin than cottage in an unpleasant part of Mount Pleasant. For the fifth day she sat beside her window looking into the fog and cracking her knuckles because she had nothing else to do. If she had owned a telephone she would have talked all day for pastime, repeating herself and driving the party line mad.

Mrs Bylow frequently sat alone and lonely. Her diurnal occupations had narrowed down to sleeping, waking to still another day, getting up, making and swallowing small meals, belching a little, cleaning up (a little), hoping, going to the bathroom, going to the Chinaman's corner store, reading the paper (and thank God for that, especially the advertisements), becoming suddenly aware again of the noise of the radio (and thank God for that, too), and forgetting again.

This, and not much more, was her life as she waited for the great dustman and the ultimate box. So Mrs Bylow's days and months slid and slid away while age—taking advantage of her solitariness, her long unemployment of vestigial brain, her

unawareness of a world beyond herself, her absence of preparation for the grey years—closed down upon her like a vice, no, more like a fog. There had been a time about ten years ago when Mrs Bylow, sitting on her small porch, beckoned to the little neighbour children who played on the sidewalk. "Come," said Mrs Bylow, smiling and nodding.

The children came, and they all went into the kitchen. There was Mrs Bylow's batch of fresh cookies and the children ate, looking around them, rapacious. They ate and ran away and once or twice a child hovered and said "Thank you." Perhaps that was not the child who said "Thank you", but parents speaking through the child ("Say Thank you to Mrs Bylow!") so the child said "Thank you" and Mrs Bylow was pleased. Sometimes the children lingered around the little porch, not hungry, but happy, noisy and greedy. Then Mrs Bylow rejoiced at the tokens of love and took the children into the kitchen. But perhaps she had only apples and the children did not care for apples. "Haven't you got any cookies?" asked a bold one, "we got lotsa apples at home."

"You come Tuesday," said Mrs Bylow, nodding and smiling, but the children forgot.

So within Mrs Bylow these small rainbows of life (children, cookies, laughing, and beckoning) faded, although two neighbours did sometimes stop on their way home and talk for a few minutes and thus light up her day. Miss Casey who worked at the People's Friendly Market and was a smart dresser with fine red hair, and Mrs Merkle who was the managing type and had eyes like marbles and was President of the Ladies' Bowling Club dropped in from time to time and told Mrs Bylow all about the illnesses of the neighbours which Mrs Bylow enjoyed very much and could think about later. Mrs Merkle told her about Mr Galloway's broken hip and Miss Casey told her about her mother's diabetes and how she managed her injections, also about the woman who worked in her department when she didn't need to work and now her kid had gone wrong and was in the Juvenile Court. Mrs Bylow was regaled by everything depressing that her two friends could assemble because she enjoyed bad news which was displayed to her chiefly against the backdrop of her own experience and old age. All these ailments, recalling memories of her own ("...well I remember my Uncle Ernest's...") provided a drama, as did the neglect and irresponsibility of the young generations. Like an old sad avid stupid judge she sat, passing judgement without ill will. It is not hard to understand why Mrs Merkle and Miss Casey, hastening past Mrs Bylow's gate which swung on old hinges, often looked straight ahead, walking faster and thinking I *must* go in and see her tomorrow.

During long periods of bad weather, as now in this unconquerable fog, time was a deep pit for Mrs Bylow. Her hip was not very good. She should have belonged to a church (to such base uses can the humble and glorious act of worship come) or a club, to which she would at least look forward. Gone were the simple impossible joys of going to town, wandering through the shops, fingering and comparing cloth, cotton and silk. Gone was the joy of the running children. Life, which had been pinkish and blueish, was grey. And now this fog.

So it was that on the fifth day of fog, Mrs Bylow sat beside her window in a sort of closed-up dry well of boredom, cracking her knuckles and looking into the relentless blank that pressed against her window panes and kept her from seeing any movement on the sidewalk. Mrs Merkle and Miss Casey were as though they had never been. I'm not surprised they wouldn't drop in, thought Mrs Bylow modestly and without rancour, it couldn't be expected, it'll be all they can do to get home; and she pictured Miss Casey, with her flaming hair, wearing her leopard coat, pushing through the fog home to her mother. Diabetes, thought Mrs Bylow, and she was sorry for old Mrs Casey. Her indulgence of sorrow spread to include Miss Casey hurrying home looking so smart. Not much in life for her, now, is there, really, she thought, rocking. Mrs Bylow peered again. She was insulted by this everywhere fog, this preventing fog. She needed a cup of cocoa and she had no cocoa. She repeated aloud a useful phrase, "The fog is lifting"; but the fog was not lifting.

Mrs Bylow creaked to her feet. She wrapped herself up well, took her walking stick and went unsteadily down her three steps. Then, not at all afraid, she turned to the left and, in a silence of velvet, she moved slowly along beside the picket fence which would guide her to Wong Kee's store. At her own corner a suggestion of sickly glow in the air told her that the street lamps were lighted. She moved on, screwing up her eyes against the greyish yellow fog that invaded eyes, nose, mouth. At last another pale high glimmer informed her that she was near Wong Kee's store and, gasping, leaning now and then against the outside wall of the store itself, she reached the door with the comfortable knowledge that, once inside, she would find light and warmth. She would ask Wong Kee for his chair or a box and would sit down and take her ease while the Chinaman went with shuffling steps to the shelf where he kept the tins of cocoa. Wong Kee was a charming old man with good cheek-bones and a sudden tired Oriental smile. After Mrs Merkle and Miss Casey he was Mrs Bylow's third friend. She pushed the door open and waddled in to where there was this desired light and warmth, puffing a little.

Something was happening inside the store, a small whirlwind and fury. Mrs Bylow was roughly pushed by large rushing objects. She lost her balance and was thrown, no, hurled violently to the ground. The person or persons rushed on, out and into the fog. The door slammed.

The store was empty. Everything was still. The old woman lay in a heap, bewildered and in pain. Gradually she began to know that someone or some people had rushed out into the fog, knocking her down and hurting her because she happened to be in the way. She whimpered and she thought badly of Wong Kee because he did not come to help her. Her body gave her massive pain, and as she looked slowly about her in a stupefied way she saw that a number of heavy cans of food had rained down upon her and lay around her. As she tried clumsily to heave herself up (but that was not possible), a customer came in.

"Well well well!" said the customer bending over her, "whatever. . ." then he straightened himself and listened.

A faint sound as of a bubbling sigh came from behind the counter on which was the till. The till was open and empty. The customer went behind the counter and again bent down. Then he drew himself up quickly. Wong Kee lay like a bundle of old clothes from which blood seeped and spread. The sound that the customer had heard was the soft sound of the death of Wong Kee who was an honest man and innocent. He had worked all his life and had robbed no one. He had an old wife who loved him. In a way hard to explain they were seriously and simply happy together. This was now over.

The customer paid no further attention to Mrs Bylow on the floor but, stepping round Wong Kee's body, reached the telephone.

A small woman parted the dingy curtains which separated the store from the home of Wong Kee and his wife. She held in her arms a bundle of stove wood and stood motionless like a wrinkled doll. Then the stove wood clattered to the ground and she dropped to her knees uttering high babbling noises. She rocked and prostrated herself beside the impossible sight of her husband's dead body and his blood. The customer regarded her as he talked into the telephone. Then he too knelt down and put his arm round her. He could find nothing to say but the immemorial "There there. . . ."

Mrs Bylow, lying neglected on the floor, endeavoured to look behind her but she had to realize as people do in bombardment, flood and earthquake that she was at the mercy of whatever should happen to her and could not do anything about it, let alone look behind her.

"They're slow coming," said the customer. "It's the fog."

The old Chinese woman wrenched herself from him. "I tarryphome," she cried out, "I tarryphome my son. . ."

The door opened and there seemed to be some policemen. The outside fog poured in with this entrance and some other kind of fog pressed down upon Mrs Bylow's understanding and blurred it. "I'm a very old woman," she mumbled to a constable who had a little book, "and they knocked me down. . .they mighta killed me. . .they shouldn't a done that. . .they've broke my hip. . .aah. . .!"

"Yes lady, we'll look after you," said the constable, "who was it?"

"It was . . ." (well, who was it?) "I guess it was some man . . . no . . ." she breathed with difficulty, she should not have to suffer so, "I guess it was a boy . . . no, two boys . . . they knocked me down . . ."

A constable at the door said to a crowd which had gathered from somewhere in the fog and now pushed against the front of the store, "Now then, you can't come in here, there's been a robbery, see? You best go on home," but someone battered on the pane with both hands enough to break it, and Miss Casey burst in at the door, her red hair wet with fog.

"She's here! Yes there she is!" said Miss Casey talking to everyone in her loud voice and bringing into the muted shop a blazing of bright eyes and hair and leopard coat and humanity, "—that's what I thought! I thought right after I left the store I'd better go in and see was she O.K. because she shouldn't be out and the fog was just *awful* and I prett' near went past her gate but I kinda felt something was wrong and my goodness see what happened. . . . Mrs Bylow honey, what happened you," and Miss Casey dropped on her knees and took Mrs Bylow's hand in hers. "Say, what's been going on around here, anyway?" she said, looking up at the constable ready to accuse.

"She's not so good," said the constable in a low tone in Mrs Bylow's dream and a high noise came into the night ("That's the syreen," said Miss Casey) and some men lifted her and took her somewhere on a bed. It did not occur to Mrs Bylow that perhaps she had been killed inadvertently by two youths who had just killed her old friend, but if a policeman had said to her "Now you are dead," she would have accepted the information, so unfamiliar was the experience of boring horizontally through a fog at top speed very slowly in a high and unexplained swelling noise. She opened her eyes and saw a piece of Miss Casey's leopard coat and so she was not dead.

"Is it reel?" she whispered, because she had always wanted to know.

"Is what reel?" said Miss Casy bending her flaming head. "Sure it's reel. The collar's reel anyway." Mrs Bylow closed her eyes again for several years and said "But I never got my cocoa." Then she began to cry quietly because she felt old and helpless and the pain was something cruel but it was good to feel Miss Casey beside her in her leopard coat. She did not know that Wong Kee was dead—slugged on the head, pistol-whipped, stabbed again and again in the stomach with a long knife—all because he had summoned his small strength and fought like a cat and defended himself for his right to his thirty dollars and some loose change and a handful of cigarettes and his life. "Well, here we are," said Miss Casey, standing up, very cheerful.

In a week or two, while she was better and before she got worse, Mrs Bylow began to remember the two boys whom she had never seen and, as she constructed their leather jackets and their faces, she said she would know them anywhere. Of course she would not, and the murderers of Wong Kee were never found but carried the knowledge of their murder into the fog with them on their way from the betrayal of their youth to whatever else they would soon violently undertake to do. When they arrived back, each at his own home, their parents said in pursuance of their habit of long years past "Where you bin?" and the hoodlums said in pursuance of their habit of long years past "Out." This satisfied the idiot parents. They said "My that fog's just terrible," and the hoodlums said "Sure is." They were excited and nervous because this was the first time they had killed, but they had the money. One of the young hoodlums did not go into the room where his parents were but went upstairs because he was pretty sure there was still some blood on his hands and so there was. Wong Kee's blood was on his parents' hands too but they, being irresponsible, did not know this. And on their hands was the blood of Mrs Bylow who was soon to die, and of Mrs Wong Kee who could no longer be said to live, and of their own hoodlum children.

Before Mrs Bylow died, wiped out by forces quite outside herself like a moth in a storm (not much more and no less), she began to be a little proud of almost being present at a murder.

"It's not everyone who's been at a murder, Miss Casey, love, is it?"

"No honey," said Miss Casey, seeing again that sordid scene, "it isn't everyone."

"I always liked that coat of yours," said Mrs Bylow.

"And then," said Miss Casey to Mrs Merkle, "d'you know what she said? She said if ever I come to die—just like she wasn't ever going to—would you please wear your leopard coat. She's crazy about that coat. And then she said she often thought of those two boys that killed the storekeeper and knocked her down and she guessed it was more their parents' fault and not their fault. It made the tears come to your eyes," said Miss Casey who was kind as well as noisy and cherished a sense of personal drama.

"Sure," said Mrs Merkle who had eyes like marbles that did not weep.

Mrs Bylow's death was obscure and pitiful. Miss Casey got the afternoon off and so there were two people at her funeral. Miss Casey wore her leopard coat as promised.

Social Credit Elected in B.C.
Lionel Kearns

Snowing, and as I enter
the corner grocery store
four local teenagers
are insulting and menacing
the Chinese shop-keeper's son
a boy about thirteen
running things alone tonight
and before I realize
what's happening they slink out
pockets full of cigarettes and candy
and he is left asking me
if that's all I want

In this almost affluent suburb
three days ago the citizens
almost unanimously endorsed
free enterprise, pavement
and the reintroduction of the strap
as a medium of education

This is Canada
true north
strong
free

They Are Burning
Fred Wah

Pitch black up the valley
in front of us twenty miles
they are burning the mountains down
the sky is that kind of orange
the hillsides are outlined to us
in just that orange horizon
which will be gone with daybreak
when the smoke of their burning
hangs over the valleys rivers and trees
drifts slowly on the contours of the land
and the deadness where no birds fly.

Yes they are burning
for it is July
and August and the nights
with no wind the darkness is cool.

What I thought would be there is not
I'm sorry to say. What I had expected
was to sleep for the ride with eyes closed
not drive into a burning mountainside.

The Medicine Cross
Hugh Brody

[In *Maps and Dreams* Hugh Brody recalls that, when he arrived to live and work among the Beaver Indians, the old chief Joseph Patsah told how his father had erected a medicine cross, "twice the height of a tall man", to confirm the potentialities of a hunting ground revealed by dreams. Later Brody was taken to the cross.]

Moose run in the autumn. You can hear the bulls; their bellowing is a hoarse and frantic gurgle. It is the one time of year that they can be dangerous. They lower their heavily antlered heads to the ground and charge any creature large enough to appear to be a sexual rival. These charges are wild and blind: once a rival is located, the bull moose rushes unseeing towards it. Some hunters take advantage of this blind haste by imitating a bull's call, luring a maddened animal to attack. A funnel of bark or cardboard or a loosely clenched fist can be used as a resonator. Joseph Patsah, however, has always used the cleaned scapula of a moose or deer. He scrapes its hard, smooth edge against the rough bark of a small pine to produce, with startling exactness, the bellow of a bull moose in rut. The real bull, angered by the sound of a rival, may charge in its direction—to be met at very close range by a carefully timed shot at the head or neck.

Joseph says he has often used this technique to good effect, but it did not work for him or any of the other men last year. Atsin tried calling through his fists, but the sound went unheeded by the bulls, whose bellows earlier in the day had echoed back and forth through the woods. In fact the rut was nearly over by the time Joseph and his family camped at Bluestone, where they hoped to prepare a supply of dry meat for the coming winter. By this time—late October—after weeks of sexual battle, bulls are exhausted and skinny—and they stink. They are not enthusiastically hunted. The hunters now concentrate their hopes on cows, which are fat from the good browsing of late summer and, with their last year's calves, are skulking among willow or poplar thickets to keep away from the excessive and violent attentions of the bulls.

In late October or early November, autumn gives way to winter. The camp at Bluestone was the last before the people moved either to their homes on the Reserve or to trapping cabins. It was at this camp that everyone felt the first bite, startling and invigorating, of the coming winter. The air had teeth and the ground a strange firmness. Each morning the ice has spread farther and thicker over the creeks. There is a new silence, yet the earth, or its covering of crusted leaves and frost-spiked grasses, crackles under every footstep. Such noise can be a disadvantage: moose might well hear a hunter's approach. But the hunter can easily see and understand tracks and droppings, dark and clear against the frost.

Despite the cold, Atsin and the younger men set up an open camp. They stretched a tarpaulin over two long poles that sloped from a high ridge pole at the front to a low ridge pole at the back. A second tarpaulin was then stretched over poles leaning in the opposite direction. The result was two open-sided tents—only roofs, really, that were held in place and at a slope by pegs and thongs along each side. If there are more than two or three hunters at one campsite, open camps are made in pairs so that everyone can sit and sleep near a central fire. Our camp at Bluestone was like that: a fire built beneath the central ridge pole, burned between two symmetrical open camps. The fire was very large; logs were over five feet long, and threw up a wall of flames between the two shelters. The sides, open to prevailing winds, were covered with spruce boughs, pieces of canvas, scraps of plastic— anything at hand. Overlapping spruce boughs covered the ground; blankets and sleeping bags were laid on top of them. The men slept parallel to the fire, two on one side, three on the other; Atsin and Thomas Fellow were nearest, the younger men farthest away.

Beside our double open camp, Joseph pitched a tent in which he and Liza and their son Tommy slept, though they shared the warmth and use of the large fire between the open shelters. Brian Akattah pitched a tent about fifteen yards away, where he, his wife Mary, and son Peter slept and ate near their own fire.

On the first morning of the hunt, the men woke long before dawn. They quickly relit the fires, brewed tea, and we ate an enormous breakfast. Soon after first light, when Liza, Mary, Tommy and Peter were only just stirring, we set out. In calm weather the coldest hour of the day is just after dawn, and for a while everyone walked fast and energetically, until we had warmed up. It was then possible to enjoy the intense well-being that sweeps through you as you feel warm, then hot, in very cold weather. Within an hour, the sun was bright, and frost gleamed on the grasses and low bushes of the hillsides. The hunters had high hopes of making a kill.

We walked far into the hills, following tracks that were many and fresh, that twisted and turned where the moose had browsed among the willows. Small heaps of round faeces here and there testified to the animals' presence. Sometimes the hunters felt them: a slight warmth shows that the moose had been there no more than an hour before: a glaze of frost means that a longer time has elapsed. All the droppings were hard and cold. The hunt was likely to be a long one.

Near the top of the first slope the willow thickets merged into a more densely forested area. At this point the four men split up, each taking his own direction. The moose we had been following had evidently moved soon after dawn from the open hillside, where the willow browse was plentiful, to the cover of the forest. Here they might continue to feed, or lie down to rest in hiding through the middle part of the day. It was going to be difficult to find them; the hunters were disappointed. Still, each selected a direction he thought was hopeful, and everyone fanned out, quickly to disappear among the trees. I followed Brian who chose a steep climb high into a stand of large firs, and then followed the hillsides several miles to the west. We saw old tracks, but no sign of any moose that Brian thought would be worth tracking. At about midday we and the others converged—as usual, and by mysterious means, within minutes of one another—and we all returned to camp. The morning's hunt had lasted a little over five hours, but no one had even had a chance of making a kill.

After some lunch and a rest sprawled beside the fire, Joseph declared that it was a good afternoon to have a look at the cross. No, it was not far, hardly more than a quick walk. This reassurance was welcome, for the morning's walk, through thickets, up steep slopes, and in dense woodland had been tiring. So we set out again, first across the ice-rimmed Bluestone Creek, and then along a trail that headed roughly north, parallel to the hills. The group included two of Joseph's nephews, Thomas Fellow and David Crown, his nine-year-old son Tommy, and eleven-year-old Peter.

"Hardly more than a quick walk" turned out to be a round-trip of fourteen miles that took four hours. The pace never altered. There is a short-stepped rhythm to Beaver walking that is fast but unhurried, and remorselessly unvaried. Sometimes Tommy had trouble keeping up with us. When he fell behind, he would run to catch up, and for spells he would jog-trot alongside David or Peter.

For the first half mile or so the trail followed a valley bottom and passed across the edge of a rancher's fields. Then it entered woodland and roamed along the side of a high bank, from which we could glimpse a succession of beaver dams. It was to this area, said Thomas, that Joseph liked to come in the spring. A mile or two beyond the dams David noticed a group of ruffed grouse perched in a high bush a short distance from our trail. He, Thomas and Peter delayed to take some shots at them—grouse are singularly unwary of hunters or even of the noise of rifle fire. As they scrambled through the dense undergrowth around the bush, David noticed another, larger group of grouse. We all hunted them for a while, but eventually cached only four birds in the grass. We would collect them on our way back to camp. A mile beyond the grouse David then spotted a rabbit, and we made a short but difficult detour in the hope of coming across more. Only one was killed, however, and it too was cached beside the trail. Except for these few shots at grouse and rabbits, we took no time to hunt. This walk was to see the cross. In its way the walk seemed to be something of a pilgrimage, a journey made necessary by Joseph's concern that our mapping be properly understood. We should see with our own eyes the emblem, or even the magic, that he had so often talked about. The importance of the cross seemed to permeate everything that he and others had been trying to explain about their feeling for and use of the land.

Yet when we finally arrived, Thomas almost immediately turned around and began to head back to camp. It was enough, he indicated, just to see the cross. Nothing actually to look at, ponder over, or make any fuss about. If Peter and Tommy had not wanted to rest a while, we should not have had even the five minutes we did spend looking at the cross itself.

In fact, the cross had rotted at its base and fallen back to lean, precarious and dilapidated, into the pines that surrounded it. The clothing and bundles its arms had supported were long gone. The panel near its base once ornamented with "all kinds of fancy", the dream inscriptions of animals the people would hunt, had fallen. Split in two pieces, it lay beside the cross's broken stump. The panel was pitted and decayed, the colour of its peeled wood now hardly any different from so many other deadfalls. It would be quite easy to pass the cross, unnoticing, so nearly did it merge with the woodland around it.

Once noticed, however, its presence could be felt. Was it because so much had been explained, and so much, therefore, anticipated? Or because in a landscape so devoid of monuments and cultural structures of any permanence, the cross had a special and remarkable significance? Though it inspired feelings of awe in me, they were subtly undermined by a dispiriting poignancy. I knew that a logging road was scheduled to be pushed along Bluestone Creek towards Quarry River. It would probably follow the trail that led us from the camp to the cross. The cross itself, so inconspicuous, blending into the trees from which the Indians had built it, would too easily be bulldozed into the ragged brush piles that lie alongside new roads on the frontier.

For a few minutes we sat there, resting and staring. No one said much. Perhaps we all felt the many possible emanations from that dilapidated symbol, or shared in some faint way the memories of it that are so central to Joseph's view of life. No doubt the others had heard him speak many times of its construction and of the dream prophesies that surround it. No doubt they also felt the new winter cold that stings the cheeks and thought it was time to hurry back to camp. Just as we were leaving, though, David did remark, "Sometime we better put up a new cross. That one's getting pretty old now."

By the time we returned it was dusk. Wood had to be cut and hauled for the night. The next day the men would try again for a moose. Should they fail, said Joseph, we might as well return to the Reserve. It was getting too cold. There was little talk of the cross. Joseph, Atsin, and the others all appeared to be satisfied that we had seen it. It is a monument in the minds of the people. Its very lack of grandeur and limited physical life signify, in ways that Joseph and Atsin would never feel needed to be stated, both the vitality of the hunter's mind and the irrelevance to it of grandiose material encumbrances. To share in this understanding is to share in the real presence of the people of the land.

The next day was colder still. Grey clouds were thick in the northwest sky. As the men set out on the hunt, Joseph said he would break camp and be ready to leave for the Reserve as soon as the hunters were back. . . . While the men were away, Joseph broke camp. He piled tarpaulins, gear, everything in readiness for the move. But late in the day Sam Crown returned with the news that he had killed a large cow moose high in the hills. He had only had time to do the butchering. We would have to stay another night. In the morning everyone would move to a trail below the hill and help pack out the meat. Camp was remade, more wood cut. . . .

It was only 3 A.M. when Brian Akkatah came from his tent and woke everyone up. He lit the fire and urged the others to get up. It was snowing. The camp was already covered. The woods were heavy with an inch of soft snow. In fresh snow, then, and with much tripping over hidden stumps and logs, we broke camp and moved to the kill. Joseph said that we should not set up a new camp, but make do with a fire in the shelter of some trees beside the trail leading up to the kill. He and Liza gathered wood, lit the fire, and brewed tea while the rest of us followed Sam to the dead moose.

The butchered carcass had to be hauled, sled-like, down the hillside. Brian roped two quarters into the hide and, single-handed, dragged this huge slithering bag over deadfalls and between tree trunks the whole distance from kill to fire. It was hard enough to pack a single quarter, and at the end of a second load everyone was hot and exhausted. By the time all the meat had been hauled and packed . . ., it was late afternoon. Along the dirt road the snow was driving towards us in hard, dry clouds, reducing the world to a small bowl of whiteness. Four months of winter had begun.

From "Some Objects of Wood and Stone"

Margaret Atwood

i   Totems

We went to the park
where they keep the wooden people:
static, multiple
uprooted and trans-
planted.

Their faces were restored,
freshly painted.
In front of them
the other wooden people
posed for each others' cameras
and nearby a new booth
sold replicas and souvenirs.

One of the people was real.
It lay on its back, smashed
by a toppling fall or just
the enduring of minor winters.
Only one of the heads had
survived intact, and it was
also beginning to decay
but there was a
life in the progressing
of old wood back to
the earth, obliteration

that the clear-hewn
standing figures lacked.

As for us, perennial watchers,
tourists of another kind
there is nothing for us to worship;
no pictures of ourselves, no blue-
sky summer fetishes, no postcards
we can either buy, or
smiling
be.

There are few totems that remain
living for us.
Though in passing,
through glass we notice

dead trees in the seared meadows
dead roots bleaching in the swamps.

The Cariboo Horses

Al Purdy

At 100 Mile House the cowboys ride in rolling
stagey cigarettes with one hand reining
half-tame bronco rebels on a morning grey as stone
—so much like riding dangerous women
          with whisky-coloured eyes—
such women as once fell dead with their lovers
with fire in their heads and slippery froth on thighs
—Beaver or Carrier woman maybe or
          Blackfoot squaws far past the edge of this valley
on the other side of those two toy mountain ranges
          from the sunfierce plains beyond

But only horses
                    waiting in stables
hitched at taverns
                    standing at dawn
pastured outside the town with
jeeps and fords and chevvys and
busy muttering stake trucks rushing
importantly over roads of man's devising
over the safe known roads of the ranchers
families and merchants of the town
                    On the high prairie
are only horse and rider
                    wind in dry grass
clopping in silence under the toy mountains
dropping sometimes and
                    lost in the dry grass
                    golden oranges of dung

Only horses
                    no stopwatch memories or palace ancestors
not Kiangs hauling undressed stone in the Nile Valley
and having stubborn Egyptian tantrums or
Onagers racing thru Hither Asia and
the last Quagga screaming in African highlands
          lost relatives of these
          whose hooves were thunder
the ghosts of horses battering thru the wind
whose names were the wind's common usage
whose life was the sun's
          arriving here at chilly noon
          in the gasoline smell of the
          dust and waiting 15 minutes
          at the grocer's

The Trans-Canada Highway, Fraser Valley east of Vancouver.

Amusement ride at the Pacific National Exhibition in Vancouver.

Lions Gate Bridge from Stanley Park in Vancouver.

Lifeguard station at Third Beach in Stanley Park, Vancouver.

Highway 3 west of Grand Forks.

Welders working amidst amusement rides at the Pacific National Exhibition grounds in Vancouver.

Fishing boats reflected in the harbour at Campbell River.

View from the wharf at Campbell River.

Part of the colourful design on Granville Island in Vancouver.

Vancouver harbour and the city from the air at sundown.

Ships at anchor at the entrance to Burrard Inlet off Vancouver.

Vancouver at night from Grouse Mountain.

Sunset over Vancouver Island from Vancouver.

Waves at Nels Bight, Cape Scott Provincial Park.

Cabins at Lake O'Hara Lodge after an autumn snowfall, Yoho National Park.

Mount Magog and Mount Assiniboine, Mount Assiniboine Provincial Park.

From Flores
Ethel Wilson

Up at Flores Island, Captain Findlay Crabbe readied his fishboat the *Effie Cee* for the journey home and set out in good spirits while the weather was fair. But even by the time he saw the red shirt flapping like mad from the rocky point just north of the Indian's place the wind had freshened. Nevertheless Fin Crabbe told the big man at the wheel to turn into shore because there must be some trouble there and that Indian family was pretty isolated. As the man at the wheel turned the nose of the boat towards the shore, the skipper listened to the radio. The weather report was good, and so he went out on the small deck well satisfied and stood there with his hands on his hips, looking at the shore where the red flag was.

The third man on the fishboat was just a young fellow. Up at Flores Island he had come down to the float with his gear all stowed in a duffel bag and asked the skipper to take him down to Port Alberni. He was an anxious kid, tall, dark, and thin-faced. He said he'd pay money for the ride and he spoke of bad news which with a young man sounds like parents or a girl and with an older young man sounds like a wife or children or a girl. Fin Crabbe said shortly that the boy could come, although the little *Effie Cee* was not geared for passengers. He didn't need to pay.

Captain Crabbe was small. He had come as an undersized boy to the west coast of Vancouver Island and there he had stayed. He had been fairish and was now bald. His eyes were sad like a little bloodhound's eyes and pink under, but he was not sad. He was a contented man and rejoiced always to be joined again with his wife and his gangling son and daughter. Mrs. Crabbe's name was Effie but she was called Mrs. Crabbe or Mom and her name had come to be used only for the *Effie Cee* which was by this time more Effie than Mrs. Crabbe was. "I'm taking home an Indian basket for Mrs. Crabbe," the skipper might say. "Mrs. Crabbe sure is an authority on Indian baskets." Fin Crabbe was his name up and down the coast but at home he was the Captain or Pop, and so Mrs. Crabbe would say, "The Captain plans to be home for Christmas. The Captain's a great family man. I said to him 'Pop, if you're not home for Christmas, I'll...!'" Thus they daily elevated each other in esteem and loved each other with simple mutual gratification. In bed no names were needed for Mrs. Crabbe and the Captain. (When they shall be dead, as they will be, what will avail this happy self-satisfaction. But now they are not dead, and the Captain's wife as often before awaits the Captain who is on his way down the coast from Flores Island, coming home for Christmas.)

Fin Crabbe had planned for some time to reach Port Alberni early in Christmas week and that suited Ed, the big crewman, too. Ed was not a family man although he had a wife somewhere; but what strong upspringing black curly hair he had and what black gambling eyes. He was powerful, not to be governed, and a heller when he drank. He was quick to laugh, quick to hit out, quick to take a girl, quick to leave her, a difficult wilful volatile enjoying man of poor judgment, but he got along all right with little Fin Crabbe. He did not want to spend Christmas in Flores Island when there was so much doing in Alberni and Port Alberni.

Captain Crabbe's family lived in Alberni proper which to the dweller in the city seems like a fairly raw small town at the end of a long arm through the forest to nowhere, and to the dweller up the coast or in the Queen Charlottes seems like a small city with every comfort, every luxury, motor cars speeding in and out by the long road that leads through the forest to the fine Island Highway, lighted streets, plumbing, beer parlours, a hospital, churches, schools, lumber mills, wharves. It lives for and on trees and salt water. Behind it is a huge hinterland of giant forests. Before it lies the long tortuous salt-water arm of the open sea.

Captain Crabbe, as the bow of the *Effie Cee* turned towards the pine-clad but desolate and rocky shore, cutting across the tricky undulations of the ocean, again gave his habitual look at the sky, north and west. The sky was overclouded, but so it usually is in these parts at this time of the year. Since these rocky shores are not protected as are the rocky shores of the British Columbia mainland by the long stretches of sweet liveable gulf islands and by the high barrier of mountainous Vancouver Island itself, the west coast of the island lies naked to the Pacific Ocean which rolls in all the way from Asia and breaks upon the reefs and rocks and hard sands, and the continuous brewing of the weather up in an air cauldron in the north seethes and spills over and rushes out of the Gulf of Alaska, often moderating before it reaches lower latitudes; but sometimes it roars down and attacks like all hell. The fishboat and tugboat men know this weather well and govern themselves accordingly. Next morning perhaps the ocean smiles like a dissolute angel. The fishboat and tugboat men know that, too, and are not deceived. So that although Fin Crabbe knew all this as well as he knew his own thumb, he did not hesitate to turn the *Effie Cee* towards the shore when he saw the red shirt flapping at the end of the rock point but he had no intention of stopping there nor of spending any time at all unless his judgment warranted it, for in this trip his mind was closely set to home.

The turning aside of the fishboat on her journey irked the young passenger very much. Since the weather report on the radio was fairly good and anyway he was used to poor weather, he felt no concern about that. But here was delay and how much of it. He did not know how often he had read the letter which he again took out of his pocket, not looking at big Ed nor at little Captain Crabbe but frowning at the letter and at some memory. He was possessed entirely, usurped, by impatience for contact, by letter, by wire or—best of all—by speech and sight and touch with the writer of this letter. Now that he had started on the journey towards her, now that he had started, now that he was on his way, his confusion seemed to clear. He read again in the letter: "Dear Jason I am very unhappy I dont know I should tell you Ive thought and thought before I wrote you and then what kind of a letter because I could say awful things and say you must come to Vancouver right away and marry me or believe me I could just cry and cry or I could write and say plain to you O Jason do I beseech you think if we couldnt get married right away. I could say I love you and I do."

The young man folded the letter again. He looked with distaste at the red flag that signified an Indian's trouble and his own delay and his mind ran backwards again. The letter had found him at last and only two days ago. He had left the camp and had crossed to Flores and there an old man with a beard had told him that Fin Crabbe was all set to go to Alberni the next morning, and he had enquired for Captain Crabbe. As he had walked up and down the float pushing time forward, sometimes a violence of joy rose in him and surprised him. This was succeeded by a real fear that something would happen to prevent the fishboat from leaving, would prevent them reaching Alberni very soon, while all the time Josie did not even know whether he had received the letter. Many feelings were induced in him by what Josie had written, and now he thought ceaselessly about her to whom, only three days before, he had barely given a thought. He unfolded the letter again.

"I gess I dont know too much about love like in the pictures but I do love you Jason and I wouldnt ever ever be a person who would throw this up at you. I dont sleep very good and some nights I threton to myself to kill myself and tho I am awful scared of that maybe that would be better and easiest for us all and next night I say no. Lots of girls go through with this but what do they do with the Baby and no real home for it and then I am bafled again and the time is going."

Jason, looking out to the ocean but not seeing it, was aware of a different Josie. If a person had told me, he thought, that I'd want to get married and that I'd be crazy for this baby I'd say they were crazy, I'd say they were nuts, and impatience against delay surged over him again. The boat neared the mouth of the bay.

"One thing I do know I couldnt go back to the prairies with the Baby," (no, that's right, you couldn't go back) "so where would the Baby and me go. Mother would let me feel it every day even if she didn't mean to tho she would take us but Father no never. Then I think its the best thing for the Baby I should drown myself its quite easy in Vancouver its not like the prairies I do mean that."

The skipper was talking back and forth to the crewman at the wheel and the *Effie Cee* slowed down. There were beams of sunlight that came and went.

"I cant believe its me and I do pitty any poor girl but not begging you Jason because you must decide for yourself. Some people would pay no attention to this letter but I kind of feel youre not like some people but O please Jason get me a word soon and then I can know what. Josie."

From the pages arose the helpless and lonely anguish of little Josie and this anguish entered and consumed him too and it was all part of one storm of anxiety and anger that she was alone and she so quiet, and not her fault (he said), and impatience rose within him to reach a place where he could say to her Don't you worry kid, I'm coming! He thought with surprise Maybe I'm a real bad guy and I never knew it, maybe we're all bad and we don't know it. He read once more: "I am bafled again and the time is going. . . . I do love you Jason." He put his head in his hands with dumb anger that she should be driven to this, but as soon as he reached a telephone in Alberni everything would be right. As he suddenly looked up he thought he would go mad at this turning off course for any sick guy or any kid who'd been crazy enough to break an arm. In his frustration and impatience there was an infusion of being a hero and rushing to save someone. Some hero, he said very sourly to himself, some hero.

The *Effie Cee* slowed to a stop and a black volley of cormorants, disturbed, flew away in a dark line. There was an Indian and an Indian woman and a little boy in a rowboat almost alongside the fishboat. The little boy was half lying down in an uncomfortable way and two rough sticks were tied to his leg. Three smaller children stood solemnly on the rocky shore looking at the two boats. Then they turned to play in a clumsy ceremonial fashion among the barnacled rocks. They did not laugh as they played.

Jason put the letter in his pocket and stood up. The rowboat jiggled in the water and Captain Crabbe was bending down and talking to the Indian. He listened and talked and explained. The Indian's voice was slow and muffled, but not much talk was needed. Anyone could see. "Okay," said the skipper and then he straightened himself and turned to look at Ed and Jason as much as to say . . . and Jason said, "Better I got into the rowboat and helped him lift the kid up," and the skipper said "Okay."

All this time the woman did not say anything. She kept her hands wrapped in her stuff dress and looked away or at the child. Jason slipped over the side and the rowboat at once became overcrowded which made it difficult for him and the Indian to lift the child up carefully without hurting him and without separating the boats. The Indian child made no sound and no expression appeared on his face so no one knew how much pain he suffered or whether he suffered at all. His eyes were brown and without meaning like the dusky opaque eyes of a fawn. The Indian spoke to his wife and she reached out her hands and held on to the fishboat so that the two craft would not be parted. Jason and the father succeeded in slipping their arms—"This way," said Jason, "see? do it this way"—under the child and raised him gradually up to where Ed and the skipper were kneeling. Everyone leaned too much to one side of the rowboat and Jason tried to steady it so that they would not fall with the child into the sea. All this time the woman had not spoken but had accepted whatever other people did as if she had no rights in the matter. When the child was safely on board, Jason sprang onto the deck and at once, at once, the *Effie Cee* turned and tore away with a white bone of spume in her mouth and a white wake of foam behind, leaving the Indians in the rowboat and the children on the shore looking after her.

"Best lay him on the floor, he'd maybe roll off the bunk," said Fin Crabbe when they had lifted the child inside. "Mustn't let you get cold, Sonny," he said, and took down a coat that swung from a hook. The child regarded him in silence and with fear in his heart. One two another white man taking him to some place he did not know.

"Make supper, Ed, and I'll take the wheel," said the skipper. The boat went faster ahead, rising and plunging as there was now a small sea running.

What'd I better do, thought Fin Crabbe and did not consult the crewman who hadn't much judgment. There were good reasons for going on through and trying to make Alberni late in the night or in early morning. That would surprise Mrs. Crabbe and she would be pleased, and the young fella seemed desperate to get to Alberni on account of this bad news; but here was this boy he'd taken aboard and the sooner they got him into hospital the better. I think it's his hip (he thought), I could turn back to Tofino but it'd be dark then and would he be any better off landing him in the dark and likely no doctor. Anyway I can make Ucluelet easy and spend the night. I don't like to take no chances but all in all I think we'll go on. And they went on.

Evening came and black night. It was winter cold outside and Jason crowded into the wheelhouse and looked out at the dark. The coming of night brought him nearer the telephone, so near he could all but touch it, but he could not touch it.

The *Effie Cee* could not make much speed now and ploughed slowly for hours never ending, it seemed to Jason, through water that had become stormy and in the dark she followed a sideways course so that she could cut a little across the waves that were now high and deep. Ed had the wheel and Captain Crabbe stood beside him. The storm increased. The boat's nose plunged into the waves and rose with the waves and the water streamed over. There was a wallowing, a sideways wallowing. The little fishboat became a world of noise and motion, a plunging, a rising, a plunging again. Jason wedged the child against the base of the bunk. The child cried out, and vomited with seasickness and fear. "Now now," said

Jason, patting him. "Try the radio again," said Captain Crabbe.

Jason fiddled with the radio. "Can't seem to get anything," he said.

"Let me," said the skipper.

"Bust," he said.

But now the storm rapidly accelerated and the waves, innocent and savage as tigers, leaped at the *Effie Cee* and the oncoming rollers struck broadside and continuously. The little boy made sounds like an animal and Jason, in whom for the first time fear of what might come had struck down all elation and expectation, took the child's hand and held it. The little plunging boat was now the whole world and fate to Jason and to Fin Crabbe and to the Indian boy but not to Ed who had no fear. Perhaps because he had no love he had no fear. Standing over the wheel and peering into the dark, he seemed like a great black bull and it was to Jason as though he filled the cabin.

Ed turned the boat's nose towards shore to get away from the broadside of the waves. Fin Crabbe shouted at him to be heard above the storm. The boat had been shipping water and Jason, crouching beside the shaking child in a wash of water, heard the words "Ucluelet" and "lighthouse" and "rocks" but Ed would not listen. The skipper went on shouting at him and then he seized the wheel. He pushed the big man with all his strength, turning the wheel to starboard. Jason and the Indian child saw the big man and the little man fighting in the small space, in the din of the ocean, the howl of the wind, for possession of the wheel. As quick as a cat Ed drew off and hit the older man a great blow. Fin Crabbe crumpled and fell. He lay in the wash of the water at Ed's feet and Ed had his way, so the fishboat drove inshore, hurled by the waves onto the reefs, or onto the hard sand, or onto the place that Ed knew that he knew, whichever the dark should disclose, but not to the open sea. Captain Crabbe tried to raise himself and Jason crawled over towards him.

The skipper could not stand in the pitching boat. He looked up at Ed who was his executioner, the avenger of all that he had ever done, driving on against death for sure.

The thought of the abandonment of Josie (for now a belief was formed terribly in him that she was to be abandoned) pierced Jason through and through and then in the immediate danger the thought of Josie was no longer real but fled away on the wind and water, and there was nothing but fear. Without knowing what he did, he seized and held the child. Never could a man feel greater despair than Jason in the walnut shell of a reeling boat soon to be cracked between land and water. Ed, bent over the wheel, knowing everything, knowing just where they were, but not knowing, looked only forward into the blackness and drove on. The sea poured into the boat and at the same minute the lights went out and they were no longer together. Then the *Effie Cee* rose on a great wave, was hurled upwards and downwards, struck the barnacled reef, and split, and the following seas washed over.

A few days later the newspapers stated that in the recent storm on the west coat of Vancouver Island the fishboat *Effie Cee* was missing with two men aboard. These men were Findley Crabbe aged sixty-five and Edward Morgan aged thirty-five, both of Alberni. Planes were continuing the search.

A day or two afterwards the newspapers stated that it was thought that there might have been a third man aboard the *Effie Cee*. He was identified as Jason Black aged twenty-two, employed as a logger up the coast near Flores Island.

On the second morning after the wreck of the *Effie Cee* the skies were a cold blue and the ocean lay sparkling and lazy beneath the sun. Up the Alberni Canal the sea and air were chilly and brilliant but still. Mrs. Crabbe spent the day waiting on the wharf in the cold sunshine. She stood or walked or sat, accompanied by two friends or by the gangling son and daughter, and next day it was the same, and the next. People said to her, "But he didn't set a day? When did he *say* he'd be back?"

"He never said what day," she said. "The Captain couldn't ever say what day. He just said the beginning of the week, maybe Monday was what he said." She said "he said, he said, he said" because it seemed to establish him as living. People had to stop asking because they could not bear to speak to Mrs. Crabbe standing and waiting on the busy wharf, paying the exorbitant price of love. They wished she would not wait there because it made them uncomfortable and unhappy to see her.

Because Josie did not read the papers, she did not know that Jason was dead. Days had passed and continued to pass. Distraught, alone, deprived of hope and faith (two sovereign remedies) and without the consolation of love, she took secretly and with terror what she deemed to be the appropriate path.

The Indian, who had fully trusted the man who took his son away, heard nothing more. He waited until steady fine weather came and then took his family in his small boat to Tofino. From there he made his way to Alberni. Here he walked slowly up and down the docks and at last asked someone where the hospital was; but at the hospital no one seemed to know anything about his only son.

A Drowning at François Lake
Andrew Wreggitt

The sun, hidden
by a dust cover of cloud
settles light
thin and cold
on the shivering grey lake
Boats are trolling
for the body of a man
suspended near the bottom
still bloated and
too heavy to rise
Grey light falls behind the mountain
where the lake
is tucked like a photograph
not wanted until now
appearing like a headline

We stare into the water
each drifting branch becomes
an arm
each shadow, a torso
chained below the surface
We sit on the shore
huddled in groups
wishing the sun would come out
wishing they would find him

At night, sitting at home
radio blaring
all the lights on
We stare into the black window
seeing faces
on the dark formless lake
where the moon
should be reflected

Mist on the River
Hubert Evans

Matt was coming down the smoke-house path. The weathered faces of the totem poles beside the river were moist from the night mist and appeared knowing and less austere against the widening translucence overhead. The air had the nose-tingling smell of the mist in it, and the sweet spice of fallen leaves. Another fine day in the making, Matt thought, a true fall day; one of the first, and in a matter of weeks the bell of the village school would ring again.

The few people now in the village had talked much about that since the Agent drove out the other day and told them that some white couple would likely be here before September was out, to open the school and live in the mission house. The final papers had not been signed, but chances seemed bright for a teacher this year, the Agent said.

Some concluded it was the man who was going to teach. Others thought it would be the woman; but you never could be sure about white people. Jonathan Tate only yesterday returned with his family from Angus, believed it would be the man, but old Minnie Moose, who had a secret way of knowing what people were up to without leaving her bed, prophesied it would be the woman. The teacher who cleared out because of the home-brew trouble had been a woman. The last man they had was young, just right for the war to take. Few, since the old, old days of Mr. Lloyd, had stayed more than a year or two, and there had been stretches when no teacher came at all.

Matt's knees were stiff and unpredictable on steep ground, but after he was below the crabapples and onto the close-cropped grass, he walked briskly, for on the level the knees were as good as anybody's. *The* knees was how he spoke of them, when the doctor down at the Junction hospital asked how he was feeling. I am a good man yet, he had told the previous doctor, and if the new one should ask he would answer the same. I am a good, strong-hearted man, he would answer, and give his chest the flat-handed, approving thump one did to a faithful horse which could always be relied on to pull its weight. Only the knees. And here Matt's curling lips and disavowing, downward glance would place the blame squarely where it belonged.

Smoke was spilling through the chinks of the family's smoke-house when Matt reached it. It took knowing to build fires that would keep in all night, one in each corner, burning low and ripening the split salmon on the racks. But Fat Marie, for all her foolish ways, was almost as good at it as Melissa. Too much wet wood and the fires went out, too much dry and you got heat which in a single night would ruin a winter's supply of fish. Some kinds of wood gave off bitter smoke, other kinds sweet. You had to be taught young to know.

Matt went to the door and peered in. Marie and Stevie were at the far end, moving back and forth below the layer of smoke. They were talking away, and in English. It still sounded strange in his ears when a child chattered like a white person, but every day he was teaching the little fellow words in their language, and it would not be long before English between them could be forgotten.

"Stevie, I am on my way to pull the net," Matt called. "Do you want to come?" He used the simplest Gitkshan words and it pleased him when Stevie understood. Matt took his hand and they walked side by side to the bank.

It was many years since the people moved to houses on the bench, but even yet the turf dipped and swelled where the earth had been banked against the walls of the old communal dwellings, in one of which Matt had been born. One of these evenings he would tell Stevie more of how it had been with their people then.

When they reached the low cut-bank Stevie took away his hand and went ahead across the shingle to the edge of the big eddy. In other places up and down the Skeena the channel changed with the years, but here it stayed the same. Things were slow in changing in this village and valley; perhaps it would be better if they did not change at all.

The mist lay close on the water, but only the outer end of the net was hidden and Matt saw that most of the floats were pulled under by the weight of fish. Fairly in the bight there was a swirling where a heavy spring salmon fought the net.

Such a fish must not be lost. "See him, young brother?" Matt asked. "Heaven is near us this morning." He went to the dugout canoe and began to drag it down, motioning for Stevie to help.

Stevie dug in his heels and tried so hard to pull that Matt's long upper lip folded in against his teeth as he suppressed a smile. "A big one, eh?" he grunted, heaving away.

"You bet." Stevie could not keep his eyes off the net. The moment the canoe was afloat he crawled to the bow and picked up the small paddle Matt had whittled for him. He was even more excited than on previous mornings.

"We go after the big one first," Matt said, as he pushed out to where he could pull the canoe hand-over-hand along the float line. "Get ready the club. This fish is yours. It is you who must kill him."

The tarred cedar floats rattled against the side of the canoe when they were over the place, and while Matt hooked his fingers into the web until he found the lead-line, he could not take his eyes from the boy. The thin little face had an eagerness which warmed Matt's heart. This was the seed of his seed and he felt an inexpressible gratitude and acceptance toward all which had gone before—Dot as she once was, and as she was now, the separation and the long, endured loneliness. No matter what she had done to put his heart in a steep place with her wild ways, he could, and did, thank her for this moment. And there would be other moments for him, years of moments, and a lifetime filled with them, in his valley and among his people, for the grandson who had come long after he had ceased to hope for one.

"I see him! I see his tail!" Stevie yelled. He gripped the raised club in both hands. Matt pretended it was all he could do to hold the net, although by the time he rolled the salmon into the canoe it actually did not have much fight left in it. But it was a good fish, close to thirty pounds, fresh-run and white bellied.

Stevie got astride it and smacked the club down on its head until a dying tremor ran along its flanks and it lay still. Then they went over the rest of the net and took twenty lesser salmon.

Back on shore, Stevie leaned against the arched bow of the canoe while they admired their catch. "Marie will have a full morning's work from this," Matt remarked, stroking his wispy moustache with his knuckles, one side and then the other.

"Say it to me in English," Stevie asked. "That's easier." He got over the side of the canoe and squatted beside his big salmon, sliding his hands proudly along its sides.

"You understand those words, surely," Matt said gently. "Morning, and work; I taught you them. Your ears are quick, and your tongue. Do not let them forget."

"I talk English and your words are hard to say, Matt." Stevie spoke impatiently but Matt let it pass. It was merely that the child was tired, which was to be expected when so small a fellow had only a street to play on. Here where he belonged, he would soon become strong and filled with life.

When Stevie got out of the canoe Matt placed a hand on his head. "They are your words, too. They are in you. They will come back."

"I'm going to tell Marie," Stevie said suddenly. He made for the cut-bank and Matt followed him but, by the time he eased first one leg and then the other over it, he decided to let Stevie go on alone. He went to the fallen totem pole of the Grouse people which lay with its rotting faces pressed into the turf and sat down stiffly on its butt, rubbing his knees and watching until Stevie went inside the smoke-house. Then he turned his face toward the river.

Soon the school would open and Stevie would have to go. They would not have much of the day together then and the learning of the little fellow's language would move more slowly. The school came first, many people said. They said education was the thing.

The mist twisted itself, devising shapes over the strongly flowing water. When he was Stevie's age he used to stand at the house door a few yards from where he now sat, watching the river on a fine fall morning such as this. Ghost faces, and the shapes of things to come, formed and swayed and dissolved there. Obscured by the white breath of *k'Shan* they performed their ritualistic dance, recalling the dead and foreshadowing the good and evil that was to be.

Presently he found he was thinking of his own first days at school. The village had no white man's houses then. The big split cedar ones, each with its group of families and often four generations under one roof, stood so close to the river that at high water the noses of the canoes were nearly inside the door openings. Mr. Lloyd, who opened the first school, had come in late summer, almost exactly at this time of year, in the moon month known as When-groundhog-goes-in-hole. The big Tsimpshean canoe had landed where the Fireweed people's pole used to stand, before they raised their new one in what was now the village.

Mr. Lloyd's wife was with him and he brought his own canoe men and a Tsimpshean interpreter. Mrs. Lloyd was small and she did not talk as much as others of the long-nose women. The Lloyds stayed a week, telling the people the Good News. Then they went away down river, but sure enough, as they promised, by the time the fattening snow was on the mountains they came back to stay.

For a time they held school in the smoke-house dwellings. You sat on the earth floor around the fire and learned to say A-B-C. If you kept at it you were given a slate to use, and later still you were taught to say words, all together, out of the reading book.

By the time the Lloyds had their own log house, the ice was on the river. The house was not much, judged by those even the native people had to-day, but it was a big thing to talk about then. It had fire in an iron box instead of on the ground, and the snow did not blow through the walls as it did through the cracks in the native ones. And that first window! People found it hard to believe you could stand inside and look through a wall. Some thought the glass was ice and expected it to melt. Mrs. Lloyd taught the little ones and showed the smartest girls how to cook, white style, and to wash with soap and understand the use of flour. A few more years and Mr. Lloyd could preach to you in your own language and Mrs. Lloyd, though she never put it to her tongue, understood every word a person let slip, make no mistake of that.

Matt got slowly to his feet and turned to see if Marie was coming to dress the fish. She had not left the smoke-house yet. He could hear the two of them inside, talking back and forth in English.

Resting on the pole again, he recalled how first one family and then another built separate houses for themselves, back from the river. That was when the mission house was built. The people liked the Lloyds because they did not act too big to learn the native language from people who could not read or write, and because they did not turn up their noses at good Indian food as most of those who came after them had.

More years. The way some people told it latterly, it was in the big 'flu that Mrs. Lloyd died, but it was before that, years before. Mr. Lloyd was getting old, but when the head men of his church wrote letters offering to send a younger man, Mr.

Lloyd said no. He said this was his home. Some of the women baked bread for him, and the men brought him fish and wild meat and shovelled his roof and paths in deep snow time.

At the last Mr. Lloyd said he was happy to go, and when they put his body beside his wife's, there in the old graveyard overlooking the river, the people built the finest grave-house, all jigsaw work, with a spindle fence and doves like from the Gospel, carved from cedar and standing on wire legs on the corner posts. Everyone put in fishing money or trapping money and bought a white, Christian gravestone.

Matthew Hecate—Mr. Lloyd had found those white man's names for him—was remembering with regretful tenderness and self-reproach that he had not gone to the grave in years. The trail became overgrown when the new graveyard behind the church was started. It was clogged with windfalls now, and, the knees being what they were, he had excused himself by believing he could not get through. Cy told him last year that the doves and the fence were down and that a spruce, big as your leg, was growing through the grave-house roof.

There had been a succession of other teachers and preachers in the old mission house, but why, Matt wondered, did the people forget most of them and still feel close to Mr. Lloyd and his quiet little wife? Was it simply because they were the first? No, there was more to it than that. Although Mr. Lloyd worked hard to turn them into Christians he did not boss or scold, but took them and liked them and spent his life among them, good and bad, just as they were. The big thing was that he had something in his heart to make an Indian feel he was as good as anybody else. But to-day very few whites could do that, for all their friendly talk.

In the sound of the water out there, swirling past under the mist, it was as if he were hearing voices: Mr. Lloyd sitting here on the grass beside you, talking to you in your language, asking the women how many fish they were putting up for winter; Mr. Lloyd in church praying for the sick ones, or his voice choking when he would be standing at the head of the grave as they buried some little child; Mr. Lloyd's voice leading with "Rock of Ages" or "Do Not Pass Me By".

But did Mr. Lloyd know how much had passed his village by since he went away? Did he know that the Better Day he was sure was coming, when he got after them to learn their letters and numbers so they would be ready, had been so woefully long in dawning?

"A better day is coming," Mr. Lloyd had promised. Yet to-day when children not much older than Stevie could do two-and-two and read out to you about Dick and Jane; when some of the people had cars and trucks and washing machines run by gas engines; when you could turn on choir and cowboy music any night in winter—with all this and more the Better Day had not dawned. Who or what was to blame? Was it government or village, the go-ahead, grasping whites or the half-ashamed, don't-care Indians? Was it too much money or not enough, too much of the white man's education or not enough of it, even yet? Or was it simply because, though his hair was as black as when he was a young cedar, he was growing old and much was happening that he did not understand.

All he was sure of, sitting here on the rotting totem pole, was that the bell soon to ring for the children of his village could not renew the hope which he had lost.

Ito Fujika, The Trapper
Howard O'Hagan

These days, seeing the name of Japan in the newspapers or occasionally hearing news of Japan over the radio, the people of Red Pass remember Ito Fujika, the trapper.

Ito, like many of his countrymen, had been a fisherman off Lulu Island on the coast of British Columbia. Two years before the war in the Pacific, wearying of the drudgery and the constant toil at the nets, he left his boat and took a train east to the Rocky Mountains, getting down at Red Pass where he planned to set himself up as a trapper. Before coming to Canada, he had trapped fur for the Emperor's Manchurian troops. He had also trapped out of his native town of Miyanoshita and now in the Rockies wished to return to his former way of living.

The people of Red Pass, a small town on the upper Fraser river, recall particularly the times when, down from his trapline, he used to sit in the beer parlor, having left his pack in the hotel room, the cheap room at the end of the hall near the toilet. They remember Ito as he sits alone and sips his one glass of beer until closing time at ten o'clock at night.

The men at other tables regard him a bit askance. They speak of him in undertones. He is like a brown wooden image, half-human in size, propped over there in the corner. The forehead protrudes. The eyes shift. Once in a while the white teeth show, as if inside of him a light flickered and was dimmed. The beer in the glass on the table, close to his chest, diminishes slowly, as by a process of osmosis, for no one notices that he raises it to his lips. There is stealth, they think, even in his drinking in a public place. Undoubtedly, though, he is alive. Life is in him. But what form of life? And what is life? Idaho Pete, a big American, himself a trapper, asks the question—naturally not aloud, to be overheard. He considers a marten in the trap, still alive. You bend over it. You put your hand around it, feeling the quick beat of the heart. Your fingers tighten until the ribs bend and break. The beat of the heart ceases. Life was there and life is gone. What is gone and where? It is a gentle way to kill, for it protects the fur from blemish. Yet is death ever gentle? Idaho Pete turns to his neighbor, forgetting death, life and Ito Fujika. He recalls the day he and his partner were drunk on the head of Calling river and chased an Indian from his trapline.

Ito, arriving at Red Pass in November, had come ready for cold weather. He had bought a muskrat cap whose untied flaps hung loose about his ears. His grey coat was knee-length. On his feet he wore overshoes. It was not a conventional outfit for mountain travel, but it kept Ito warm. And at Red Pass, he realized he had come to the place he sought. Here were the mountains, higher than those around Miyanoshita, and as at Miyanoshita the sound of falling water. Across the lake was the green forest.

Shortly before six in the afternoon, Ito showed himself in the log cabin which was Mr. Scroggins' store. He was polite. His English was good. He replied, when asked, that he was going trapping and wanted food, and a packsack to carry it in.

Mr. Scroggins, who was tall, pale and excessively lean—Ito was puzzled that one should be so lean when food was stacked around him on the shelves—had a cuspidor behind the counter. He leaned over it and spat before studying again the man before him.

"Where do you figure on going trapping?" he asked.

Ito made a gesture with his arm towards the door, indicating the lake, beyond it the gap through the mountains. "Up there," he said, "and build a cabin."

"You had better wait until tomorrow," Mr. Scroggins said, as he went about closing the store. That night Ito sat under a spruce tree at the east end of the town. He caught two trout, with the line and hook and piece of red flannel he always had with him, and ate them raw.

In the morning he came again to the store.

"You won't have to build a cabin," Mr. Scroggins told him. "There's one up there already."

Ito bowed his head, smiled. He wrung his hands. If there was a cabin up there already, he suggested, then someone else must be trapping in that part of the country?

"Someone else was," Mr. Scroggins said. "He isn't trapping there any more. He's gone away."

It was in this fashion that Ito came into possession of John Flaherty's cabin. The cabin, being built on Crown land, was there for anyone to use it. Ito did not know this and was convinced of his bargain when Mr. Scroggins threw in the entire outfit—traps, two axes, pots and pans, sleeping bag—of Mr. Flaherty who had left for elsewhere. Mr. Flaherty, a man of temperament, had not done well in his trapping and one by one had surrendered his belongings to Mr. Scroggins whom he owed for a year's grubstake. Ito paid for the outfit more than twice its worth when new, taking three hundred dollars from a belt about his middle. Again he was in ignorance and was pleased at the charity offered him, a newcomer of alien race.

The cabin was no more than a day's travel into the hills. Ito made several round trips to carry in his equipment and grub. On the last trip he carried in, strapped to his packboard, the Number 6 trap. This was a beartrap, weighing about forty pounds, of which he was proud.

The cabin itself was hardly a basis for this emotion, being no more than a lean-to against a cliff. During cold weather it frosted at night and sweated when the stove was lit by day. In the thaws the roof leaked. Still, for all that, Ito was happy, having owned nothing of the sort so substantial in his life. He laid out his trapline, following, to some extent, Mr. Flaherty's old blazes. In town in December he bought heavier socks, moosehide moccasins and a pair of snowshoes. He retained the long grey coat and tied the flaps of the fur cap under his chin.

Ito's success as a trapper that first winter was not marked. His traps yielded a marten, three weasels, a mangy fox. The lack was due partly to ineptitude, but mostly to the valley, close to the railroad, having been pretty well cleaned of fur. Notwithstanding, the fur he caught gave him sensuous delight. He knew that it would become a portion of a woman's garment and touching it felt that he was in a way touching the women of this strange land who would wear it. These caresses became a secret ecstasy, consummated in the lantern light of the wind-battered cabin.

In the spring, when the snow had seeped into the ground, but before the willows were leafed, he set out the beartrap above the cabin at the foot of a slide. Just beyond it he put his bait, a slab of rancid bacon. Four or five days later, returning to the trap, he found, clamped within its jagged jaws, the forepaw and arm of a grizzly bear. Tendons, ripped from the shoulder, hung from the upthrust arm. The grizzly, great in strength and rage, had broken away. That, however, was not Ito's fault, nor did it denote a failure of the trap called "Number 6." The trap had held. The weakness was in the bear himself. If his arm had been as strong as the trap his sixty-pound hide would now have been in Ito's keeping.

When he next went down to Red Pass he took the arm and paw with him to demonstrate that he, Ito Fujika, formerly a catcher of small fur in Japan, had trapped a grizzly bear, the mighty animal of the Rockies. He laid the hairy and frozen limb on the counter of Mr. Scroggins' store and was astonished when a woman customer ran out screaming and when Mr. Scroggins seized the trophy, strode to the door and threw it across the road.

Aside from such small affairs and the occasion when, on the edge of town, bowing to impulse, he was discovered trying to strangle the schoolteacher's Airedale, Ito got on well with the people. In the summer he worked on the railroad section-gang and was accounted a good worker. After the snow flew again, he appeared and reappeared from his trapline, walking across the frozen lake, his feet deep-sunk on their snowshoes, so that he seemed to be walking on his knees. On the coldest day he would come in smiling, washing his mittened hands—not as the other men, whose understanding of the country and unconfessed affection for it, permitted them to curse the wind and snow and the awful silence which was about them like the threat of a word unuttered.

The night in late February when Idaho Pete crossed the floor of the beer parlor to Ito Fujika's table, it was cold outside and still. Now and again the logs of the building cracked, as if that cold and stillness bore upon it.

Idaho Pete—who had never been in Idaho, but who, coming from the States, had been given his name because he talked of it as the state where one day he would like to "settle"—explained, before leaving those at his own table, that he was inclined "for a bit of fun with the little Jap."

"Well, Fuzzy," he said, seating himself by Ito, "how's tricks?"

Ito receded deeper into his corner. His muskrat cap was on the chair beside him and his close-cropped hair stood stiff as quills.

His teeth flashed. He made a sound. He lisped, nodded his head to lend emphasis to his good will.

Idaho Pete leaned closer. "They tell me," he said, "that fur is running good up in that valley of yours." He twisted in his chair to wink at his friends.

Ito said nothing.

"Well, Fuzzy," the other continued, "I figure I need a change of scenery. Things are awful dull out on my trapline. Maybe in a day or two I will be up there to call on you and if I like the look of things, I'll be there to stay. See?"

Ito uttered one word: "No!"

He uttered it without thinking, instinctively. His cabin, his traps, his trails to be given up to another man? He said "No!" again, more softly.

Idaho Pete shrugged his broad shoulders, blinked his eyes. He turned to the table he had left. "He says 'No!'" he shouted across the room. He laughed. His drinking companions laughed. Idaho Pete slapped the table so that Ito's glass jumped, fell to the floor, shattered.

Idaho Pete rose. He said from his height, "I'll be seeing you, brown eyes. Watch for me. I'll wear a red mackinaw so you'll be sure to know me when I come up the trail."

Ito sat for a few minutes, listening to the other table. "He believed me!" Idaho Pete said. Then there was more laughter. Someone else said, "Why that country was cleaned out years ago. No white man—remember Flaherty had to clear out. Only a Jap could make a living up there." They laughed again. They were laughing at him—at Ito Fujika who had ancestors, at Ito Fujika, son of the Emperor, to whom they were properly servants. They laughed at Ito Fujika, who now owned his cabin in the mountains.

The next morning Ito left the hotel earlier than was his custom, without breakfast, while it was still dark. Soon after noon he reached his cabin.

When the next day he had set the beartrap—the Number 6 trap, the one which had wrenched the arm from the grizzly bear—he returned to Red Pass. He had set the trap two miles below his cabin in a depression in the trail where anyone, traveling into the cabin from the railroad, would have to pass. He had sunk it in the snow, dusted snow over the marks of his work. Now, as he neared the town, snow fell in slow, wide flakes from the heavy sky, a final seal upon his efforts.

Ito had come to a decision. He would go down to the Coast to visit his cousin. He mentioned this to Mr. Scroggins in the afternoon. He would wait in town overnight for the train.

Walking about the town, observing the snow fall, he reasoned that if, in his absence, the big man in the red mackinaw became entangled in the trap, Ito Fujika could not be blamed. Ito Fujika was absent on family business. Perhaps, not expecting to be back until the spring, he had put out the trap there on the chance of catching a bear when his fur was prime. That is to say, when the bear was fresh from his den. At any rate, no one had a right to go up to his cabin when the owner was not at home. The trap, indeed, was no more than a lock upon the cabin door.

It was probable, too, that weeks would pass before anyone learned of what had taken place. The wide jaws of the trap would seize the man just below the knee. They would crush the bone. If he freed himself, which was not likely, for a lever was required to pry those jaws apart, where would he go, and how far could he go in deep snow with a shattered leg and in cold which split trees and caused the very lake to groan? Drowsy with pain and cold, he would fall asleep. He would not awaken.

When someone passed by, or when word, in its mysterious course, reached the town, he, Ito, would be far away, possibly in the United States—for means existed of crossing the border—or with the fishing fleet in Alaskan waters.

Ito, of course, regretted the necessity of leaving. He would have preferred to be on hand when the trap was sprung, out of view among the spruce trees above it, watching. When he thought of the scene, the red mackinaw like a huge spot of blood on the snow, his skin tightened, his scalp puckered, a tingling and a warmth suffused his limbs, his breath came quickly.

No one passing him now as he walked towards the beer parlor in the twilight, seeing him smile and nod, would have guessed at this hatred which he had for the big man in the red mackinaw. He felt himself surrounded by big men, by coarse laughter, by big feet waiting to trample upon him, by big hands eager to take from him, as from his people, everything that they had. The man in the red mackinaw was the type of all he feared. He went to the beer parlor, not because he wished to meet Idaho Pete again, but to nurture hatred for him and also because it was wise to be seen by as many as possible a day's travel from his cabin.

In the beer parlor, before Idaho Pete had appeared, Ito was restless. He drank his glass of beer. Without thought, he had a second. From that it was easy to go on to the third, and after the third to another.

When Idaho Pete came in, it seemed to Ito, his vision not as steady as it was before, that they were acquaintances of long standing. Idaho Pete stood for half a minute inside the door, feet apart, hands in his pockets, hat cocked back from his forehead, looking about the smoky room. Ito recalled then foreigners he had seen on the streets in Tokyo. Idaho Pete's eyes were cold, blue, assured like those of a man on a hilltop. He walked to the table where his friends were sitting. Seated, he glanced at Ito. He winked. Ito's neck was scalded with a hot rush of blood. He smiled at Idaho Pete, ran his tongue around his lips.

He could not look at the other man without thinking of the trap under its blanket of snow on the trail. Thinking of the trap, he questioned if it were set in exactly the right place, if there might be a chance of a man passing without stepping on its sensitive "paw," if, in other words, it were set in the narrowest part of the trail. It seemed now that it would have been wise to have put the trap just a bit higher, where the ground sloped more sharply away to the valley. This was the last touch that was needed. If he hurried, and was without the encumbrance of a pack, he decided he would have time to go up there and still return to take the next afternoon's train—if he hurried, if he used the darkness.

Ito left the beer parlor through the side door, swiftly, like a shadow sucked through the wall into the lobby of the hotel. He found his snowshoes, went out, crossed the railroad tracks. There, tying on his snowshoes, he began the crossing of the lake. The wind, newly risen, jolted him, but feeling carefully with his feet he kept to the hard hump of the trail made by his previous crossings. On either side the vast snowfield stretched away, like mist waiting to engulf him. The wind, shifting to the east, was sharp enough to peel flesh from bone.

For hours, having crossed the lake, Ito struggled and panted upwards in the timber. His chest heaved, his heart pounded, and his head, with the beer he had drunk, was as in a vise of steel. Here in the forest where the snow was softer he floundered off the trail, ran his face against trees, caught his webbed snowshoes in the branches of fallen logs, fell and got to his feet. Darkness was the always yielding wall against which he pressed.

Lost in the furious treadmill of the night, in the frozen mountains whose valleys, he sensed, were made for giants to walk in, he commenced to wonder how far he had come, if he were close to the trap or still miles from it. Soon each step was taken in apprehension of the hungry jaws hidden ahead underneath the snow. It was even possible, he reasoned, that wandering from the trail in the dark and back onto it, he had passed the trap. Ahead of him, now it was also behind.

He stopped. His mind urged him on, but his vulnerable legs faltered, refused, remaining unmoving in the snow. He looked down, and in the darkness, unable to see his feet, was overcome with dizziness, like a man who fronts an abyss. Sweat broke out over Ito's body, coursed down the small of his back, and his racing blood made the roar of a waterfall between his ears.

He thought he would find a stick, a sapling, to prod the snow before him. He held out his arm, took a step. He touched a young balsam. He tried to bend its trunk, to break it off. It was young enough to bend, too old and strong to break. He wrestled with it, fought its roots. His fury mounted against this thing which gave and would not yield. He sobbed. Foam flew from his lips. He took out his knife, hacked at the thin trunk. In final impatience, he climbed into its branches until his weight bent its tip into the snow. There, leaning on it, he began to whittle again at the trunk. Slowly, as if with a will of its own, with a strength beyond his strength—already numbed with cold—the balsam slipped from his grasp. Suddenly it flew upright, intent on its business of growing, slapping him across the face, throwing him on his back into the snow.

Ito did not at once get up. He was tired, his energies were spent. He thought he would rest a minute, pillowed on the snow. He shivered, his teeth chattered, his breath hissed faintly in the snow. He curled his knees into his chest, his head fell onto his arm and Ito was asleep.

He was still asleep when, six weeks later, a sergeant of the provincial police came up to investigate the cause of his absence, for Ito had left his packsack and trail axe uncalled for, and at the hotel they were not sure whether he had gone to the Coast or returned to his trapline. The thaw had come and the sergeant, before reaching him, had found the Number 6 trap revealed through the snow on the trail. He sprang it, hooked it on the branch of a tree. Ito had circled the trap and was above it. What was left of him, a pair of martens having been to him before the sergeant, was only a hundred yards from his cabin door.

Today in Red Pass, some people will still tell you of Ito Fujika, the trapper, who was new to the mountains, and who set a beartrap in dead winter and then grew weary and slept on the way back to his cabin. Others, for no cause that they can state, at mention of his name will wag a head, spit and walk away.

Nausikaa, Vancouver Island

Theresa Kishkan

I

I found you curled like a dead seal
kelp-weed hiding your nakedness
small fish swimming in your eyes.

I come to this beach for the artefacts:
    legendary fishing globes; serpent shapes in rootwood
    sea-onion Medusa heads; starfish, purple and fat.

You were too large for my bucket of lucky stones and clamshells;
I stretched you like a skin between two logs
I made a fire to dry your bones.

II

In our island wanderings we find whale skeletons.
You choose a breastbone, you string it with seaweed.
The fires die to a glowing brand
your hand is sure on this harp
and your song is a cycle of sea and land
                    storm and calm.

Smoke rises like a flower from what's left of a fire
separating thinly, then drifting away.

III

This is a wet island of enormous trees
a mist that never rises but settles instead
on the green, muting it, making it shine.

    (You tell me about Ithaka:
     cypress trees that cling to the hills
     clouds that roar with the voice of Zeus
     a blue Adriatic filled with fish)

We go to a forest and stand in the heart, listening
to a wind rushing like a fury through a thick green weave.

IV

You are leaving, you tell me a woman waits
in a bed you made to hold both your weights:
you don't want her alone in that bed for too long.
It is a secret thing of olive trunk
strung with oxhide and covered with blankets
she weaves on an all-night loom.

    There was not time between us for secrets
    for pledges or your handiwork;
    there was not an olive trunk in sight on this beach
    only cedar logs cured in salt.

So you're leaving, you've mended your boat
I've lent you a compass, a book about stars.
I must return to the waiting
for a stranger to rise from the waves.

He shall be perfect, and a bringer of gifts.

Bushed

Earle Birney

He invented a rainbow but lightning struck it
shattered it into the lake-lap of a mountain
so big his mind slowed when he looked at it

Yet he built a shack on the shore
learned to roast porcupine belly and
wore the quills on his hatband

At first he was out with the dawn
whether it yellowed bright as wood-columbine
or was only a fuzzed moth in a flannel of storm
But he found the mountain was clearly alive
sent messages whizzing down every hot morning
boomed proclamations at noon and spread out
a white guard of goat
before falling asleep on its feet at sundown

When he tried his eyes on the lake   ospreys
would fall like valkyries
choosing the cut-throat
He took then to waiting
till the night smoke rose from the boil of the sunset

But the moon carved unknown totems
out of the lakeshore
owls in the beardusky woods derided him
moosehorned cedars circled his swamps and tossed
their antlers up to the stars
Then he knew   though the mountain slept   the winds
were shaping its peak to an arrowhead
poised

And now he could only
bar himself in and wait
for the great flint to come singing into his heart

At Sechelt

Dorothy Livesay

Sea is our season; neither dark nor day,
Autumn nor spring, but this inconstancy
That yet is continent: This self-contained
Organic motion, our mind's ocean
Limitless as thought's range, yet restrained
To narrow beaches, promontories
Accepting her in silence; the land's ear
Forming a concave shell along the sands
To hear sea's shuffle as she leaps in gear
Spuming her poems upon our ribbéd hands
Crying against our poor timidity;
O come to bed in bedding water, be
Swept to these arms, this sleep, beloved and proud!
You'll need no linen; nor, thereafter, any shroud.

2
Now that I walk alone along the stones
I am compelled to cry, like the white gull
Light as snow on the undulating wave
Riding, lamenting. Though he lie
Forever feasting on the sea's blue breast
And I am shorebound, sucked to the hot sand
Crunching the mussels underfoot, scuttling the crabs
And seared by sun—still we are, each one,
The bird, the human, riding the world alone
Calling for lover who could share the song
Yet bow to the denial; laugh or be mute;
Calling, and yet reluctant to forego
For otherness, the earth's warm silences
Or the loquacious solace of the sea.

Seashelter

Dorothy Livesay

The houses last longer
than those who lived there
who hammered 2 by 4's
wainscotted, plastered walls
unfrantically
painted them pink or blue
(never a green wall)

This shingle house was made
high on a mountain
                        when the crew went in
to heave and haul
                    the forest
tame it down
with donkey engine
then the stripped bark
and logs rolled
lumbering   down
                        (the land left bleeding)

When they cleared out they hoisted houses high
on sledges over barren forest rubble
and tumbled them to the sea
to be towed down to the quiet beaches
Porpoise Bay
and landed.

House weather-stained
with leaking roof
        wind-beaten
                water-soaked
house lived in
                locked box where
I saw your faded photograph
in an old trunk

The cracking walls
still stood—
but you
had gone.

Ted's Wife
Audrey Thomas

It was Phyllis Keeping who first called Ted's wife, "the alternate selection." It was at the Garwood's annual Christmas party. There was a lull in the conversation and Phyll, who seemed to be listening intently to something old Mrs. Garwood was saying, suddenly looked up and asked in a loud, clear voice (as though she'd been waiting to say it, thought more than one person, later): "Well, where's Ted, and, oh dear, what's her name? I always think of her as the alternate selection." No one actually gasped—Phyll was known for her wicked tongue—and one or two people laughed; but Anne Garwood, who had been busy passing around the hot hors d'oeuvres (the party was still thought of as Belle Garwood's Annual Do, although Anne and Jim really gave it, did all the preparations, and, for the last two years, opened their own home, rather than have Belle breathe in all that stale smoke the next day), said quietly and firmly ("Really," she thought to herself, "that woman is too much!"): "Ted and *Helen*," letting her voice underline the word, "are coming on the 6:15. I imagine that it's late."

"Helen!" cried Phyll, as though only just remembering it. "*Helen.* Of course!"

People went back to talking in little groups, admiring the Christmas tree, which, this year, had been decorated entirely with things from the island: long chains of scarlet arbutus berries, shells, gilded pine cones. It really was pretty. ("Although you have to be one of the island Raj," Phyllis would say, the next day, "to get away with decorating your Christmas tree with clam shells. I was surprised that there wasn't a gilded starfish on the top.")

"Peace on earth, good will to men—which we must assume includes women, too," Anne said to Jim, as they were cleaning up. "You'd think that woman would lay off, in honour of the season, if not out of some feeling for Ted. Of course, her remarks will be all over the island tomorrow."

"I doubt if Ted will hear it, or, if hearing, care."

"*She* may. Helen. Both hear it and care. I think Phyll Keeping gets more and more like some horrid character out of *Volpone*."

"She drinks too much at parties."

"She drinks too much all the time, but sometimes I think that the drinking is just a cover."

He shook his head at her, not quite sure what she meant. His mouth was full of the last of the smoked salmon.

"Well, if she drinks too much, she can always use that as an excuse for the kind of thing that she says. So can other people—and do. 'Oh, you know Phyll,' they say. I suspect that she's just naturally vicious and the drinking is really an excuse to be vicious in public and get away with it. When Ted and

Helen finally did arrive, you saw what happened—how everyone stopped talking, except your mother, who hadn't caught Phyll's remark. That's the trouble with that kind of wit—it's far too clever—you don't forget what's been said. She would probably have been terrific in advertising."

"Putting down the other product."

"Yes, you're right. Well, she certainly has it in for Helen."

"That's understandable."

"She wanted Ted all to herself."

"To herself and Dave."

" 'To herself and Dave,' yes. One tends to forget that Dave's involved in this. I'm always surprised that he puts up with her behaviour."

"Maybe she wasn't always this way."

"She certainly has never been quite so bad."

"Well, her remark says it all. It was clever, but not really apt, now, was it?"

"You mean, 'the alternate selection' to whom?"

"Exactly. People won't get it—most people. It will just stick in their minds in connection with Helen."

"But then, they'll start asking themselves what Phyll meant."

"And wonder if she—"

"Yes. And she, not being free—." He broke off. "Bloody woman. Let's go to bed. She's managed to be the centre of *our* attention for far too long."

It was a strange remark and people did comment on it. Most of Phyll's remarks were as obvious as they were witty—calling the fat couple who'd been staying with the Mackenzies, "Babar and Celeste," or the visiting minister, "Extreme Unction." You got that right away (or as soon as you'd seen the couple or talked to Reverend Manly for more than five minutes). But Ted had not run away from or divorced his wife; she had died, very suddenly, after a brief illness. And they had been devoted to one another. So, "the alternate selection" to whom? In the following weeks, there developed two schools of thought about this remark: one was that Phyll had unconsciously revealed that she and Ted had a "thing" for one another, but as she was married to Dave (and again, in a very happy marriage), she was not free to go to Ted when Mary died; the other was that the remark was *very* conscious and that it was precisely what Phyll wanted people, including Helen, to think.

Phyllis had been awfully helpful after Mary died and this seemed only natural at the time. The two couples had been friends for years and Dave and Ted worked in the same department, although in different fields. When Ted asked for a six-month leave of absence, so that he could go abroad and do some research, busy himself, so that he wouldn't brood after Mary's death, it was Dave and Phyllis who backed him up and urged him on, and Phyll, in particular (because she was on the island all the time), who promised to feed the cats and check in on his house every day. Phyll had even thrown a small farewell party at Madrona Inn and had given Ted a blank book in which to keep a journal. A whole bunch of them went down to see him off at the ferry the day that he left for London. Dave was driving him in, as Ted's car had been put up on blocks until his return. It had been a beautiful morning in early June and Ted seemed touched that so many people would get up at such an early hour (the ferry left at 8 a.m.) to wish him well. Phyll said later that she thought that he looked awfully frail, that he seemed to have aged terribly in the last three months. She wondered if going abroad and away from all his friends was such a good idea after all. On the island, she had made a special point of kissing both Ted and Dave as they came off the ferry on Friday nights during the term, and insisted on driving him back to his house (where the lights had already been put on and the refrigerator checked for ice). You could see her at the farmer's market on Fridays ("Well, we're all dressed like farmers at least," Phyll said once, laughing as she waited her turn, "although what I see in front of me is a poet; and in front of him, a renegade engineer; and in front of *him*, a superannuated hippie") buying a few extra goodies for Ted, along with her own weekend purchases. And she always invited him for at least one meal, even though she didn't see Dave from Monday to Friday and they always enjoyed their time alone together. When Ted protested about the loaves of fresh bread, the flowers on his bedside table (for of course she had a key to his place and could come and go as she chose), she asked him what he thought friends were for? And it was she who helped him go through Mary's things, her only sister being 4,000 miles away, putting them in cardboard boxes and taking them in, depending upon their age and condition, to the Sally-Ann or the New-to-You shop in Victoria. Ted had been going to offer everything to the thrift shop on the island, until Phyll said, in horror, "Do you really want to see your wife's dresses coming at you along the road? Or her shoes on someone else's feet?" ("At which point, he looked at me blankly and said, 'Oh, no, of course not,' and promptly burst into tears. I could've bitten off my tongue.")

Ted and Mary had been on the island longer than Dave and Phyll; indeed, it was an invitation to their friends' house on a crisp October weekend that made them fall in love with the place and eventually buy. That was when land was still relatively cheap, just before this particular island became one of *the* places to buy (Phyll called it "The Last Resort")—and they found a glorious acreage, right up above the Pass, that was an easy, pretty walk from Ted and Mary's. They kept their apartment in town, even after they renovated the old farmhouse on their property. Dave had ten more years until retirement, and Ted, five; both of the wives opted for living on the island more or less fulltime and the men arranged their schedules so that their teaching was fitted into four days, which gave them from Friday night until Monday night

(sometimes even Tuesday morning) at home. The two men actually got on somewhat better than the two women. For one thing, Mary was much older than Phyll; and she was a painter. She had a small studio on the very edge of their property and she went there every weekday, rain or shine, when Ted wasn't home. She laughed at her paintings and called herself "the eternal amateur," but really, they were quite good, abstract without being blobs, and the colours were bold and brilliant, quite unlike what you would imagine a frail, rather conservative person like Mary would produce. She was beginning, finally, to have a "name," at least in British Columbia, when she dropped dead, literally, one Sunday evening. ("We were sitting around the fireplace, laughing at some silly story that Ted was relating, when Mary got up and said, 'Excuse me, but—' and fell over. She died before we were really out of our seats. Ted kept saying, 'Mary, Mary?' the way you do on a telephone when the line suddenly goes dead. Finally, the Hovercraft came and took them away—he, walking by the stretcher, still holding her dead hand; Dave, on the other side, holding him. I went back into the house and there was the fire, still crackling, and Mary's wine glass at the edge of the carpet where it had rolled, and a big wine stain that had spread like blood. I washed up and tidied the sitting room, and scrubbed the carpet as best I could, and then, I just sat there, wondering what it would be like to go like that, to feel suddenly strange—you know, she'd had a bad heart for years—and stand up, try to say something, and just be struck down, wham, your life slammed shut. I knew that Ted and Dave probably wouldn't be back until the morning, so I went home and went to bed and lay there, absolutely rigid with fear, the way I used to lie when I was a child so that 'THEY' wouldn't know that I was awake and come out of the corners and murder me. I imagined the most horrible scenes of Mary—who was so elegant, you know, and so private—being un-dressed and put on one of those tables, cut into, explored and examined like a piece of defective machinery, her heart held up to the light. By the time they returned on the regular ferry, the next morning, I was almost catatonic. And Ted—well! It was Dave who kept us all going through the next few days.")

But Phyll hadn't really known Mary all that well. The "age" thing and the "painting" thing (Mary wasn't interested in coffee mornings or the Golf Club), and a certain general reserve which she had, made it awfully difficult for Phyll to get through to her. It was not as though Mary were thorny, like a hedge of the wild roses that grew everywhere on the island, but rather, that she was distant. It was as though there were a long forest path between her and a woman like Phyll. And maybe the path was like one of those old logging trails, which led nowhere in the end, after you'd been stumbling along it for what seemed like hours. Despite this, Mary was more relaxed on the weekends, when Ted was there, and the four of them often ate together, or played silly games like Clue or Risk on long rainy Saturday evenings. Ted was reserved himself, but he was a wonderful storyteller and mimic. He had travelled quite a lot as a young man and could do killing imitations of border officials, policemen giving directions, lonely old ladies at English seaside resorts complaining about the soup. Phyll said once that he should have been an actor, not a scholar, and people still talk about his performance as Scrooge, some years before. Phyll pouted a little because there weren't any meaty women's parts in that dramatization and she nearly voted against it, but she was the first to rush up and kiss Ted and tell him how absolutely wonderful he had been. (But she got her own back when her Puck was praised in the island paper, *The Barnacle*, the next spring.)

Phyll's days were very busy. She had a huge successful vegetable garden, which everyone told her was like a painting or a tapestry, for she planned it for eye appeal as well as for nutrition. She typed Dave's papers for him, and sometimes Ted's as well. And she did her share of volunteer work, driving old ladies and gentlemen to the outpatients' clinic in Victoria or on Salt Spring Island, driving the same people to the corner store or the farmers' market on Fridays. "Hither and yawn," as she sometimes called it. ("My God, how they do run on about food and ailments! I'm tempted sometimes to get earplugs. I hope when I get like that, they shoot me!")

She liked opera and went into the city regularly in the winter, meeting Dave on the mainland, for a change, and they would have a nice dinner, either before or after the opera, and perhaps see friends. Sometimes, they made up a foursome with Ted and Mary and they went to see a play.

"People ask me what I *do* over here," Phyll would complain laughingly to weekend guests. "To me, there never seems to be enough hours in the day." They would marvel at her big wood-stove, on which she had just cooked a wonderful meal, and they would get up the next day to breakfast on her homemade bread and jam and freshly ground coffee. She would show them where to empty the compost bucket and take them on nature walks. She saw to it that they returned to the mainland dazzled. (Although, sometimes, she complained to Dave that she wondered if they were running a convalescent home. At which point, he would laugh and say, "Well, don't do it then," knowing full well that she thrived on it. "What a Queen you are, Phyll," he said to her once. She was quite annoyed. "I don't feel much like a queen when I'm emptying all those ashtrays or running the last of the guests' sheets through the washing machine." "Oh yes, you do," he said. "You feel more like a queen than ever—a queen in exile. One of those royal persons who would be a queen if the monarchy hadn't been overthrown." "I don't think that you're very nice," she said, really hurt by his remarks. "Most of them are *your* friends or *your* students, after all." But he simply picked up the garbage can with a smile and said, "But *your* invitations," and he went outside.)

After Ted went away on leave, she discovered that she missed him far more than she missed Mary, but she would never have told anyone that—not even Dave. She had always had a suspicion that Dave was just a tiny bit jealous of her friendship and rapport with Ted—they got on so well and so easily together. Mary was ten years older than Ted and she coddled him to such a degree—or so it seemed to Phyll—that Phyll admitted that she'd been shocked to discover some beautiful nightdresses ("Real silk, my dear, and dripping in lace. The kind of thing that you're given, not the kind of thing that you buy") among Mary's clothes. She never before thought of their relationship as sexual. ("I felt as though I'd caught him sleeping with his mother!") Now, she imagined how Ted would make love—with great gentleness and wit, she thought. She envied Mary those nightgowns, for they could only have come from Ted. But with her bad heart? Had he ever been able to let himself go? Wouldn't he always have to be thinking of her, of whether or not he was too heavy on her, or if he were asking too much? (But he was actually very tall and thin—he would probably hardly be any weight at all.) What did he do now that Mary was dead? Did he miss her *physically*? (She had been cremated; there was no gravestone.) But she must have been over seventy! How often would a seventy-year-old woman want to make love, especially if her heart were bad? Phyll took away the nightgowns and burnt them. It would be wrong for anyone else to wear them.

At first, Ted had written regularly—at least once a week. He rented a flat in London and was doing some work at the British Museum, something to do with *Beowulf* and the Sutton Hoo Ship Burial. The letters came to Dave, of course, as was only proper, but they were addressed to them both inside, "Dear Dave and Phyll," and she was sure that a lot of the descriptions of people and places were for her benefit. He was having some trouble sleeping, he said, and he had taken to getting up very early and going for long walks, when all the rest of the city was asleep. He stood on Westminster Bridge at 5 a.m., waiting for Big Ben to strike. He walked to the new Covent Garden at Vauxhall and loved all the vegetables and flowers, as gorgeous as ever, but missed "the noise and disorder and confusion of the old." He described the warnings, everywhere, about unattended parcels, and the "Arabs running around Harrod's in their white nighties." "And the famous London taxicab is no longer as black and uniform as the businessman's umbrella. I have seen maroon cabs, blue ones, even a white cab! But just when I think London—never mind London Bridge—is falling down, falling down, I see a sign from the top of a bus on Regent Street. I suppose that I think of it now because it was a shop that specialized in those wonderful black umbrellas. Running around the top of the windows, in discreet gold lettering on black, the store announced that it also sold 'life preservers, sword canes and dagger cases.' The Empire is not dead yet (at least on Regent

Street).” He enclosed, however, a Bird’s custard label with the instructions in English, French and Arabic.

“Bird’s custard!” Phyll said. “Whatever is that poor man eating?” She began to think about the kind of meals that she would prepare for him when he returned. Thick fish chowders and pot roasts that were marinated in wine. Grilled salmon. *Crisp* vegetables. Blackberry-and-apple pies. She imagined herself down on the dock meeting him, in the new wine-coloured cardigan that she was knitting (somehow Dave was never there with them.) She copied out a line of *Beowulf* and memorized it: “Waes þu, Hrothgar, hal!” She could see his face light up with happiness. And back at the house, waiting, she would have hot apple juice and rum, and some of her famous fruitcake. He had promised that he would return before Christmas and that he would spend the holidays with them.

At the end of October, he suddenly decided to go to Greece. “I know I won’t get a ‘beaker of the warm south’ at this time of the year—half a glass, if I’m lucky—but my work here is nearly done, and looking at the Elgin Marbles the other day, I suddenly had a great longing, since I’m more than halfway there, to see the Parthenon at sunset. It was something Mary and I always intended to do, but we never got around to it. Maybe I want to see it for her as well, who knows? Anyway, I’m off tomorrow, just like that, leaving all my academic paraphernalia with my landlady, who shakes her head over the whole business (‘And ’im, such a proper gentleman too!’), but who has promised to keep it in her box-room until I pick it all up on the way home.”

Phyll thought that for all the lightness of the tone, he sounded very melancholy, maybe suicidal, although Dave couldn’t see how she was getting that out of the letter at all.

“Well, I just *feel* it, the reference to Mary and sunsets and rushing off so suddenly.”

“I think that it sounds very healthy myself.”

“You think that everyone’s healthy unless they’re actually broken open and bleeding. *I* think that he’s very lonely and unhappy. I’m even toying with the idea of flying out to join him for a week or so.”

Dave looked at her. “Leave him alone. He knows what he’s doing.” (But, what Dave didn’t know, what she had never told him—or anyone, in fact—was that, when Ted had broken down that afternoon over Mary’s clothes and shoes, she had reached out her arms to him and had rocked him against her, as he wept, saying over and over again, “Oh my dear, my dear.” Something had passed between them that day, something very rare and very fine; their friendship had entered a new and deeper stage. It would never be spoken of or acted upon unless Dave—. But that was silly; they loved each other very much. And besides, he was as strong as an ox.)

She didn’t go, of course. That would have been too risky all round. But she did fret about him and wrote him even longer, wittier letters than ever before, one a day on the days

that Dave wasn’t there, usually late in the afternoon when she had just come in from her walk and her cheeks were still damp and alive from the wind and the sea air. She would build up the fire, get out the sherry and begin. “Time spent with you,” she wrote him in one letter, “it makes me feel very close. Is the Greek light all that it’s cracked up to be?”

He found rooms, after a week, in a kind of pension in what had been the old Turkish quarter, “with the Hill of the Muses and Philopappou just above me. I climb there every day, just before sunset, lean against the monument, and look across at the Acropolis. As the wonderful honey-coloured light flows down, I forget all about the pollution, the incessant noise of the automobiles, the horrible lumps of grilled meat that are cooking in the over-priced taverns—all the crass commercialism of this city. It’s erased in an instant and I come as close to a mystical experience as I’m ever likely to get.”

The weather, surprisingly, held. And in the *Pension Olympia*, “congenial strangers” came and went. “I feel that I’m beginning to re-cover or un-cover, or something, and I even wish that I’d become a classical scholar, instead of immersing myself in the cold northern waters of Early English.” He began to talk of a trip, to Delphi, Meteora and Thessalonika, that he was planning to take “with one or two others.” After that, it was only postcards (“Don’t worry, I’m keeping a journal and taking pictures, you shall see and hear it all later”) until, one day, in late November, Dave brought over an air-letter which said that he would be arriving, as planned, in a couple of weeks, and that he would phone them from the airport. “Don’t bother to meet me. There are one or two things I must do in town, and, by the way, I shall be bringing someone with me.” It was a typical November night and the rain drummed against the roof and hurled itself at the window panes. Any minute now, they’d have a power failure. Phyllis willed herself to sit still on the couch and sip at her drink while Dave read the letter aloud, as was his custom. When he finished, he handed the letter to her with a smile.

“I wonder who ‘someone’ is?” she said, trying to keep her voice steady. “‘Stoke the fire and kill the fatted calf.’ It must be someone special. I never thought of Ted as sly before.”

“How about shy, instead of sly? Maybe he’s fallen in love.”

“At his age? He’s an old man!” She poured herself another drink.

“Not really, and even if he is—in the eyes of this youth-oriented culture anyway—what would it matter? He sounds happy. Aren’t you happy for him?”

“Oh yes, of course.” She was terrified that she was going to burst into tears at any minute. Who? Who? How dare.... “Only if he were happy and it was all right wouldn’t he write reams and reams about it, the way all lovers do? No,” she said, “there’s something strange, when ‘someone’ doesn’t even have a name.” She poked at the fire and smiled. “Unless...”

“Unless what? What are you grinning at?”

"Unless 'someone's' name would indicate that she's a he."

Phyllis had long since ceased to shock him. Or so he thought.

"That's ridiculous!"

"Is it? *Is* it? He always seems to have a following of earnest young men. And he was a confirmed bachelor until he was well over thirty. Then, he married an older woman." (Mentally, she rearranged the evidence of the nightgowns. Not gifts from a lover consumed with passionate intensity, but desperate purchases by a middle-aged woman yearning to be held and entered.)

Dave laughed.

"We all have followings of earnest young men. Earnest young women too. That's part of the whole mystique. Ted may have more men than women, simply because his field seems to attract more men than women."

"Why?"

"Why? I don't know why. Perhaps because you get a lot of pedants in Early English—or used to. It's all changing."

Phyllis smiled again. "Do I make up one bed or two, I wonder?" The three of them sitting around a log fire had become four, one of them a handsome young Greek of about twenty-seven, a poet perhaps. His white teeth gleamed, as he smilingly struggled to follow the conversation. This was a picture, a rearrangement that she could accept. So long as she did not dwell on what the two of them did when they were alone. She accepted that kind of thing, of course, but she didn't really like to think about men—about Ted and his Greek friend—fucking each other in the ass.

"Listen," Dave said. "Don't go around speculating aloud, will you?"

"About what?"

"You know, 'about what.' About Ted coming back with a man."

"Ah ha! So you think I might be right?"

"I don't know. You have an awful way of getting to the heart of the matter. But, I think that, in fairness to Ted, you might keep your thoughts to yourself."

"Do you think that he would be ostracized? People on this island are pretty sophisticated, you know."

"No. . . . I don't know. People on this land—your crowd, anyway—pretend to be sophisticated. I think that they are actually conservative."

"Oh, very well. My lips are sealed. But I bet I'm right!"

And at first glance, it looked as if she *were* right. The night that Ted arrived was dark and stormy, and the ferry was late getting in. They didn't see him in the first rush of foot passengers and they were wondering whether or not he'd missed the boat after all, when Dave shouted, "There he is!" and began to wave.

"Look at 'someone,'" Phyll said triumphantly, "he looks positively delicious."

"Look again," Dave said, laughing. "I hate to spoil your fantasy, Phyll, but look again."

And it wasn't a boy. It was definitely a girl, a young woman, with her hair tucked up in a knitted cap, who was holding onto Ted's gloved hand, and pulling behind them one of those wheelie-carts that was piled high with luggage. Dave rushed forward to help them, but Phyllis just stood there, while men, women, children and dogs hurried past her, up the wharf. Her heart was beating so fast and so hard that she was sure that everyone could hear it. She thought of the chaste bed that she'd made up in Ted's spare room. How they would laugh about that! She thought of how hard she'd worked the past few days to make the place sparkle and shine; she thought of the loaf of sourdough rye that she put on the kitchen table, the jar of her apple butter beside it and the bottle of Ouzo chilling in the fridge. She thought of the special trip that she'd taken to Victoria to get *that*, and to look up the words, "welcome home," in Greek at the public library. And the present under his pillow, with the note saying, "My dear, now I will feel complete again." The note was the worst thing of all.

And the shock of it all, the rage—and what a fool he'd turned out to be. So that, when Ted and Helen gave a *Twelfth Night* party, and Ted, at the end of the feasting, tapped on his wine glass and said shyly, "Well, we've decided to make it legal," Phyll's voice, drunken, but high and hard and clear, cut across the congratulations and applause with her best line yet.

"What are you going to do," she cried, "adopt her?"

Finches Feeding
P. K. Page

They fall like feathered cones from the tree above,
sumi the painted grass where the birdseed is,
skirl like a boiling pot
or a shallow within a river—
a bar of gravel breaking the water up.

Having said that, what have I said?
Not much.

Neither my delight nor the length of my watching is
                        conveyed
and nothing profound recorded, yet these birds
as I observe them
stir such feelings up—
such yearnings for weightlessness, for hollow bones,
rapider heartbeat, east/west eyes
and such wonder—seemingly half-remembered—as they rise
spontaneously into air, like feathered cones.

By the River

Jack Hodgins

But listen, she thinks, it's nearly time.

And flutters, leaf-like, at the thought. The train will rumble down the valley, stop at the little shack to discharge Styan, and move on. This will happen in half an hour and she has a mile still to walk.

Crystal Styan walking through the woods, through bush, is not pretty. She knows that she is not even a little pretty, though her face is small enough, and pale, and her eyes are not too narrow. She wears a yellow wool sweater and a long cotton skirt and boots. Her hair, tied back so the branches will not catch in it, hangs straight and almost colourless down her back. Some day, she expects, there will be a baby to play with her hair and hide in it like someone behind a waterfall.

She has left the log cabin, which sits on the edge of the river in a stand of birch, and now she follows the river bank upstream. A mile ahead, far around the bend out of sight, the railroad tracks pass along the rim of their land and a small station is built there just for them, for her and Jim Styan. It is their only way in to town, which is ten miles away and not much of a town anyway when you get there. A few stores, a tilted old hotel, a movie theatre.

Likely, Styan would have been to a movie last night. He would have stayed the night in the hotel, but first (after he had seen the lawyer and bought the few things she'd asked him for) he would pay his money and sit in the back row of the theatre and laugh loudly all the way through the movie. He always laughs at everything, even if it isn't funny, because those figures on the screen make him think of people he has known; and the thought of them exposed like this for just anyone to see embarrasses him a little and makes him want to create a lot of noise so people will know he isn't a bit like that himself.

She smiles. The first time they went to a movie together she slouched as far down in the seat as she could so no one could see she was there or had anything to do with Jim Styan.

The river flows past her almost silently. It has moved only a hundred miles from its source and has another thousand miles to go before it reaches the ocean, but already it is wide enough and fast. Right here she has more than once seen a moose wade out and then swim across to the other side and disappear into the cedar swamps. She knows something, has heard somewhere that farther downstream, miles and miles behind her, an Indian band once thought this river a hungry monster that liked to gobble up their people. They say that Coyote their god-hero dived in and subdued the monster and made it promise never to swallow people again. She once thought she'd like to study that kind of thing at a university or somewhere, if Jim Styan hadn't told her grade ten was good enough for anyone and a life on the road was more exciting.

What road? she wonders. There isn't a road within ten miles. They sold the rickety old blue pickup the same day they moved onto this place. The railroad was going to be all they'd need. There wasn't any place they cared to go that the train, even this old-fashioned milk-run outfit, couldn't take them easily and cheaply enough.

But listen, she thinks, it's nearly time.

The trail she is following swings inland to climb a small bluff and for a while she is engulfed by trees. Cedar and fir are dark and thick and damp. The green new growth on the scrub bushes has nearly filled in the narrow trail. She holds her skirt up a little so it won't be caught or ripped, then runs and nearly slides down the hill again to the river's bank. She can see in every direction for miles and there isn't a thing in sight which has anything to do with man.

"Who needs them?" Styan said, long ago.

It was with that kind of question—questions that implied an answer so obvious only a fool would think to doubt—that he talked her first out of the classroom and then right off the island of her birth and finally up here into the mountains with the river and the moose and the railroad. It was as if he had transported her in his falling-apart pickup not only across the province about as far as it was possible to go, but also backwards in time, perhaps as far as her grandmother's youth or even farther. She washes their coarse clothing in the river and depends on the whims of the seasons for her food.

"Look!" he shouted when they stood first in the clearing above the cabin. "It's as if we're the very first ones. You and me."

They swam in the cold river that day and even then she thought of Coyote and the monster, but he took her inside the cabin and they made love on the fir-bough bed that was to be theirs for the next five years. "We don't need any of them," he sang. He flopped over on his back and shouted up into the rafters. "We'll farm it! We'll make it go. We'll make our own world!" Naked, he was as thin and pale as a celery stalk.

When they moved in he let his moustache grow long and droopy like someone in an old, brown photograph. He wore overalls which were far too big for him and started walking around as if there were a movie camera somewhere in the trees and he was being paid to act like a hillbilly instead of the city-bred boy he really was. He stuck a limp felt hat on the top of his head like someone's uncle Hiram and bought chickens.

"It's a start," he said.

"Six chickens?" She counted again to be sure. "We don't even have a shed for them."

He stood with his feet wide apart and looked at her as if she were stupid. "They'll lay their eggs in the grass."

"That should be fun," she said. "A hundred and sixty acres is a good-size pen."

"It's a start. Next spring we'll buy a cow. Who needs more?"

Yes who? They survived their first winter here, though the chickens weren't so lucky. The hens got lice and started pecking at each other. By the time Styan got around to riding in to town for something to kill the lice a few had pecked right through the skin and exposed the innards. When he came back from town they had all frozen to death in the yard.

At home, back on her father's farm in the blue mountains of the island, nothing had ever frozen to death. Her father had cared for things. She had never seen anything go so wrong there, or anyone have to suffer.

She walks carefully now, for the trail is on the very edge of the river bank and is spongy and broken away in places. The water, clear and shallow here, back-eddies into little bays where cattail and bracken grow and where water-skeeters walk on their own reflection. A beer bottle glitters where someone, perhaps a guide on the river, has thrown it—wedged between stones as if it has been there as long as they have. She keeps her face turned to the river, away from the acres and acres of forest which are theirs.

Listen, it's nearly time, she thinks. And knows that soon, from far up the river valley, she will be able to hear the throbbing of the train, coming near.

She imagines his face at the window. He is the only passenger in the coach and sits backwards, watching the land slip by, grinning in expectation or memory or both. He tells a joke to old Bill Cobb the conductor but even in his laughter does not turn his eyes from outside the train. One spot on his forehead is white where it presses against the glass. His fingers run over and over the long drooping ends of his moustache. He is wearing his hat.

Hurry, hurry, she thinks. To the train, to her feet, to him.

She wants to tell him about the skunk she spotted yesterday. She wants to tell him about the stove, which smokes too much and needs some kind of clean-out. She wants to tell him about her dream; how she dreamed he was trying to go into the river and how she pulled and hauled on his feet but he wouldn't come out. He will laugh and laugh at her when she tells him, and his laughter will make it all right and not so frightening, so that maybe she will be able to laugh at it too.

She has rounded the curve in the river and glances back, way back, at the cabin. It is dark and solid, not far from the bank. Behind the poplars the cleared fields are yellowing with the coming of fall but now in all that place there isn't a thing alive, unless she wants to count trees and insects. No people. No animals. It is scarcely different from her very first look at it. In five years their dream of livestock has been shelved again and again.

Once there was a cow. A sway-backed old Jersey.

"This time I've done it right," he said. "Just look at this prize."

And stepped down off the train to show off his cow, a wide-eyed beauty that looked at her through a window of the passenger coach.

"Maybe so, but you'll need a miracle, too, to get that thing down out of there."

A minor detail to him, who scooped her up and swung her around and kissed her hard, all in front of the old conductor and the engineer who didn't even bother to turn away. "Farmers at last!" he shouted. "You can't have a farm without a cow. You can't have a baby without a cow."

She put her head inside the coach, looked square into the big brown eyes, glanced at the sawed-off horns. "Found you somewhere, I guess," she said to the cow. "Turned out of someone's herd for being too old or senile or dried up."

"An auction sale," he said, and slapped one hand on the window glass. "I was the only one there who was desperate. But I punched her bag and pulled her tits; she'll do. There may even be a calf or two left in her sway-backed old soul."

"Come on, bossy," she said. "This is no place for you."

But the cow had other ideas. It backed into a corner of the coach and shook its lowered head. Its eyes, steady and dull, never left Crystal Styan.

"You're home," Styan said. "Sorry there's no crowd here or a band playing music, but step down anyway and let's get started."

"She's not impressed," she said. "She don't see any barn waiting out there either, not to mention hay or feed of any kind. She's smart enough to know a train coach is at least a roof over her head."

The four of them climbed over the seats to get behind her and pushed her all the way down the aisle. Then, when they had shoved her down the steps, she fell on her knees on the gravel and let out a long unhappy bellow. She looked around, bellowed again, then stood up and hightailed it down the tracks. Before Styan even thought to go after her she swung right and headed into bush.

Styan disappeared into the bush, too, hollering, and after a while the train moved on to keep its schedule. She went back down the trail and waited in the cabin until nearly dark. When she went outside again she found him on the river bank, his feet in the water, his head resting against a birch trunk.

"What the hell," he said, and shook his head and didn't look at her.

"Maybe she'll come back," she said.

"A bear'll get her before then, or a cougar. There's no hope of that."

She put a hand on his shoulder but he shook it off. He'd dragged her from place to place right up this river from its mouth, looking and looking for his dream, never satisfied until he saw this piece of land. For that dream and for him she had suffered.

She smiles, though, at the memory. Because even then he was able to bounce back, resume the dream, start building new plans. She smiles, too, because she knows there will be a surprise today; there has always been a surprise. When it wasn't a cow it was a bouquet of flowers or something else. She goes through a long list in her mind of what it may be, but knows it will be none of them. Not once in her life has anything been exactly the way she imagined it. Just so much as foreseeing something was a guarantee it wouldn't happen, at least not in the exact same way.

"Hey you, Styan!" she suddenly calls out. "Hey you, Jim Styan. Where are you?" And laughs, because the noise she makes can't possibly make any difference to the world, except for a few wild animals that might be alarmed.

She laughs again, and slaps one hand against her thigh, and shakes her head. Just give her—how many minutes now?—and she won't be alone. These woods will shudder with his laughter, his shouting, his joy. That train, that kinky little train will drop her husband off and then pass on like a stay-stitch thread pulled from a seam.

"Hey you, Styan! What you brought this time? A gold brooch? An old nanny goat?"

The river runs past silently and she imagines that it is only shoulders she is seeing, that monster heads have ducked down to glide by but are watching her from eyes grey as stone. She wants to scream out "Hide, you crummy cheat, my Coyote's coming home!" but is afraid to tempt even something that she does not believe in. And anyway she senses—far off—the beat of the little train coming down the valley from the town.

And when it comes into sight she is there, on the platform in front of the little sagging shed, watching. She stands tilted far out over the tracks to see, but never dares—even when it is so far away—to step down onto the ties for a better look.

The boards beneath her feet are rotting and broken. Long stems of grass have grown up through the cracks and brush against her legs. A squirrel runs down the slope of the shed's roof and yatters at her until she turns and lifts her hand to frighten it into silence.

She talks to herself, sings almost to the engine's beat—"Here he comes, here he comes"—and has her smile already as wide as it can be. She smiles into the side of the locomotive sliding past and the freight car sliding past and keeps on smiling even after the coach has stopped in front of her and it is obvious that Jim Styan is not on board.

Unless of course he is hiding under one of the seats, ready to leap up, one more surprise.

But old Bill Cobb the conductor backs down the steps, dragging a gunny sack out after him. "H'lo there, Crystal," he says. "He ain't aboard today either, I'm afraid." He works the gunny sack out onto the middle of the platform. "Herbie Stark sent this, it's potatoes mostly, and cabbages he was going to throw out of his store."

She takes the tiniest peek inside the sack and yes, there are potatoes there and some cabbages with soft brown leaves.

The engineer steps down out of his locomotive and comes along the side of the train rolling a cigarette. "Nice day again," he says with barely a glance at the sky. "You makin' out all right?"

"Hold it," the conductor says, as if he expects the train to move off by itself. "There's more." He climbs back into the passenger car and drags out a cardboard box heaped with groceries. "The church ladies said to drop this off," he says. "They told me make sure you get every piece of it, but I don't know how you'll ever get it down to the house through all that bush."

"She'll manage," the engineer says. He holds a lighted match under the ragged end of his cigarette until the loose tobacco blazes up. "She's been doing it—how long now?—must be six months."

The conductor pushes the cardboard box over against the sack of potatoes and stands back to wipe the sweat off his face. He glances at the engineer and they both smile a little and turn away. "Well," the engineer says, and heads back down the tracks and up into his locomotive.

The conductor tips his hat, says "Sorry," and climbs back into the empty passenger car. The train releases a long hiss and then moves slowly past her and down the tracks into the deep bush. She stands on the platform and looks after it a long while, as if a giant hand is pulling, slowly, a stay-stitching thread out of a fuzzy green cloth.

Christ Walks in This Infernal District Too
Malcolm Lowry

Beneath the Malebolge lies Hastings Street,
The province of the pimp upon his beat,
Where each in his little world of drugs or crime
Moves helplessly or, hopeful, begs a dime
Wherewith to purchase half a pint of piss—
Although he will be cheated, even in this.
I hope, although I doubt it, God knows
This place where chancres blossom like the rose,
For on each face is such a hard despair
That nothing like a grief could enter there.
And on this scene from all excuse exempt
The mountains gaze in absolute contempt,
Yet this is also Canada, my friend,
Yours to absolve of ruin, or make an end.

Blue River; Clearwater
Tom Wayman

Driving north in October to the Yellowhead
in the afternoon, passing through the wooded valleys of the
    North Thompson
arriving at dusk in Blue River.
Find the motel in the cold air, under the dark mountains.

A walk in the town: the last yellow-orange sunlight
catches the snow high up on the eastern peaks.
Everything is still. These are the villages
of five jobs: CNR, Hydro, local sawmill, local logging, BC Tel
plus gasoline and oil. The small wooden railway houses
are waiting for winter: this one has built
miniature pointed roofs above the shrubbery in the yard
ready to take the weight of the snows.
Smoke goes up over the first lights
into the perfectly clear sky. Throb and hum of a distant diesel
pulling through the forest canyons, on into the cold.

And returning, a night in Clearwater:
walking down through the evening to see the river;
local sawmill, local logging, fuel oil, Hydro and the CNR.
Here are houses where the owners
ran out of money before they could put up siding.
Tarpaper, or black sheets of insulation paper
look out at the black hills. The wrecks of eight cars
surround this place—with old packing boxes,
odd tires, a child's swing and a broken tricycle.
Here is a sign saying this house is also the chain-saw dealer.

My hands are chilled, as are the sides of my head.
The river swirls quickly and heavily, while indoors
is the heat of babbling television.

These towns trouble me
like the cry of a young man in the night.
Which of us will have to work here?
These are the hardest times I have seen in my life.

Autumn
Rona Murray

We walked the hill
and watched the hawks
    cutting down   swinging round
    making unbird cries

    being born or dying noises
    in throats of birds
    whose sky   moved
                with clouds
    and the world was
                burning larch and birch
                and fields of brittle umber grass
                    exhaling the ghost

Almost
    we could see it leaving

    we not knowing
              not knowing if. . . .
Knowing mountains were hung

    already hung between us
    with white on their crowns
          white scattered thin like salt

       on trees guarding the passes

Hagar's Escape
Margaret Laurence

The girl behind the wicket at the bank seems awfully young to handle so much cash. How many ten-dollar bills must rush through her fingers in a day? It doesn't bear thinking about. What if she questions me? Asks why Marvin isn't bringing the check in this time? I'm all in a lather, and can feel the perspiration making my dress sodden under the arms. I'm not used to so much standing. The woman in front of me is taking such a long time, and seems to have a dozen transactions to perform. All kinds of papers she's handing in, pink ones and white, green checks and small blue books. She'll never be finished. My legs hurt—it's the varicose veins. I despise those elastic stockings and won't wear them. I should have worn them today. What if I fall? Someone will cart me home, and Doris will be so cross. I won't fall. I refuse to. Why doesn't the wretched woman hurry? What's the bank girl doing, that takes her so infernally long? What if she questions me?

It's my turn, suddenly. I mustn't look agitated. Do I appear quite steady, confident, casual? I know she'll look at me suspiciously. I can just see the look she'll give me, the minx—what does she know of it?

She doesn't even look up. She takes the check and counts out the bills and hands them over without a murmur. What a civil girl. Really, a most civil girl, I must admit. I'd like to thank her, tell her I appreciate her civility. But she might think it odd. I must be careful and quiet. I take the money and go, as though this sort of thing were a commonplace. I don't even look behind to see if their eyes are following. There. I did that quite well. I can manage perfectly well. I knew I could.

Now the hard part. If only my legs hold out. I took a two-ninety-two before I left, from Doris's hoarded stock, and so the awkward place, the spot soft as a fontanel under my ribs, isn't acting up too badly. The bus stop is right outside the bank. Doris and I come here when we go to the doctor's. I'm sure this is where we catch the bus to downtown. It must be. But is it?

There's a bench, thank God. I sit down heavily and try my level best to compose myself. Let's see—have I got everything? The money's in my purse. I peek, to make sure, and sure enough it's there. I'm wearing an old housedress, beige cotton patterned perhaps a little bizarrely in black triangles. A good dress was out of the question. Doris would have wondered, and besides, this one's more suitable for where I'm going. I have my special shoes on, hideous they are, with built-in arches, but they do give good support. I've worn my blue cardigan in case of chill. It has a mended spot on one cuff, but possibly no one will notice. My hat's my best one, though, shiny black straw with a nosegay of velvet cornflowers blue as a lake. Everything's all right. I think I've got everything I

require. When the bus comes, I'll just ask the driver where I can get an out-of-town bus to—where?

Drat it, the name's gone. I shan't know. He'll say *Where?* And I'll be standing there like a dummy, without a word. What shall I do? My mind's locked. Easy, Hagar, easy. It will come. Just take it easy. There, there. Oh—*Shadow Point.* Thank the lord. And here's the bus.

The driver helps me on. A nice young man. I ask the crucial question.

"I'll let you off at the bus depot downtown," he says. "You can catch the bus for Shadow Point there. You alone, lady?"

"Yes. Yes. I'm alone."

"Well—" Does he sound dubious? "Okay, then."

He's not starting the bus, though. He looks at me, even after I've managed to sit down in the nearest seat. What is it? Will he make me go back? Are others staring?

"The fare, ma'am, please," he quietly says.

I'm humiliated, flustered. I open my purse, and grope, and finally thrust it into his hands.

"Yes, yes. I'm sorry. You'll find the money there."

Whistling through his teeth, he picks a bill and puts back some change.

"Okay, here you are."

Rigid as marble I sit, solid and stolid to outward view. Inwardly my heart thunders until I fear other passengers may hear. The ride is interminable. Buildings rush by, and cars, and each time the bus stops and starts it jerks me like a puppet.

"Depot," the driver intones. "Okay, lady, here you are. You just go in there. The ticket wicket's straight ahead. You can't miss it."

In the bus depot millions of people are yelling and running, toting suitcases. Everyone knows where to go, it seems, except myself. *Shadow Point?* Whatever happens, I must not forget. Where is this wicket he spoke of?

She's very young, and wears her hair coiled on top of her head—how on earth does she keep it up there? It looks as though it's built around a mold, or a wire frame, like Marie Antoinette's. And yet her face is not unlike my Tina's—a tanned skin, clear and free of blemishes, so simple and vulnerable. Maybe all girls her age look that way. I did myself, once. And wouldn't she be horrified to know that? Perhaps she'll glide away, with that haughtiness only the young can muster, not wanting to be bothered.

"Sure," she says. "It's right over there. Look—that way. Here—come on, I'll show you."

She takes my arm, shrugs in the same embarrassment as the driver, when I try to thank her. She doesn't know she'll ever be in need, but something unacknowledged in her knows, perhaps. And off she goes, to heaven only knows what events, what ending.

Now the ticket is in my hand, and paid for, and I board a bus, having been steered by someone, I don't know who. I'm getting rather tired. It's taking so much longer than I thought it would. I sit, at last, and rest.

Whoom! An explosive noise, and whir of wheels. What's happening? And then I see the bus is whirling along a road, and we're on the way. I doze a little, and after a while we're there, at Shadow Point.

Deposited by the roadside, I stand and stare after the bus. I'm here, and astonished now that the place looks ordinary. And yet—I'm here, and made it under my own steam, and that's the main thing. The only trouble is—can I find the steps, the steps that lead down and down, as I seem to recall, to the place I'm looking for? The sky is a streaky blue, like a tub of water that a cube of bluing has been swirled in. I'm here all by myself.

A service station beside the road has a small store attached to it. How fortunate I happened to notice it. I must have provisions, of course. As I push open the screen door, a bell clonks tiredly. But no one appears. I select my purchases with some care. A box of soda biscuits, the salted kind—Doris always buys those bland unsalted ones that I don't like. A little tin of jam, greengage, my favorite. Some large bars of plain milk chocolate, very nourishing. O—here's a packet of those small Swiss cheeses, triangles wrapped in silver paper. I like them very much, and Doris hardly ever buys them, as they're an extravagance. I'll treat myself, just this once. There. That'll do. I mustn't take too much, or I won't be able to carry it all.

A dun-haired and spectacled woman slouches in from some back room and stands waiting behind the counter. She has deplorable posture. Someone ought to tell her to straighten her shoulders. Not me, though. I must watch what I say. Already she seems to be looking at me half suspiciously, as though I were an escaped convict or a child, someone not meant to be out alone.

"That be all?" she enquires.

"Yes. Let's see now—yes, I think so. Unless you happen to have one of those brown paper shopping bags, the kind with handles—you know the sort I mean?"

She reaches out and now I see a pile of them directly in front of me on the counter.

"They're a nickel," she says. "That be all, now? That's three fifty-nine."

So much for these few things?

Then I see from her frown that a terrible thing has occurred. I've spoken the words aloud.

"The bars are twenty-five apiece," she says coldly. "Did you want the ten-cent ones?"

"No, no," I can't get the words out fast enough. "It's quite all right. I only meant—everything's so high these days, isn't it?"

"It's high all right," she says in a surly voice, "but it's not us that gains, in the smaller stores. It's the middlemen, and that's for sure, sitting on their fannies and not doing a blame thing except raking in the dough."

"Oh yes, I'm sure you're right."

In fact, I haven't the foggiest notion what she's talking about. I hate my breathless agreement, but I've no choice. I mouth effusive thanks, unable to stop myself.

"Don't mention it," she says in a bored voice, and we part. The screen door slams behind me. It creaks open again immediately, the bell jangling.

"You forgot your parcel," she says accusingly. "Here."

At last I'm away, and walking down the road. The shopping bag feels heavy. The air is uncomfortably warm with that oppressive mugginess we get here in summer, close to the sea. In Manawaka the summers were all scorchers but it was a dry heat, much healthier.

A sign with an arrow. *To the Point.* Well, there's a sign that's very much to the point. The silly pun pleases me and lightens my steps. My legs are holding out well. It can't be much further. How shall I find the stairs? I'll have to ask, that's all. I shall simply say I'm out for a walk. There's nothing odd about that. I'm managing admirably. I'd give anything to see Doris's face when she gets back from shopping. I have to chortle at the thought of it, for all that my feet are hurting rather badly now on this rough gravel road. A jolting sound, a cyclone of dust, and a truck pulls up.

"Want a lift, lady?"

Fortune is with me. Gratefully, I accept.

"Where are you going?" he asks.

"To—to the Point. My son and I—we've rented a cottage there."

"Well, lucky for you I happened by. It's a good three miles from here. I'm turning off at the old fish-cannery road. Okay if I let you off there?"

"Oh yes, that would be just fine, thanks."

That's the very place. I'd forgotten, until he said it, what the place was and what it used to be, but now I recollect Marvin's explaining about it that day. Doris said it still stank of fish and Marvin said that was just her imagination. It couldn't, he said, for it hadn't been in use for about thirty years, having gone out of business in the depression.

"Here you are," the driver says. "So long."

The truck bounces away, and I'm standing among trees that extend all the way down the steep slopes to the sea. How quiet this forest is, only its own voices, no human noises at all. A bird exclaims piercingly, once, and the ensuing silence is magnified by the memory of that single cry. Leaves stir, touch one another, make faint fitful sounds. A branch rasps against another branch like a boat scraping against a pier. Enormous leaves glow like green glass, the sunlight illuminating them.

Tree trunks are tawny and gilded. Cedar boughs hold their dark and intricate tracery like gates against the sky. Sun and shadow mingle here, making the forest mottled, changing, dark and light.

The stairway's beginning is almost concealed by fern and bracken, tender and brittle, green fish-spines that snap easily under my clumping feet. It's not a proper stairway, actually. The steps have been notched into the hillside and the earth bolstered at the edges with pieces of board. There's a banister of sorts, made of poles, but half of them have rotted away and fallen. I go down cautiously, feeling slightly dizzy. The ferns have overgrown the steps in some places, and salmonberry bushes press their small needles against my arms as I pass. Bushes of goatsbeard brush satyr-like against me. Among the fallen leaves and brown needles of fir and balsam on the forest floor grow those white pinpoint flowers we used to call Star of Bethlehem. I can see into cool and shady places, the streaks of sun star-fished across the moist and musky earth.

I'm not weary at all, nor heavy laden. I could sing. I'm like Meg Merrilies. That's Keats, and I can remember parts of it still, although it must be forty years or more since I laid eyes on it. If that isn't evidence of a good memory, I don't know what it is.

> Old Meg she was a gipsy,
> And lived upon the moors;
> Her bed it was the brown heath turf,
> And her house was out of doors.
> Her apples were swart blackberries,
> Her currants pods o' broom;
> Her wine was dew of the wild white rose,
> Her book a churchyard tomb.

I see some blackberry bushes here. They have berries on them all right, but not swart enough, I fear, and they won't be changing from hard emerald for another month. As for her wine, those roses must've been a giant breed. You'd not quench your thirst to any extent by sipping dew out of the wildflowers that grow hereabouts.

Then it strikes me suddenly, a stone pelted at my gaiety. I haven't brought any water. I haven't anything to drink, not a mouthful, not even an orange to suck. Oh, what was I thinking of? How could I have neglected that? What shall I do? I'm nearly at the bottom of the steps. There must be several hundred of them, in all. I can't face climbing them. I'm all at once tired, so tired I can barely move one foot and then another.

I go on, step and step and step, and then I'm there. The gray old buildings loom around me. I don't even look at them closely, for the full weight of my exhaustion presses down upon me now that I'm really here. I'm limp as a dishrag. I don't even

feel specific pain in my feet or under my ribs now—only a throbbing in every part of me.

A door's ajar. I push it and walk in. I set my shopping bag on a floor richly carpeted with dust. Then, unthinking, unaware of anything except my extremity of weariness, I hunch down in the dust and go to sleep.

I waken famished, and wonder for the moment when Doris will have the tea ready and whether she's baked today or not, for I seem to recall her mentioning that she intended to make a spice cake. Then I see beside me on the floor my summer hat, the cornflowers dipped in dust. What on earth possessed me to come here? What if I take ill?

One day at a time—that's all a person has to deal with. I'll not look ahead. I shall be quite comfortable here. I'll manage splendidly. I root in my paper bag, and when I've eaten I feel restored. But thirsty. There's no water—none. How has it happened? I'd give almost anything right now for a cup of tea. I seem to hear Doris laughing—*Serves you right, for dumping it down the sink.* Oh, I never did—how can you say it? It wasn't I. You're mean, Doris. How can such meanness flourish?

She's not here. What can I have been thinking of? I'll look around. Perhaps there's a well. Now I'm certain there must be, if only I can find it. What would a fortress be without a well?

A manager or owner must have lived here once, I think, when this place was used. The windows are broken and when I look outside I see a larger building a short distance away, right beside the sea. It's been washed and warped by salt water and the soft-water rain, and some of its boards are loose. That'll be the cannery, where the boats used to come in all weathers, bringing their loads of scaled and writhing creatures shining with slime, and the great clams with fluted shells pried from the sea.

This house of mine is gray, too, as I see when I poke my head a little further out of the window. So far from bothering me, I find a certain reassurance in this fact, and think I'll feel quite at home here. How Marvin would disapprove. He's mad on paint. That's his business, selling house paint, and he claims to know as much about it as any man alive. Probably he does, if that means anything. You'll see him sometimes poring over his sample charts, memorizing the names of the new colors. Parisian Chartreuse or Fiesta Rose. But this is my house, not his, and if I choose not to tint and dye it, that's my affair.

Now for the rooms. The living-room is empty, only the puffs and pellets of dust like shed cat's hair or molted feathers tumbling lightly in corners as the breeze sweeps at them. There was a fireplace, but the grate has fallen in and only a rubble of broken brick remains. In the bay window, perhaps draperied once with tasseled velvet, there's a built-in wooden bench. It's the kind that lifts up like a chest-lid and you store the family albums or unused cushions inside. I lift and look. Within is an old brass scale, the kind they used for weighing letters or pepper. It tips and tilts to my finger, but the brass weights are lost. Nothing can be weighed here and found wanting.

Kitchen and scullery have been camped in, it appears, by tramps or fugitives at some time. This revelation startles me. I'm not the only one who knows this place. Of course not. May they not come again? What would I do? Perhaps they'd be harmless, only seeking shelter. I can't lock my castle any more than I could my room at home. Well, this is a joke on me all right. I'll not anticipate. I'll meet it when it comes. But this is only brave prevarication, for I'm feeling nervous.

The wooden table is black and sour with spilled grease, and it has been hacked at and initialed by more knives than one. On it sits squatly an empty gallon jug with a label that reads Dulcet Loganberry Wine. There's a paper plate that once held fish and chips—whose mouth were they stuffed into, I wonder, and where's the person now, and was it long ago or only yesterday? The sink is stained with rust and dirt, and the taps are gone. On the floor stands an Old Chum tobacco tin, containing three cigarette butts. That's all. Nothing else here.

The banister on the hall stairs is fumed oak, with a carved newel post. Slowly, I mount. One step at a time. Another and another. Then it's done, and up here I feel somehow more barricaded, safer. The rooms are empty, except for the tumbleweed dust. No—not quite. In one bedroom there's a brass four-poster, and incredibly the mattress is still on it. Delighted, I pat it. My room had been prepared for me. The mattress is mildewed, it's true, and musty from never being aired. But it's here and mine. From the bedroom window I can look out to the darkening trees and beyond them to the sea. Who would have thought I'd have a room with a view? Heartened, I plod back down the stairs, and then return, bearing my bag and my hat.

To move to a new place—that's the greatest excitement. For a while you believe you carry nothing with you—all is canceled from before or cauterized, and you begin again and nothing will go wrong this time.

November Day on Howe Sound
George Woodcock

The best of all Novembers
as the mountains shout
when that low-slanted sun
lights them within,
igniting from grey stone
alchemic vividness:
vermilion, rust, fire orange,
viridian, copper-blue,
faded Prussian, moss
green, arbutus bronze.

Rock slide and mountain wall
glistening in cascade spray:
at level-rayed evening
exploding into gold:
in autumn fire haze
distancing amethyst.

Last leaves burn on trees
stripped to bone of life
or dance down wind,
bright dying butterflies
asserting mortal splendour
at the year's end of life
framed by the glistening
indifferent sea.

O mountains shout again
and gold leaves die in flight
on that bright day you
sing me into night.

Closeted

David Watmough

It was the kind of late February afternoon that can send Vancouverites mad with boasting. The temperature had been up in the high teens for nearly two weeks, with the bonus of an accompanying sun and cloud-enlivened skies. The rhythms of spring had thus settled upon us, with the early multi-colors of the bulbs, the hyacinths and crocuses, already pushed out of the way, mainly by the yellows from daffodils, forsythia, laburnum and broom. It was, in fact, the time of our west coast joy and complacency when we become buoyantly introverted in the face of grim weather bulletins still persisting from beyond the mountains to the east.

I parked the Peugeot outside the tennis courts where several young couples were playing—and paused to enjoy the exposed flesh before attending to my business in the building opposite. There was one pair in particular which held my attention. The girl was wearing a shirt and shorts. The boy was naked to the waist. Neither of them could have been a day over eighteen.

I didn't exactly sigh over the allure of youth—I wasn't feeling *that* old—but the gap of roughly twenty years between us was certainly sufficient to prompt a stab of nostalgia for that energy and freedom from wrinkle or blemish which adolescence can sometimes so beautifully demonstrate.

The two of them were intense in their performance and fairly equal in prowess. There was a lot of volleying and a few wasted shots. Not unnaturally, his service was the more powerful, and from time to time, during the few minutes I stood observing them, the ball from his far side of the court would elude her and end up by the plastic green meshing which separated the hardtop from the narrow earth bed on my side which was seasonally adorned with vermilion camellias with their background of dark green leaves.

When I finally turned away to attend to my concerns, it was with a welcome sense of satisfaction. The sun, the bright-colored camellias, the young exposed skin, all melded into a major constituent of the euphoria which enveloped me as I crossed the street into the sharp shadows from the lofty portals of the senior citizens' residence where I had come to read.

I had no sooner entered that antiseptic-smelling hallway milling with white-coated women, looking so briskly purposeful, than the world of color and young life I had just vacated became something of a desperate counterpoint to my suddenly failing spirits. It was always the same. Buoyed by the belief I was doing something worthwhile in reading a story or part of a novel to whichever group of old people requested it, I would forget the previous experience of a Senior Citizens' Home—either private or run by the city—and suppress the unwelcome recollection of stale urine, the savage impact of age represented in calloused flesh, bent backs and skinny arms and legs. In answering the phoned request to read for a brief while in this facility or that, I refused to think of the caustic waves of the years, smothering wits, feeding the ache of arthritis, blotting out sight: the harvest from strokes in distorted voices and crippled gait. And above all, the loneliness of those who had lived on after their loved-ones and friends, and now shared the remnant of years with total strangers.

But it came to me, as I followed Miss Moberly, the Social Events Director at Grassmere Long Term Care Facility, to where she had deposited her circle of ancients, just how frail and frightened I was over the geriatric horrors surrounding me. Involuntary droolings from worn-out orifices merged obscenely with the tang of disinfectant; and the sound of a crone crying as she waited vainly for a visitor—these monstrous ikons of age depressed the hell out of me.

There was certainly no sense of moral smugness at this essay in good works. Only a glum acceptance of my selfish inability to cope with it all. When I had first agreed to give a reading of my work before an old people's group I had mentioned it to several friends, particularly fellow-writers, in the hope that they, too, would be persuaded to do likewise. But that gesture soon evaporated in the light of bleak experience. Now I told no one. It wasn't just that I wished to conceal that grotesque sense of depletion that so often accompanied my foraging into that kingdom of the old. I was also ashamed.

Miss Moberly's senescent congregation was seated in the vicinity of the tall windows through which the bright sun streamed. One or two old women knitted or talked or did both, but for the most part they sat silent, perhaps shaking from an infirmity such as Parkinson's disease, or hunched in one of the velvet green armchairs in a position which allowed them most relief from the problem of thin flesh as scanty relief from sharp bones. Many had canes by their chairs, several muttered quietly to themselves, one preferred to stand in her chromium walker, and another, wearing a pink cardigan and with an arcane strip of metal across her head which thus flattened her yellow-white hair, was stretched out on a sofa and gazed across at the tennis players clearly visible through the leafless trees over the street. There was one old man.

Miss Moberly began by leaving the "t" off my surname of Bryant and went on to describe me as primarily an author of children's books dealing with animals. It was at that juncture that I testily decided to change the story I was going to read them, from a ghost story set in Cornwall which I had initially intended, to a more somber one that dealt with sexual ambiguity and which had not the vaguest reference to pets and would certainly not be construed as having an appeal to the juvenile market.

Just as the Social Events Director concluded her erroneous remarks, the old lady in the pink cardigan screamed out angrily from her window seat. "Those kids are naked over there. Someone should call the police!"

One of the nurses crossed quickly to her, for the tempestuous grimalkin had grabbed her cane and was thudding angrily with its rubber ferrule at the glass pane.

"That's all right, Nelly. It's just the tennis players. It is much warmer out there than you might suspect. And then for hot-blooded youngsters—with all that activity . . ."

"It's just to spite us. I know what they're at. I've seen that little slut out there before."

"She's hardly naked, dear," the uniformed woman said soothingly.

But Nelly was not to be deflected so facilely from her protest.

"Well *he* is! Look at that creature—flaunting his ugly body to upset all of us."

The interchange was brought to a halt by another diversion. I was turning to the apposite page in my short-story volume when the old man spoke up.

"I can't hear the speaker from here," he whined. He was sitting in proximity to the fiery critic of the young tennis players.

"How do you know, Herb? He hasn't said anything yet!" The new voice belonged to a tall, birdlike woman sitting immediately in front of me. She seemed, at least from her features, to be full-witted and even smiled encouragingly at me from behind steel-framed spectacles.

"Herb is a bit of a complainer," she explained, in a firm voice quite loud enough for him to hear.

"Can I come and sit on the other side of you, Sir," he said in his high tremolo. "My best ear's that side, you see."

It occurred to me that I'd never get started at all if this interrupting continued. "Come on over, then," I said loudly—too loudly—"It'll be nice to have a bit of male back-up with all these lovely ladies around me."

That brought the expected titter from most of my audience but it was lost on the Grassmere inmate sitting opposite.

"You'll only start grumbling about your darned eyes if you do, Herb." Adding as she continued to look directly at me. "He's got a cataract problem. He's always moaning about the light. That's why we stuck him up near Beverly with his back to the window, isn't it Miss Moberly?"

But he was already tottering unsteadily in my direction, leaning heavily on his walking stick. I eyed him as he approached. One of the nurses immediately hurried from her seat to aid him in his erratic progress. He stuck out an elbow for her to support. Herb, I noticed, was a little man, perhaps an octogenarian. His eyes were watery and weak under close-cropped white hair. He was cleanshaven although whoever

had shaved him hadn't done too neat a job, judging by the patches of silvered whiskers about his cheekbones and chin. His neck was a wattle of red flesh and seemed hardly firm enough to support the rather large head. Below all that he was even more of a mess—what with the foodstains down his rumpled shirt and old grease patches shining from a virtually buttonless vest that he wore under a too large, brown jacket which looked itself like a Goodwill reject. I had often noticed at other such geriatric institutions that the few old men they contained looked infinitely scruffier and frailer than their female counterparts. But Herb had a dishevelled quality all his own.

No sooner had he sat down on my right than the prophecy of the old girl facing me was vindicated.

"The light hurts me eyes a bit. I can't see you but perhaps I can hear if you speaks up. Most of 'em don't, you know. That's why I don't usually come to these reading things."

"Shut up!" said another woman whom I hadn't noticed hitherto.

Miss Moberly recognized a newcomer slowly approaching on the arm of yet another white uniform. "This way, Agnes, he hasn't started yet. He's still talking to Herb."

I decided to change the situation then and there. They'd be bellyaching and interrupting for the rest of the afternoon if I didn't get things under way. "This story is from my book *Love & The Waiting Game*," I began, and started to read my rather inappropriate tale in the confessional idiom, of a Cornish sex scandal on a farm which involved a middle-aged invert. The story was entitled "Cousin Petherick & The Will."

Halfway through my narrative Ms. Pink Cardigan informed us all that she could now observe more nude tennis players and a hitherto silent member of my elderly audience announced that she, too, had visited Galiano Island where part of my story was located. But such minor interruptions were not unusual and after an encouraging smile and slight pause, I rammed fresh color into my voice and continued as if nothing had happened.

It was with the conclusion of the tale, with its grim revelation of a man's embarrassing affection for another that unusual things began to happen. They started with old Herb, when I had concluded with my standard invitation for questions or comments.

"Was—was that man—that Cousin Petherick—real?" he asked quietly.

The hag across from me glared through her thick glasses.

"He was disgusting, that's for sure!"

Herb ignored her and her displeasure.

"A farmer, you say. A farmer like me. More like me than you might all think. Only I was down there to California. Apple orchard we had in the Pajaro Valley, down there near Santa Cruz."

"Young man," said the hag, "you seem clean-living and that. Why do you dredge up all that kind of filth, eh? Don't you ever spare a thought for the beautiful things of life?"

By now I was wishing that I had not succumbed to that fit of perversity and had read a different, more innocuous story. Not that I was ashamed of this one—or reluctant to account for my literary products. But I was hardly demonstrating courage or candour before these old things who had enough to do to hang onto life when at the clammy brink of death, than to wrestle with the problems of the sexually persecuted, the woes of those thrust by the vortex of procreation to the circumferences of life. Or so I thought. And so, seemingly, did Miss Moberly who was calling for general attention prior to thanking me and bidding me farewell. But not old Herb.

He wasn't holding up his shaking hand to protect his bleary eyes from the light any more. He was addressing his Grassmere sisters.

"That—that man he was talking about? The fat one who made the will? That could've been me!"

"I didn't know you were *Cornish*, Herb," the advocate of Life's Beauties snapped. "In any case, you were a widower before you joined us here. You told me yourself. No children, I understood, but a widower nevertheless."

But he didn't seem to connect with her words. Either that or he was indifferent to them. "Mr. Bryant took me back long before that," he said slowly. "Long, long before Marjorie and Vancouver. Down there to California it was. Off the old Aptos Road we had our place. Charley Parkhurst and me. We used to watch the trains go through to Santa Cruz. The Southern Pacific that was. We'd take the buggy over to Soquel and then on to Capitola in the cove. Jest Charley and me that was. Went swimming from the Ocean View Hotel in Aptos, too. We'd lie in the sun and listen to the sealions—when there wasn't no fog, that is."

"Mr. Bryan doesn't want to hear your old stories, Herb," Miss Moberly remonstrated, a smile etched with the severity of the Mt. Rushmore carvings across the lower half of her powdered face.

"He's senile, that's what Herb is," contributed an unnamed other.

"We're all senile, aren't we Miss Moberly? Only we don't want to believe it." This time a tiny woman, almost hairless, piped from the very back row of the gathered horseshoe.

"Speak for yourself, Kitty," called out my witch adversary of the steel-rimmed glasses—without bothering to turn her head to recognize the voice's owner. "Anyway," she continued, "I want to ask Mr. Bryant about Devonshire cream. My husband, the late Mr. Arthur Weston, was from Torquay and always used to go on so about the clotted cream and how delicious it was."

I drew breath willingly; only too ready to switch the topic

and *always* primed to give my mini-spiel on the subtle but major differences between English Devon and Celtic Cornwall. But my only peer of gender in the lounge of The Grassmere Long Term Care Facility wasn't about to be deflected.

"Your man, that Cousin Petherick, he never knew about himself, really, did he? I mean he put all that in his will about liking the other chap and leaving his money to him. But they didn't . . . they weren't . . ."

It wasn't just because of the pain of his faltering, but the sheer misery of the old man's appearance that firmed up my resolve. He was salivating freely now and his head rocked wildly—like one of those plastic caricatures of birds that keep dipping huge heads into empty tumblers—in the windows of some sleazy stores. "They weren't really lovers," I announced distinctly. "You're right, they were not exactly that."

"We were," Herb said to the burgeoning silence. "Charley and me was what you could call lovers. Out on the beach the first time. In public you might say."

"I don't see why we have to sit here and listen to unbridled filth," said the steel spectacles, sitting, if it were humanly possible, even more upright. "Miss Moberly, where is my wheelchair? I've got to go you-know-where."

"Just one moment, Nora. Now before we all have our tea and cookies, I just want to say to Mr. Bryan—"

But like old Herb, I, too, was beyond niceties. "Why *now*?" I almost yelled at him. "Why do you have to tell all this *now*?"

He had to struggle with that—as if the problem was of such magnitude it would only yield to immense effort. If that awful head shook any more, I told myself, it was bound to fall off. It was only then I realized the old man was quite devoid of teeth. But quiver and shake, lick lips without managing to contain his drool, finding it terribly hard to shape words in that ever-shrinking palate—in spite of all such obstacles of his dotage, he was determined to strive for the words which he had eluded or repressed for so long.

"That Petherick was a kind of virgin, weren't he? Not me. Charley and I had it off. Not just the once but two times. But you see we never *talked* about it. And no one thought of will-making down there in California. But we should have spoked, I reckon. If I'd told him what I'm telling you then it would've all been different mebbe. Not all wasted like for that Petherick of yours and his Jimmy Tehiddy. There would have been no Marjorie, come to think of it. Fancy that! Not if the two on us had come clean about what we felt for each other when we had the apple orchard."

"I understand," I told him, although I really didn't.

"In any case," said Miss Moberly, now physically standing between us so that we could only converse through the unrelenting white of her uniform, "teatime is hardly the appropriate occasion for *that* kind of talk. Goodbye, Mr.

Bryan, on behalf of all of us at Grassmere. And thank you so much for your odd little tale."

"My pleasure," I replied mechanically.

"Old Charley," said Herb, "fancy my remembering old Charley after all these years. Handsome one he was, you know. But proud! No one took no liberties with Charley Parkhurst. Punch you in the teeth if you was to call him some name what he didn't like."

I stood up to go, squeezing past Miss Moberly for a final word with the old chap. "After that I should level with you," I said to him in a lowered voice. "I'm gay myself, of course. But for us it's easier than back when you were talking about. Anyway, goodbye," I said, holding out my hand. He took it and we shook together, symbiotically, for a few seconds. He was patently summoning up a fresh spurt of words.

"Gay was you? Course it wasn't so happy a time then. It was all uphill work in the Twenties and then the Depression right after. Jesus, the work on that orchard was hard for just two guys what couldn't afford no help. No, I can't say we was gay exactly. But we had our fun and that. We made our own bed, you now. All the furniture in the shack, come to that. Then Charley was some carpenter. And I was o.k. at the rough stuff."

"What—what happened to Charley, Herb?" I asked—really anxious to be on my way but wishing also to do the polite and kind thing.

"Dunno," he said, for him quite sharply. "Dunno what happened. Probably married and settled down like me and Marge. He was originally from New Hampshire. May have made his way back there. Long dead and gone now, I expect."

Then Herb smiled broadly, revealing gums from which the pink had almost disappeared. "I sure got it all right in this place," he said. "What with just me and all the women falling over me—got it made I have!"

I gave his arm a nudge, and felt only bone. "It comes to us all," I told him with a jocularity that was absolutely false. Then I smiled inanely at my erstwhile audience of oldsters whose combined age covered centuries—before fleeing their patient presence for the easier deceptions of the tennis-court world outside.

Lardeau/Summer, 1964
Fred Wah

I said we slept in a shack
at the bottom of the valley
watched the sun set after supper
over an ice field to the north
an unnamed glacier, then
the mountains about us
left white by the moon.

And I said it was a hot day
where we were I had a headache
at noon the blue above turned
to a green blur of moving trees
the felled log rolled under me
and we began the afternoon's cruise
looking at ourselves in the forest.

About the Lardeau?
There is little to say.
It is green, it rains
often, the mountains
are very beautiful,
there is a moon at night,
the unnamed glacier is the shape
of a bird in flight, with stars
in its eyes, my logging boots
make me feel strong
but too heavy to use strength,
the rivers and creeks
flow south to the lake,
there are mosquitoes, the name
is Marblehead.

At the end of it
it was all a dream
I said from looking up
up an eighty-foot pole
at lunch and he:
well, I'll be here all winter
and the cruising's easy on snowshoes
though this summer has been a nice one
gotta get that left shock fixed next time in town
I said
you must be finishing labor
at the top of Meadow Mountain
for she was born at 9:15
and we neared the top then too
I had pains in my stomach.

Notes on Contributors

Margaret Atwood is a leading Canadian writer in many fields, including fiction with her novels like *Surfacing* and *Lady Oracle*, poetry, of which she has published many volumes, the most important being *Selected Poems*, and criticism with her fine study of Canadian writers, *Survival*.

Eric Ivan Berg was born in the Cariboo and died in a logging accident in 1977. As well as being a logger, he worked as a disc jockey, a radio producer, and a security guard. His poems were collected posthumously in *Cariboo Country Poetry*.

Earle Birney has published many volumes of poetry since his first, *David and Other Poems*, appeared in 1942. His *Collected Poems* was published in 1976. He has also written two novels, *Turvey* and *Down the Long Table*.

M. Wylie Blanchet's *The Curve of Time*, describing summers spent as a widow with small children exploring coastal waters in a small boat, is one of the travel classics of British Columbia.

Franz Boas was one of the first anthropologists to do field work in Canada, beginning with the Inuit and then, in 1886, devoting himself to the Indians of the North Pacific. He published several collections of Indian tales and a seminal book on coast culture, *Primitive Art*.

George Bowering, born in the Okanagan, became a member of the group that produced the influential poetry magazine, *Tish*, from Vancouver in the 1960s. His many books of verse include *Touch*, *In the Flesh*, and *George, Vancouver*.

Hugh Brody is an anthropologist whose *Maps and Dreams* tells of a period he spent among the Beaver Indians of the Peace River country helping them counter the threat to their hunting grounds posed by pipeline construction.

William Francis Butler, an Irish-born soldier, served in Canada against the Fenians in 1867, took part in Wolseley's expedition to the Red River, and in 1870 and 1872 undertook two investigative expeditions, which gave him the material for his two travel classics, *The Great Lone Land* and *The Great North Land*.

Jacinto Caamano was one of the Spanish captains who explored the coast of present-day British Columbia during the late eighteenth century, a time of rivalry between the Spanish and British.

Emily Carr made a singular contribution to Canadian painting in her canvases and gouaches of Indian villages and forest scenes. Her achievement, however, was only recognized late in her life. She also wrote a series of brilliant autobiographical works, including *Klee Wyck*, *Growing Pains*, *The Book of Small*, and her journal, *Hundreds and Thousands*, published posthumously.

Ken Cathers is a young Vancouver Island poet whose work has appeared in journals like *Tamarack Review* and *Malahat Review*.

Roy Daniells headed the English departments at the University of Manitoba and the University of British Columbia. He was a distinguished Miltonist and published two books of verse, *Deeper into the Forest* and *The Chequered Shade*.

Born in 1892 and still writing, **Hubert Evans** is the dean of Canadian novelists. His first books appeared in the 1920s, but *Mist on the River*, published in 1954, is his best-known novel, dealing with the Indian villages of northern British Columbia in which Evans lived during the 1940s.

A partner in the North West Company, **Simon Fraser** was sent to the Rocky Mountains in 1805, and established a series of posts in northern British Columbia. Then in 1808 he made the difficult descent of the Fraser River through the mountains to the sea. He believed it was the Columbia he was following.

Gary Geddes is a widely published poet and an anthologist. He is also the founder of Quadrant Editions, an unusual publishing house that issues to subscribers books of selective appeal.

M. Allerdale Grainger left King's College, Cambridge to join in the Klondike gold rush, worked on the river boats, placer mined, and fought in the South African War before he took to logging, which is the subject of his only novel, *Woodsmen of the West*, written before he became Chief Forester of British Columbia in 1916. He died in 1941.

Roderick Haig-Brown combined the life of writing with the occupation of stipendiary magistrate in the little Vancouver Island town of Campbell River. He had been a logger, trapper, and guide before he began to write the books on fishing and outdoor life that made him celebrated and the splendid essays collected in volumes like *Measure of the Year*.

John Sebastian Helmcken arrived in Victoria as doctor for the Hudson's Bay Company in 1850. He took an active part in British Columbian politics during the colonial period, but after Confederation withdrew to his practice. His *Reminiscences* were published in 1975, fifty-five years after his death.

Charles Hill-Tout was a pioneer field anthropologist in British Columbia, where he settled in 1891. He was a remarkable self-taught scientist who forced the grudging respect of his academic rivals. His papers and translations of Indian tales were published in four volumes in 1978 under the title of *The Salish People*.

Edward Hoagland is an American novelist who in 1966 spent three months wandering in the northern wilderness of British Columbia, and out of the experience wrote a vivid journal, *Notes from the Century Before*.

Jack Hodgins was born and grew up in the small logging communities of Vancouver Island. For eighteen years he was a high school teacher, but since 1979 he has been writing full-time. His novels, *The Invention of the World* and *The Resurrection of Joseph Bourne*, and the short stories he has collected in *Spit Delaney's Island* deal with the eccentric world of far western Canada as invented by Jack Hodgins.

Bruce Hutchison has followed a double career of distinction, as newspaper editor (of the *Winnipeg Free Press*, the *Victoria Times* and the *Vancouver Sun*) and as a writer of informal histories, including *The Unknown Country*, *The Fraser*, and his book on Mackenzie King, *The Incredible Canadian*.

John R. Jewitt was made captive by the chief Maquinna when the *Boston*, the boat on which he was armourer, was attacked by the Indians and all except Jewitt and one other seaman were massacred. He shared the life of the Indians for two years until he was finally rescued.

In 1846 **Paul Kane** set off on the journey from Toronto to the Pacific Coast that he describes in *Wanderings of An Artist*. From the sketches of Indians and landscape he made then, he painted ambitious academic canvases, but it was his sketches, which survive, that were most vivid in their documentation of dying cultures.

Lionel Kearns, who teaches English at Simon Fraser University, is a poet frankly concerned with social protest, yet at the same time a dedicated craftsman, as his books like *Pointing*, *About Time*, and *Practicing Up to be Human* clearly show.

Theresa Kishkan, who lives in Vancouver, has published in many magazines, and her book of poems, *Ikons of the Hunt*, appeared in 1978.

Born in Vancouver of Japanese descent, **Joy Kogawa** in her delicately visual poems continues Asian traditions in a western language. Her poems are collected in books like *A Choice of Dreams* and *Jericho Road*.

Patrick Lane went from school to a series of labouring jobs in the interior of British Columbia where he had been born. When he eventually began to write poetry it was coloured by these experiences, and he has moved from stark narrative verse to poetry of growing complexity. *Beware the Months of Fire*, *Unborn Things*, and *Selected Poems*.

Margaret Laurence may well be Canada's most important novelist. Her earlier books—*This Side Jordan*, *The Tomorrow Tamer*, *The Prophet's Camel Bell*—reflect the African experiences that helped shape her as a writer, but her most important books are the Manawaka cycle set largely in the prairies: *The Stone Angel*, *A Jest of God*, *The Fire Dwellers*, *The Diviners*.

The New Englander, **John Ledyard**, went to England in 1774, and in 1776 enlisted as a marine on the *Discovery*, taking part in Cook's last voyage. In 1783 he wrote his recollections of it, *A Journal of Captain Cook's Last Voyage*.

Charles Lillard was born in California, was brought up in Alaska, and later moved to British Columbia. He has worked a great deal in the bush, but he has also taught at the universities of British Columbia and Victoria before liberating himself to become a free lance editor and writer. His books of verse include *Drunk on Wood* and *Voice, My Shaman*.

Dorothy Livesay's poems first began to appear in the 1920s. In the 1960s she began to write and publish again with great vigour, so that she is not only one of the first Canadian modernists, but also, in her seventies, among our best contemporary poets. *Collected Poems: The Two Seasons* reflects this remarkable double career.

Malcolm Lowry, the English writer, lived in Canada from 1939 to 1956. Here he completed his masterpiece, *Under the Volcano*, and wrote a number of books sensitively attuned to the Canadian environment, notably his novel, *October Ferry to Gabriola*, and his volume of short stories, *Hear Us O Lord from Heaven Thy Dwelling Place*.

Daphne Marlatt was born in Australia and spent part of her childhood in Penang before moving to British Columbia. She was poetry editor of the *Capilano Review* and wrote *Steveston Recollected: A Japanese Canadian History*. *Net Work: Selected Writing* is the best collection of her prose, which always hovers near poetry.

Michael Mercer is a prolific writer of radio and television drama, of which many examples have been broadcast over CBC networks. He is currently completing his first novel.

Rona Murray was born in England and spent much of her childhood in India, coming to Canada in her teens. Her work has appeared widely in England and the United States as well as Canada. Her *Selected Poems* appeared in 1974 and her most recent volume is *Journeys*.

Susan Musgrave has lived in the Queen Charlottes, Ireland, and England, but now she is in Victoria where she spent her childhood. She has published a novel and several volumes of poems, of which the most representative is *Selected Strawberries and Other Poems*.

Howard O'Hagan is one of the most unjustly neglected of Canadian writers. His novel, *Tay John*, has a fine mythic quality, and he has also collected his stories in *The Woman Who Got On at Jasper Station and Other Stories*. After an active life in Australia, California, and Sicily, he lived in Victoria until his death in 1982.

Margaret Ormsby, formerly head of the Department of Histroy at the University of British Columbia, is a noted writer on the past of the Pacific Coast. Her most important work is *British Columbia: A History*.

P. K. Page was one of the group of young poets who established the historic poetry magazine *Preview* in 1942. Her early books were *As Ten as Twenty* (1946) and *The Metal and the Flower* (1954), as well as a novel, *The Sun and the Moon*. In the 1950s she lived in Australia, Mexico, and Brazil and became an accomplished artist as P. K. Irwin. Returning to Canada, she began to write poetry again and, like Dorothy Livesay, has enjoyed a fine second career, exemplified in books like *Poems Selected and New* and *Evening Dance of the Grey Flies*.

Marjorie Pickthall was one of the transitional writers who spanned the period between the Confederation poets and the modernist poets of the 1930s. Born in England in 1883, she came to Toronto as a child, was educated there, worked as a librarian at the University of

Toronto, and spent her last years in Vancouver, where she died in 1922. As well as poems, she wrote children's novels and historical romances. The best of her work was collected by Lorne Pierce in *Selected Poems of Marjorie Pickthall* (1957).

Al Purdy is one of the most vigorous and prolific of recent Canadian poets. After a varied life of hard work and rough living, including riding the rods in the Depression, he now devotes himself entirely to writing. The essence of his many books can be found in two selective volumes, *Being Alive: Poems 1958–78* and *Bursting into Song: An Al Purdy Omnibus*.

Bill Reid, a modern master of Indian carving, is descended from the famous Haida carvers Charles Edenshaw and Charles Gladstone. He has created gold and silver jewellery and carved fine poles in the classic Haida tradition, and is the most important of contemporary Indian sculptors.

Kevin Roberts, Australian by birth, combines salmon trolling with teaching creative writing at Malaspina College in Nanaimo. His poems have appeared in many magazines and his books include *West Country* and *Deepline*.

Robin Skelton's varied career has encompassed the founding and editing of the internationally prestigious *Malahat Review*, scholarly studies of Irish literature and of poetics, a book on spells, and many volumes and brochures of verse, including *The Hunting Dark*, *Timelight*, and *Landmarks*. He is chairman of the Writer's Union of Canada for 1982–83.

Born in Binghamton, New York, **Audrey Thomas** has lived for many years in British Columbia, with interludes in West Africa. Her books—novels and short stories—include *Mrs. Blood*, *Songs My Mother Taught Me*, *Blown Figures*, and *Real Mothers*.

David Thompson began his exploring career as a surveyor for the Hudson's Bay Company, but it was after he joined the North West Company in 1797 that he made his most important travels and discoveries, establishing a trading post on the Columbia in 1807 and descending the river to the sea in 1811. In all he surveyed and mapped nearly five million square kilometres of North America, and left a fine narrative of his explorations and adventures.

Peter Trower writes his poems about the logging camps and the mean city streets out of a hard experience of the working man's life. His books include *Moving through the Mystery* and *Ragged Horizons*.

Captain George Vancouver sailed with Captain Cook on two voyages and on the second of them, in 1778, made his first landing on Vancouver Island. In 1791 he returned in the *Discovery* to establish the British presence on the north Pacific Coast and to survey the inlets and islands of the region.

Born in Saskatchewan, **Fred Wah** grew up in the Kootenay country of British Columbia about which so much of his poetry has been written. He was one of the founding editors of *Tish* in Vancouver and, after an interlude in the United States, returned to the Kootenays. His most comprehensive volume is *Loki is Buried at Smoky Creek: Selected Poems*.

David Watmough was born in London, of Cornish ancestry, migrated to the United States in 1952, and in 1959 reached Vancouver, where he has remained ever since. Many of his fictions are written for reading aloud, as monodramas. His books include *Love and the Waiting Game* and *No More into the Garden*.

Tom Wayman, born in Toronto, has spent most of his life in British Columbia. He has taught English in schools and universities, but has also worked on construction and in a motor truck factory, and many of his poems reflect the struggles of the workers against employers and bureaucrats, though others poignantly evoke the western landscape. *Waiting for Wayman* and *For and Against the Moon* are two of his collections.

Though **Ethel Wilson** lived into her nineties, her writing career was relatively brief, beginning with the publication of *Hetty Dorval* in 1947 and virtually ending with the appearance of *Mrs. Golightly and Other Stories* in 1961. She died after a long illness in 1981, but her five novels remain among the best written in British Columbia.

Born in Winnipeg, educated in Britain, **George Woodcock** returned to Canada in 1949, settling in British Columbia where, except for travels in Asia, Oceania, and Europe, he has remained ever since. He founded *Canadian Literature* in 1959 and edited it to 1977, and has published many books—verse, biography, history, travel, criticism, belles-lettres.

Andrew Wreggitt was born in Sudbury in 1955, but for the greater part of his life has lived in northern British Columbia and Vancouver. He now lives in Prince Rupert. He has contributed stories and poems to many magazines, and has published a book of verse, *Riding to Nicola Country*.

Dale Zieroth was born in a small Manitoba town, and some of his best poetry inimitably evoked the way of life in such communities. Later he moved to a mountain community in British Columbia and eventually to North Vancouver. In his volume *Clearings* he talks of the transition between such different western homes; in *Mid-River* his poems are about the life of a land dominated by mountains.